First World War
and Army of Occupation
War Diary
France, Belgium and Germany

42 DIVISION
127 Infantry Brigade
Manchester Regiment
1/7th Battalion
24 February 1917 - 28 March 1919

WO95/2661/1

The Naval & Military Press Ltd
www.nmarchive.com
Published in association with The National Archives

Published by

The Naval & Military Press Ltd

Unit 10 Ridgewood Industrial Park,

Uckfield, East Sussex,

TN22 5QE England

Tel: +44 (0) 1825 749494

www.naval-military-press.com

www.nmarchive.com

This diary has been reprinted in facsimile from the original. Any imperfections are inevitably reproduced and the quality may fall short of modern type and cartographic standards.

© **Crown Copyright**

Images reproduced by permission of The National Archives, London, England, 2015.

Contents

Document type	Place/Title	Date From	Date To
Heading	WO95/2661/1 1/7 March.R Mar'17-Mar'19		
Heading	42nd Division 127th Infy Bde 1-7th Manchester Regt. Mar 1917-Mar 1919		
Heading	War Diary Of 1/7th Manchester Regt Vol 3 March 1st 1917 To March 31st 1917		
War Diary	Moascar	01/03/1917	02/03/1917
War Diary	Alexandria	03/03/1917	03/03/1917
War Diary	Ralyan S.S	03/03/1917	06/03/1917
War Diary	Troopship Kalyan	07/03/1917	09/03/1917
War Diary	From Marseilles Train	10/03/1917	12/03/1917
War Diary	Merelessart	13/03/1917	14/03/1917
War Diary	Liercourt	15/03/1917	29/03/1917
War Diary	Dompierre	30/03/1917	31/03/1917
Miscellaneous	Organisation Of Infantry Battalion. Appendix I		
Heading	War Diary Of 1/7th Manchester Regt From-April 1st 1917 To April 30th 1917 Vol IV		
War Diary	Dompierre	01/04/1917	08/04/1917
War Diary	Peronne	09/04/1917	27/04/1917
War Diary	Villers Faucon	27/04/1917	28/04/1917
War Diary	Epehy	29/04/1917	30/04/1917
Miscellaneous	To H.Q 127th. Brigade. Appendix 1	01/05/1917	01/05/1917
War Diary	149th. Inf. Brigade.	24/02/1917	24/02/1917
Miscellaneous	Special Training	14/04/1917	14/04/1917
Miscellaneous	Permanent Regimental Employ. Appendix III	19/04/1917	19/04/1917
Miscellaneous	France Appendix IV		
Heading	War Diary Of 1/7th Bn. Manchester Rgt For May-1917 Volume V		
War Diary	Epehy & In Trenches	01/05/1917	08/05/1917
War Diary	Villers Faucon In & In Trenches	09/05/1917	11/05/1917
War Diary	Brown Line & F 27 Caurd	12/05/1917	15/05/1917
War Diary	K.11.a.7.7	16/05/1917	16/05/1917
War Diary	P.32. B (57e S.E.)	17/05/1917	17/05/1917
War Diary	Vallulart Wood	18/05/1917	18/05/1917
War Diary	P.18. B.2.7 [Battn. H.Q.	19/05/1917	23/05/1917
War Diary	P.18.B.2.7	24/05/1917	31/05/1917
Operation(al) Order(s)	Operation Order No. 1 Appendix I	02/05/1917	02/05/1917
Miscellaneous	Battalion By Lieut. Colonel A.E. Cronshaw. Appendix I	02/05/1917	02/05/1917
Miscellaneous	Battalion Orders By Lt. Col. A.E. Cronshaw In The Field Appendix II	06/05/1917	06/05/1917
Miscellaneous	Battalion Orders By Commanding. Lt. Col. A.B. Cronshaw. In The Field Appendix III	08/05/1917	08/05/1917
Miscellaneous	Battalion Orders By Commanding. 1/7th. Manchester Rgt. Appendix IV	14/05/1917	14/05/1917
Miscellaneous	Battalion Orders By Major J.H. Allan. Appendix V	16/05/1917	16/05/1917
Miscellaneous	Appendix VI		
Miscellaneous	Battalion Orders By Major J.H. Allan In The Field Appendix VIII	26/05/1917	26/05/1917
Miscellaneous	H.Q Officers		

Miscellaneous	Battalion Orders By Major J.H. Allan. In The Field Appendix VII	26/05/1917	26/05/1917
Operation(al) Order(s)	Operation Order No. 6 Appendix IX	31/03/1917	31/03/1917
Miscellaneous	Appendix X		
Heading	War Diary Of 1/7th Bn. Manchester Regt. From June 1st 1917 To June 30th 1917 Volume VI		
War Diary	J.36.d.9.1	01/06/1917	19/06/1917
War Diary	P.15.B.8.7 Royal Court	20/06/1917	27/06/1917
War Diary	J.36.d. 9.5	26/06/1917	30/06/1917
Operation(al) Order(s)	Operation Order No. 10 By Lieut Colonel A.E. Cronshaw. Appendix I	07/06/1917	07/06/1917
Operation(al) Order(s)	Operation Order No. 10 By Lieut. Colonel A.E. Cronshaw. Appendix I	08/06/1917	08/06/1917
Operation(al) Order(s)	Addenda No. 2 Operation Order. 10 Appendix I	08/06/1917	08/06/1917
Miscellaneous	A Form Messages And Signals. Appendix II		
Miscellaneous	Appendix III		
Operation(al) Order(s)	Operation Orders No. 12. Appendix IV	13/06/1917	13/06/1917
Miscellaneous	1/7th. Bn. Manchester Regiment. Appendix VI	14/06/1917	14/06/1917
Miscellaneous	1/7th. Bn. Manchester Regt. Appendix VI	14/06/1917	14/06/1917
Heading	War Diary For 1st July To 31st July 1917 1/7th Bn. Manchester Regt. Vol VII		
War Diary	J.36.d.9.5	01/07/1917	07/07/1917
War Diary	Ytres	08/07/1917	08/07/1917
War Diary	Barastre	09/07/1917	09/07/1917
War Diary	Achiet Le Petit	10/07/1917	13/07/1917
War Diary	Camp At Achiet Le Petit	14/07/1917	14/07/1917
War Diary	Achiet Le Petit	15/07/1917	31/07/1917
Miscellaneous	Report On Raid 2nd /3rd July, 1917	02/07/1917	02/07/1917
Operation(al) Order(s)	127th Brigade Operation Order No. 31. Appendix I	01/07/1917	01/07/1917
Miscellaneous	Appendix "A" Artillery Programme. Appendix I		
Operation(al) Order(s)	Operation Orders by 2/Lt. a. Hodge. commanding No. 9. Platoon. Appendix I (b)		
Miscellaneous	Raid on Wigan Copse. Appendix I (C)	03/07/1917	03/07/1917
Miscellaneous	Raid On Wigan Copse. Appendix I	03/07/1917	03/07/1917
Miscellaneous	Appendix I		
Miscellaneous	Copy Of Routine Order No. 380. By Major General B. R.Mitford C.B., C.M.G., D.S.O. Appendix I		
Operation(al) Order(s)	Operation Order No. 19. Appendix II	07/07/1917	07/07/1917
Operation(al) Order(s)	Addendum To Operation Order No. 19	08/07/1917	08/07/1917
Miscellaneous	1/7th. Manchester Regt. Appendix III	13/07/1917	13/07/1917
Miscellaneous	Exercise No. 1. Ref. Map Bucquoy Scale 1:20,000. Fifth Army (B). Appendix IV	17/07/1917	17/07/1917
Heading	War Diary Of 1/7th Bn. Manchester Rgt. From 1st Aug 1917 To 31st Aug. 1917 Volume VIII.		
War Diary	Achiet Le Petit	01/08/1917	20/08/1917
War Diary	Bouzincourt	21/08/1917	22/08/1917
War Diary	Hopoutre L.15.b.9.1	23/08/1917	30/08/1917
War Diary	Brandhoek G.18.a.2.6	31/08/1917	31/08/1917
Miscellaneous	Battalion Orders By Lieut Col. A.E. Cronshaw., T.D. Appendix I	20/08/1917	20/08/1917
Operation(al) Order(s)	Operation Order No. 19 Appendix II	22/08/1917	22/08/1917
Miscellaneous	Battalion Orders By Lieut Colonel A.E. Cronshaw T.D. Appendix III	30/08/1917	30/08/1917
Miscellaneous			
Heading	War Diary 1/7th Bn. Manchester Regt. From 1st Sept. 1917. To 30th Sept 1917. Volume. IX.		

War Diary	Brandhoek E.18.a.2.6	01/09/1917	06/09/1917
War Diary	I.11.b.15.6 Bn. H.Q.	07/09/1917	08/09/1917
War Diary	I.6.b.5.12	09/09/1917	11/09/1917
War Diary	I.11.b.15.6	12/09/1917	14/09/1917
War Diary	Sheet 28 N.M 1:20,000	15/09/1917	15/09/1917
War Diary	Toronto Camp	16/09/1917	16/09/1917
War Diary	G.14.a.1.5	17/09/1917	18/09/1917
War Diary	L.15.b.6.4 Sheet 27	19/09/1917	19/09/1917
War Diary	J.4.b.7.6	20/09/1917	21/09/1917
War Diary	Coyyde	22/09/1917	24/09/1917
War Diary	R.27.c.3.3	24/09/1917	30/09/1917
Miscellaneous	Appendix II		
Miscellaneous	Appendix III		
Operation(al) Order(s)	Operation Order No. 25. Appendix I	07/09/1917	07/09/1917
Heading	War Diary Confidential Of 1/7th Manchester Regt. Period Oct. 1st To Oct 31st. 1917 Vol X		
War Diary	R.33.A.2.9 Middlesex Camp	01/10/1917	01/10/1917
War Diary	M.19.a.1.9 Left Sub Sector of Nieu Port Bains Area	02/10/1917	03/10/1917
War Diary	M.19.a.1.9	04/10/1917	06/10/1917
War Diary	La Panne	07/10/1917	19/10/1917
War Diary	Sheet 12 S.W. 1/20,000 Nieuport M.28.c.8.8	20/10/1917	24/10/1917
War Diary	M.28.b.5.2	25/10/1917	28/10/1917
War Diary	Redan [Nieuport	29/10/1917	31/10/1917
Operation(al) Order(s)	Operation Orders No. 39 Appendix I	02/10/1917	02/10/1917
Miscellaneous	Warning Order. Appendix I	01/10/1917	01/10/1917
Miscellaneous	Defence Orders. Appendix III		
Operation(al) Order(s)	Operation Order No. 40 Appendix IV	06/10/1917	06/10/1917
Miscellaneous	Move Order No. 41. Appendix V	19/10/1917	19/10/1917
Operation(al) Order(s)	Addenda To Move Order No. 41 Appendix V	19/10/1917	19/10/1917
Miscellaneous	Appendix VI		
Map	Appendix VII		
Map	Identification Trace For Use With Artillery Maps. Appendix III		
Heading	War Diary (Confidential) Of 1/7th Manchester Regiment Period Nov 1st To Nov. 30th 1917 Vol 10		
War Diary	Redan Nieuport	01/11/1917	01/11/1917
War Diary	M.28.b.5.2	02/11/1917	06/11/1917
War Diary	Canada Camp Coxyde	06/11/1917	16/11/1917
War Diary	Teteghem	17/11/1917	17/11/1917
War Diary	Esquelbecq	18/11/1917	18/11/1917
War Diary	Wemaers Cappel	19/11/1917	19/11/1917
War Diary	Wallon Cappel	20/11/1917	20/11/1917
War Diary	Mazinghem	21/11/1917	26/11/1917
War Diary	Oblinghem	27/11/1917	27/11/1917
War Diary	A.14.a.9.9	28/11/1917	30/11/1917
Operation(al) Order(s)	Operation Order No. 46. Nov. 15th. 1917	15/11/1917	15/11/1917
Operation(al) Order(s)	Operation Order No. 47. Nov. 16th. 1917	16/11/1917	16/11/1917
Operation(al) Order(s)	Operation Order No. 48	17/11/1917	17/11/1917
Operation(al) Order(s)	Operation Order No. 49	18/11/1917	18/11/1917
Operation(al) Order(s)	Operation Order No. 50	19/11/1917	19/11/1917
Operation(al) Order(s)	Operation Order No. 51	25/11/1917	25/11/1917
Operation(al) Order(s)	Operation Order No. 52	26/11/1917	26/11/1917
Heading	War Diary (Confidential) Of 1/7th Manchester Regt. Period Dec. 1st To Dec 31st. 1917. Volume 2		
War Diary	Givenchy A.14.a.9.9	01/12/1917	02/12/1917
War Diary	A.8.d.85.45	03/12/1917	08/12/1917

War Diary	Gorre	09/12/1917	14/12/1917
War Diary	A.8.d.85.45	15/12/1917	21/12/1917
War Diary	E.17.b.9.9.Bethune	22/12/1917	28/12/1917
War Diary	Ferme Du Roi E.6.C.7.4	29/12/1917	31/12/1917
Map	Appendix IX		
Miscellaneous	Givenchy Front Right Battalion Subsector. Appendix II	06/12/1917	06/12/1917
Miscellaneous	Report On Firetrench West Of The Craters. Appendix II		
Heading	War Diary (Confidential) Of 1/7th Bn. Manchester Rgt. Period January 1st To January 31st 1918 Volumn 1		
War Diary	Bethune	01/01/1918	02/01/1918
War Diary	Kingscllere A.I5.C.65.23	03/01/1918	08/01/1918
War Diary	Woburn Abbey A.20.b.8.3	09/01/1918	14/01/1918
War Diary	Kingsclere A.15.e.65.23	15/01/1918	21/01/1918
War Diary	Le Preol F.15.d.05.90	22/01/1918	28/01/1918
War Diary	Hingette	29/01/1918	31/01/1918
Map	Canal (4) Appendix I		
Heading	War Diary (Confidential) Of 1/7th Battalion Manchester Regt. Period 1st Feb.1918 To 28th Feb. 1918 Volume 2		
War Diary	Hingette	01/02/1918	12/02/1918
War Diary	Burbure	13/02/1918	28/02/1918
Heading	42nd Division 127th Infantry Brigade. 1/7th Battalion Manchester Regiment March 1918		
Heading	War Diary Confidential Of 1/7th Manchester Rgt. From 1st March 1918 To 31st March 1918 Vol III		
War Diary	Burbure	01/03/1918	03/03/1918
War Diary	Busnes	04/03/1918	21/03/1918
War Diary	L'Ecleme	22/03/1918	22/03/1918
War Diary	Ayette Lens 1/100,000	23/03/1918	23/03/1918
War Diary	800 Yds S. of Gomiecourt	24/03/1918	25/03/1918
War Diary	57D.N.E 1/20,000 Bn. HQ F.22.C.9.2	26/03/1918	26/03/1918
War Diary	F.22.E.9.2	26/03/1918	28/03/1918
War Diary	F.20.D. 1500 Yks N.W. Of Bucquoy	29/03/1918	31/03/1918
Heading	127th Inf. Bde. 42nd Div.1/7th Battn. The Manchester Regiment. April 1918		
Heading	War Diary No 4 Ape 1st 1918 To Ape 30th 1918. 17th Bn. Manchester Regt. Vol 15		
War Diary	F20 b and d	04/04/1918	04/04/1918
War Diary	F21, 22 & 27	05/04/1918	06/04/1918
War Diary	Gommecourt	01/04/1918	02/04/1918
War Diary	F20 b and d	03/04/1918	03/04/1918
War Diary	F22 & 23	07/04/1918	07/04/1918
War Diary	Vauehelles	08/04/1918	08/04/1918
War Diary	Louvencourt	09/04/1918	16/04/1918
War Diary	Hebuterne	17/04/1918	24/04/1918
War Diary	Jbd	25/04/1918	28/04/1918
War Diary	Gommecourt	29/04/1918	30/04/1918
Heading	War Diary (Confidential) Of 1/7th Battalion Manchester Regt. Period May 1st To May 31st 1918. Volume. 5		
War Diary	Gommecourt	01/05/1918	05/05/1918
War Diary	Henu	06/05/1918	31/05/1918
Heading	War Diary (Confidential) Of 1/7th Bn. Manchester Regiment. Period June 1st To June 1918 Volume 6		
War Diary	Henu	01/06/1918	06/06/1918
War Diary	Hebuterne	06/06/1918	14/06/1918
War Diary	Sailly Au Bois	15/06/1918	23/06/1918
War Diary	Colincamps	24/06/1918	30/06/1918

Type	Description	Date 1	Date 2
Map			
Miscellaneous	127th Infantry Brigade.	16/06/1918	16/06/1918
Operation(al) Order(s)	Operation Order No. 77	12/06/1918	12/06/1918
Operation(al) Order(s)	Corrigenda To Operation Order No. 77	12/06/1918	12/06/1918
Operation(al) Order(s)	Code Referred To In Operation Order No. 77 Issued To O.C Operations	11/06/1918	11/06/1918
Miscellaneous	Raid Orders For Centre Party Lieut Col. B"V" Manger Commanding "C" Battalion.	12/06/1918	12/06/1918
Miscellaneous	Raid Orders For Right Party By Lieut, Col. E.V. Manger Commanding "C" Battalion.	12/06/1918	12/06/1918
Miscellaneous	Raid Orders For Covering Party By Lieut. Col. E.V Manger Commanding "C" Battalion.	12/06/1918	12/06/1918
Miscellaneous	Raid Orders For Left Party By Lieut. Col. E.V. Manger Commanding "C" Battalion.	12/06/1918	12/06/1918
Miscellaneous	Artillery. T.M. And Machine Gun Barrage.	12/06/1918	12/06/1918
Miscellaneous	Appendix "A" Table Of Tasks For 18 Pounders.		
Miscellaneous	Appendix "B" Table Of Tasks For Howitzers.		
Miscellaneous	Copy Of Telegram Received From 127th. Brigade Dated 16.6.18	16/06/1918	16/06/1918
Miscellaneous	127th. Inf. Brigade.	16/06/1918	16/06/1918
Heading	War Diary Of 1/7th Battalion Manchester Regiment July 1st To July 31st 1918 Volume 7		
War Diary	Colincamps	01/07/1918	10/07/1918
War Diary	Bus	11/07/1918	18/07/1918
War Diary	Colincamps	19/07/1918	31/07/1918
Operation(al) Order(s)	C. 127 Operation Order No. 19	18/07/1918	18/07/1918
Operation(al) Order(s)	C 127 Operation Order No. 20	20/07/1918	20/07/1918
Miscellaneous	Report On Operation-July 19th. To 21st 1918. 1/7th. Bn. Manchester. Regt.	19/07/1918	19/07/1918
Miscellaneous	Copy of Congratulatory Messages From Brigadier General A. Henley Comdg. 127th. Brigade. (Acting G.O.C. 42nd. Div.)	20/07/1918	20/07/1918
Miscellaneous	127th. Inf. Brigade.	27/07/1918	27/07/1918
Miscellaneous	Copy Of Wire From 42nd Division	20/07/1918	20/07/1918
Miscellaneous	Copy Of Congratulatory Messages	31/07/1918	31/07/1918
Heading	War Diary (Confidential) Of 1/7th Bn. Manchesters. Period August. 1st 1918 To August 31st 1918 Volumn. 8		
Miscellaneous	1/7th Manchester Regt.	03/08/1918	03/08/1918
War Diary	Colincamps	01/08/1918	03/08/1918
War Diary	Louvencourt	04/08/1918	11/08/1918
War Diary	Collincamps	12/08/1918	31/08/1918
Map			
Map	Part Sheet 57d N.E.		
Operation(al) Order(s)	Operation Order 107	16/08/1918	16/08/1918
Heading	War Diary (Confidential) Of 17th Battalion Manchester Regt Period Sept 1st 1918 To Sept 30th 1918 Volumn 9		
War Diary		01/09/1918	17/09/1918
War Diary	M.5.a	18/09/1918	20/09/1918
War Diary	J.27.d	21/09/1918	30/09/1918
Miscellaneous	Adjutant Vege App. V		
Miscellaneous	App VI		
Miscellaneous	To Adjt C/124 App VII		
Miscellaneous	To Vege App VIII		
Miscellaneous	Reported B.C.T.D. For Information. App IX		
Miscellaneous	To Vege App. X		

Miscellaneous	O.C.A. B.C.D. Coys App XI		
Miscellaneous	Copy Of Order To C Avd D Coys "A" Battalion App XII		
Miscellaneous	7th. Bn. The Manchester Regt. App XIII		
Map	Part Of Sheet No. 57c Ne & Se Scale 1:20,000		
Miscellaneous	A Platoon In Line Appendix I		
Operation(al) Order(s)	Operation Order 69 No. By Officer Commanding C.U.B.	15/09/1918	15/09/1918
Miscellaneous	Tactical Demonstration		
Operation(al) Order(s)	Operation Order No. 72 By Commanding "C" Battalion, App III	26/09/1918	26/09/1918
Heading	War Diary (Confidential) Of 7th Bn. Manch. Rgt. Period Oct. 1st To Oct 31st 1918 Volumn 10		
War Diary		01/10/1918	21/10/1918
War Diary	Beaurois	22/10/1918	31/10/1918
Operation(al) Order(s)	7th Battalion Manchester Regiment. Operation Order No. 10. Appendix I	16/10/1918	16/10/1918
Operation(al) Order(s)	7th Bn. Manchester Regiment Operation Order No. 74. Appendix II		
Operation(al) Order(s)	Operation Order No. 74	19/10/1918	19/10/1918
Map	Part Of Sheet 57b Ne.		
Miscellaneous	Notes On Operation.	04/10/1918	04/10/1918
Miscellaneous	42nd (East Lancashire) Division.	21/09/1918	21/09/1918
Heading	War Diary (Confidential) Of 16th Bn. Manch. Rgt. Period Nov 1st To Novsolt 1918 Volumn 11		
War Diary	Beauvois	01/11/1918	04/11/1918
War Diary	M30	05/11/1918	06/11/1918
War Diary	Le Carnoy	07/11/1918	07/11/1918
War Diary	Vieux Mesnil	08/11/1918	12/11/1918
War Diary	Hautmont	13/11/1918	30/11/1918
Heading	War Diary (Confidential) Of 7th Bn Manch. Regt. Period Dec. 1st To 31st 1918 Volume 12		
War Diary	Hautmont	01/12/1918	14/12/1918
War Diary	Assevent	15/12/1918	15/12/1918
War Diary	Merbes Site Maielle	16/12/1918	16/12/1918
War Diary	Leval Trahegnies	17/12/1918	19/12/1918
War Diary	Fleurus	20/12/1918	31/01/1919
Heading	War Diary (Confidential) Of 7th Manchester. Regiment. Period. Feb. 1st To Feb. 28th Volume.2		
War Diary	Fleurus	01/02/1919	28/02/1919
Heading	War Diary 1/7th Manchester Regt. 1st-31st March 1919 Volume 3		
War Diary	Fleurus	01/03/1919	06/03/1919
War Diary	Charleroi	07/03/1919	28/03/1919
Map			

WO 95/2661
1/7 Manch. R
Mar '17 — Mar '19

WO 95/2661
1/7 Manch. R
Mar'17 – Mar'19

42ND DIVISION
127TH INFY BDE

1-7TH MANCHESTER REGT.
MAR 1917-MAR 1919

SECRET.

War Diary
of
1/7th MANCHESTER REGT

— VOL 3 —

MARCH 1ST 1917   TO

   MARCH 31ST 1917.

Mar '17
Mar '19

WAR DIARY or INTELLIGENCE SUMMARY

Army Form C. 2118

1/7th Bn Manchester Regt

Place	Date	Hour	Summary of Events and Information	Remarks and references to Appendices
MOASCAR	1/3/17		Battalion total strength officers 37, other ranks 970. Marching out strength officers 36, other ranks 918. The difference is principally accounted for by 2 Advance parties totalling 6 officers and 36 O.R. Beside these 3 officers and 6 other ranks are in 2 attached to Northern H.Q. (WOODWARD and M. NORBURY). Received orders to entrain tomorrow but	
	2/3/17		embark at ALEXANDRIA for S.S. KALYAN on 3rd. Camp struck & cleaned up. Bttn entrains & starts for ALEXANDRIA 1835. 8th Manchesters leave on train 1 hour later. Parties, F.A. &c on arrival more train. The last of the 42nd Div. leaves today. Entraining strength 25 officers, 878 O.R. 2 Lt. D. NORBURY and 5 O.R. go with horses, 36 O.R. sent to Base MUSTAPHA.	
ALEXANDRIA	3/3/17		Arrive 0140. Everyone embarked (S.S. KALYAN) by 0345. The 8th (D.+O.) Gunners, R.A.M.C. &c also embark same ship. 200 mules Coy. About 2000 troops on board. Ship sails about 1700 escorted by 2 destroyers. Ship very full. Everyone to wear life belts & keep them by them at night. Warm stormy afternoon.	g/c
"KALYAN" S.S.	4/3/17		Fine weather. 1600 Practise alarm turn out.	g/c
	5/3/17		No sign of submarines	g/c
	6/3/17		Another fine day. Practise turn out at 1045 & again 1700.	g/c

WAR DIARY / INTELLIGENCE SUMMARY

Army Form C. 2118

1/7 5th Bn. Manchester Regt

Place	Date	Hour	Summary of Events and Information	Remarks and references to Appendices
Tamba hills KATHAN	7/3/17		Turned windy & rough in afternoon; slanting destroyer had a bad time heading into the wind; steamer altered course to get wind behind.	gre
- " -	8/3/17		Wind & sea got up again in afternoon & evening; became very rough. The following figures refer to "other ranks" now present with Battn:—	
			1) Number who came out with Battn in 1914 231	
			2) No: of Para 1 who have never away from Battn .... 51 (none except on leave or on course)	
			3) No: of Para 1 who have been away once (wounded) 102	
			4) No: of Para 1 who have been away twice 77	
			5) Remainder of Para 1 who served in Gallipoli 190	
			6) No: of Para 5 who have been twice wounded 19	
			7) No: of Para 5 — do — — sick 90	gre
	9/3/17		Anchored in Gulf of MARSEILLES about 1145. Stayed on board all day. The whole Battn and some other "details" entrained in afternoon with 3 days Rations. Train	gre
From MARSEILLES Train	10/3/17		moved at 1736. Lt. Col. A.E. CRONSHAW C.B. from "Halte Repos" at ORANGE	gre
- " -	11/3/17		about 2330. Hot tea for battalion at all "Haltes Repos" en route.	gre
- " -	12/3/17		"Halte Repos" MACON, LES TUMES, LOUVRES. PONT REMY and detrained 1520. Battn marched about 7 miles S. JUVISY, LAROCHE, PONT REMY and detrained 1520. Battn marched about 7 miles S. & billeted at MERELESSART where it arrived about 2330 and goes into billets.	gre

ABBEVILLE 14 / 1
DIEPPE 16 / 150,000
2 A & D

Army Form C. 2118

WAR DIARY
of 1/7th Battn Manchester Regt
INTELLIGENCE SUMMARY
(Erase heading not required.)

Instructions regarding War Diaries and Intelligence Summaries are contained in F.S. Regs., Part II. and the Staff Manual respectively. Title Pages will be prepared in manuscript.

Place	Date	Hour	Summary of Events and Information	Remarks and references to Appendices
MERELESSART	13/3/17		Billets accommodation very fair. Bn. H.Q. at YONVILLE about 2 miles away. Other Battns of Brigade in villages at varying distances. Bn. Coy. fit, below est. on roll.	gre
	14/3/17		Received orders to move to LIERCOURT tomorrow. No time to settle down yet.	gre
LIERCOURT	15/3/17		Battn moved to LIERCOURT 0900 and arrived 1130. Accommodation not very good and billets scattered. Some entered into village of DUNEA. Battn is now in area of 125th Brigade which has been created by them. Lt. Col. C. CRENSHAW is Commandant of this area. Battn is now complete with 1st line transport. Battn drew rifles (Mark III*) bayonets, Aldershot helmets, box helmets and a second canister.	gre gre
	16/3/17			gre
	17/3/17		2nd Lt. L.G. HARRIS and 2 N.C.Ops proceed to FRIEVAL Grenade School. Lt. Col. A.E. CRENSHAW, Capt TINKER and RSM LUCAS in an order to front line trenches the 21/3/17. Major J.H. ALLAN takes over temporary command of Battn. Along with 5 officers & 11 O.R. officers Lt. MARSHALL 2/4th L.F. BURN 2/4. W.T. THORPE, 2/4. GRESTY and 2/4. WILKINSON	gre
	18/3/17		2/Lt A. HODGE and 2/Lt E. TAYLOR join Battn on 12.5.	gre
	19/3/17		Lt MARSHALL goes on 7 days leave to LYONS. Men progressing during week to course of training. 2/Lt. A. HODGE and 2/Lt E. TAYLOR arrived & FLIXECOURT for course of Rifle Grens. A.D.S.S. Commences hot baths Battn at HALLENCOURT.	gre gre

MAPS ABBEVILLE 1/40000
DIEPPE 1/60000

WAR DIARY

1/7th Batt'n Manchester Reg't

INTELLIGENCE SUMMARY
(Erase heading not required.)

Army Form C. 2118.

Place	Date	Hour	Summary of Events and Information	Remarks and references to Appendices
WERCOURT	20/3/17		2/Lt F.G. BURN proceeds to PARIS for 3 days on Signalling duty. M.O. C/O Lt. Musketry & Lt. Bayonet fighting proceed to School of Instruction MONTIGNY. Received Orders re of new attack formation (from trenches) used in France from G.H.Q.	
	21/3/17		Lt D. NORBURY, 2/Lt R. NORBURY, 2/Lt J.G. CHATTETON and 2/Lt L. TAYLOR and 391 O.R. proceed for 6 days instruction in Musketry to School PONT REMY.	
	22/3/17		Lt Col A.E. CRONSHAW, 2nd/Lt A.R. TINKER and party return from Front Line and Lt Col CRONSHAW assumes command of Bath. Cold weather and snow.	
	23/3/17		2/Lt F.G. BURN returns. Gen Marjorie, Gen V. ORMSBY C.B. and to have a both at the Bath and L. Brigade Major, Capt S. TUITE DALTON, also Staff Capt, Capt W.T. WOODS. Frost & snow very bad.	
	24/3/17		Lessons & organization of new formation continue. 6th formation of Platoon, are now brought up to a large extent. See Appendix I. At 11 p.m. clocks were advanced to summer time.	I
	25/3/17		Had frost cold. Two NCOs proceeded on GAS course to MONTIGNY. 7 O.R. (the first party to leave France) went to ENGLAND on leave for 10 days. Weather as yesterday.	MTB.
	26/3/17		Capt T.R. CRENSH proceeded to 127 Bde HQ to relieve the Brigade Major, 2/Lt M.H. BARRATT appointed acting Adjutant in his absence. 2/Lt W.T. THORP and batman went on Lewis Gun course to ETAPLES. 2 NCOs arrived and gave recruits Demonstration on use of the P.H. Helmet. Lt Col A.E. CRONSHAW gave	MTB

MAPS ABBEVILLE 14 } 1:100,000.
DIEPPE 16
FRANCE 62C 1:40,000.

WAR DIARY
or
INTELLIGENCE SUMMARY.
(Erase heading not required.)

1/7th Batt.
of Manchester Regt

Army Form C. 2118.

Place	Date	Hour	Summary of Events and Information	Remarks and references to Appendices
LIERCOURT	26/3/17		A Lecture to Officers Kept on "Preparation for Active Operations." Wet and milder.	MB
	27/3/17		Capt MIDD went to MONTIGNY on a Course re "New Formations." 2/Lt HEATHCOTE-HACKER and NCO went on General Course to FLIXECOURT. The Maj Gen'l Comm'g 6's Division attended Rgt Gen'l B.R. MITFORD. C.B. DSO. called to inspect the Batt'n during training. Wet and bleak.	MB
	28/3/17		1st Line Transport moved out at 9.am Capt. WARD JONES in charge of Adv. Column 2/Lt T.C. CHATTERTON and 7 O.R. left for leave to England. 2/Lt R.T.R. BAKER followed with Train Transport to join M Line. Batt'n moved from HERCOURT by rail to CHUIGNES. Left 8.35 am — arrived 1.30 p.m. Marched 5 miles	MB
	29/3/17		village of DOMPIERRE. Bad quarters they took on arrival. Heavy baggage right through on motor lorries by road. 2/Lt JESSOP remained behind to clear up Billeting etc with 2 O.R. Men for next returning.	MB
DOMPIERRE	30/3/17		2/Lt H.R. KAY proceeded to 42nd Div. School MONTIGNY. M Line Transport. Capt MARD JONES and 2/Lt R.T.R. BAKER arrived about 4 p.m. Parties for right outside the village. Still stormy centre.	MB
	31/3/17		Capt TOWNSON left for III Corps School. Coy Comm'rs 7 days course. 2/Lt T.C. MORTEN took over the duties of Imm Major at HERBECOURT. 3 Coys went out road making. 2/Lt TAYLOR appointed temporarily as Transport Officer. 10 O.R. reinforcements arrived from Egypt.	MB

A. Gorman
LIEUT-COLONEL
COMMANDING 7TH BATT'N MANCHESTER REGT.

APPENDIX I.

PRECIS of O.B. 1919.

ORGANISATION OF INFANTRY BATTALION.

(I) BATTALION. H.Q.
  and 4 Companies
    of 4 Platoons
      of 4 Sections.

Personnel additional to War Establishment attached to Battn. H.Q. for administrative duties will be temporarily detached from Companies but remain on establishment of Companies for accounting purposes.

A H.Q. Coy. as such will not be formed.

This personnel of Battn H.Q. is divided into fighting portion and administrative portions. The former will be grouped into sections, each under a Commander.

(II) COMPANY. — H.Q. not to exceed 14 other Ranks composed entirely of fighting troops formed as a section under a Commander.

(III) PLATOON — The minimum strength of a platoon will not be allowed to fall below 28 and the maximum strength will normally not exceed 44 other ranks.

Platoon H.Q. will not exceed 4 other ranks.

The composition of sections is given in S.S. 144.

(IV) If casualties reduce the strength of platoons below 28, the necessary numbers will be obtained by temporary amalgamation of Companies or Platoons or Sections in the Company.

(V) BATTALION H.Q.

FIGHTING PORTION.	ADMINISTRATIVE PORTION
Sergt. Major.	Q.M.S.
Clerks.	C.Q.M.S.
Gas Personnel.	Storemen
Signallers	Transport Estb.
Runners	Shoemakers.
Pioneers	Tailors
Stretcher Bearers.	Butchers
Cooks.	Cooks.
Batmen.	Grooms.
	Batmen
	Instructional Estb.
not to exceed 70.	not to exceed 80.

Establishment of Battalion — 971 other ranks.

Battn Hdqrs.	FIGHTING.	ADMINIS-TRATIVE.	FIGHTING.	ADMINISTRATIVE
Fighting Portion	70.		70	
Administrative "		80		80
4 Coys. H.Q. at 14	56.		56	
16 Platoons at 44	704		at 28. 448	
Sicks, extra regt'l employ and other non-effectives.		61		317.
	830	141	574	397.

The above figures include those who must be left behind when the Battn. takes part in an attack.

Original

Vol 3

CONFIDENTIAL —

WAR DIARY
OF
1/7th MANCHESTER REGT

From — APRIL 1st 1917   To — APRIL 30th 1917

VOL. IV

WAR FRANCE. 62C. 1:40000.

1/7th Battalion
of
Manchester Regt.

Army Form C. 2118.

Original

WAR DIARY
INTELLIGENCE SUMMARY.
(Erase heading not required.)

Instructions regarding War Diaries and Intelligence Summaries are contained in F.S. Regs., Part II. and the Staff Manual respectively. Title pages will be prepared in manuscript.

Place	Date	Hour	Summary of Events and Information	Remarks and references to Appendices
DOM PIERRE	1/4/17		Capt A.T. WARD JONES appointed Bgde Transport Officer, by previous orders of the G.O.C. 2/Lt B.G. TAYLOR appointed as T.O (Temp). 2/Lt R.J.R. BAKER and 25 O.R. attached to 429th F.C. R.E. for instruction. The whole Batt'n proceeded to Dist'd Enghoshoe to have new Box Respirators fitted and tested. MMB. Lt. T. SIVEWRIGHT arrived from the base and taken on the strength.	
	2/4/17		2/Lt S.T. WILSON and 69 O.R. went to PORT REMY Musketry Camp, proceeding by barge. Capt H.H. MIDD rets from MONTIGNY Schools. 2/Lt G. JESSOP rejoins having completed the work of Rear party, Billeting Officer at LIERCOURT. 47 O.R. arrived from the base. 2/Lts M. BATEMAN and G.H. FRANKLIN arrives from leave to England. 2 O.R. went to Batam's.	MMB
	3/4/17		3 Coys occupied on road repairing, between HERBECOURT and BIACHES. 8 O.R. left for leave to England. 2/Lt G.H. FRANKLIN appointed Transport Officer.	MMB
	4/4/17		2/Lt C.S. MOOD proceeds as Town Major to MERICOURT. 2/Lt M.T. THORP returned from Course at LE TOUQUET. The Sergeant Leytherne as in force in 42 SD Div. is adopted for all working parties and futilities. Details as per attached appendix I.	APPENDIX I MMB.
	5/4/17		The whole Batt'n on road making. Capt C.E. HAHAM went on 3 weeks Officers leave to England.	MMB.
	6/4/17		The whole Batt'n on road making. Capt A.H. TINKER went on Stamp Course to MONTIGNY. Capt E. TOMSON returned from the Stamp Course at MONTIGNY.	MMB.
	7/4/17		Maj. J. SCOTT and 19 O.R. went on 10 days leave to England. 2/Lt G. JESSOP a.D. 11 O.R. went on 2 wks lve. Bombing Course to Dist. School at MERICOURT. 2/Lt F. GREY BURY appt. B.G.Q.M. Ordees rec'd to move at once to PERONNE. Main body moved of at 9.30 a.m. 1 hire Transport of.	MMB
	8/4/17	10.40 a.m.	Rear party to bring rest of baggage release 2/Lt M.T. THORP R. left behind under 2/Lt M.T. THORP. Rear party to England arrived back to march to PERONNE. Main body + Rhine T arrives at 2.45 p.m. and Billeted at FARM COURT. Good Billeting + well concentrated. Weather good.	MMB
PERONNE	9/4/17		The whole Batt'n went to LA CHAPPELLETTE on railway work. Communication established with Bgde Through P.S. Rifle. 2/Lt T.R. WILKINSON + 2 O.R. ret'd from Telescopic Sight Schools. Weather good.	MMB
	10/4/17		The railway work was discontinued and fund repairing carried on under the C.R.E. of the Div'n. 2/Lt T.C. CHATTERTON ret's from leave in England.	MMB.

1577 Wt. W10791/1773 500,000 1/15 D. D. & L. A.D.S.S/Forms/C. 2118.

MAP. FRANCE 1:40000. 62C.

Army Form C. 2118.

WAR DIARY of 1/7 Battalion MANCHESTER REGT.
INTELLIGENCE SUMMARY.
(Erase heading not required.)

Instructions regarding War Diaries and Intelligence Summaries are contained in F.S. Regs., Part II. and the Staff Manual respectively. Title pages will be prepared in manuscript.

Place	Date	Hour	Summary of Events and Information	Remarks and references to Appendices
PERONNE	11/4/17		Batt's place on board refraining. 2/Lt T.BAKER and 19 O.R. went on leave to England. Night working parties commenced. Hours 6670 and 10 to 2am. 2/Lt C.R.THORPE arrived from England and fallen on the strength accordingly.	MRB
	12/4/17		Routine as usual, including night work. Lt J.T. MARSHALL Maximum proceeded to III Corps School. 2/Lt H.N.KAY rett from 42nd Div School.	MRB
	13/4/17		MONTIGNY and Capt A.H. TINKER rett from Same School. 2/Lt C.S. WOOD returned from MERICOURT having handed over the duties of Town Major there.	MRB
	14/4/17		Routine as usual, without night work. 2/Lt S.T.MILSON and 69 O.R. returned from Musketry and Lewis Gun Courses commenced for Bombers, Rifle Grenadiers & Bayonet Fighters at PONT REMY.	APPENDIX II MRB
	15/4/17		Smaller working parties for the morning, but Herschele Batts out on route training in the afternoon. Capt A.H. NIDD and 19 O.R. Proceeded to England on Leave. 2/Lt J.C.CHATTERTON H1. NCO to Glag Course to Div: School MERICOURT. A Sprcins demonstration of the Platoon in new attack formation, given by a Platoon of 126 15 Regt. All batts available went to witness the demonstration. Lt. Col A.E.CRONSHAW and Capt E.TOMSON went with a 127 Bgde party to make a reconnaissance forward address same night.	MRB
	16/4/17.		Batts work over work on 60cm railway at BIACHES. (2½ Corps) Remainder on embroidering Stores etc. Bad weather. Snowing and wet.	MRB
	17/4/17.		Same routine as for previous day. 2/Lt J.C.CHATTERTON rett from Course to Bri. School. Lt W.T. SIVEWRIGHT went on Lewis Course 15 MONTIGNY.	MRB MRB.
	18/4/17		Same as for previous day. Lt J.MARSHALL rett from MONTIGNY.	MRB.
	19/4/17		Routine same as for previous day. 2/Lt T.P.WILKINSON and 16 O.R. proceeded to England on leave. Special new list of Promanent Employed Men handed in to Bgde for the confirmation of the Q.C.C. Details as per Appendix III attached.	Appendix III MRB.

MAP. FRANCE. 1:40000 Sheet 62C.
1:20000
57C. SE
62C. NE

Instructions regarding War Diaries and Intelligence Summaries are contained in F.S. Regs., Part II. and the Staff Manual respectively. Title Pages will be prepared in manuscript.

3

WAR DIARY
or
INTELLIGENCE SUMMARY
(Erase heading not required.)

of The 1/7th Battalion
of Manchester Regt.

Army Form C. 2118

Place	Date	Hour	Summary of Events and Information	Remarks and references to Appendices
PERONNE	20/4/17		Routine same as for previous day. 7 O.R. arrived from Base and sent to their Coys.	MHB.
	21/4/17		Routine Same as for previous day. Lt. W.J. SIVEWRIGHT returned from MONTIGNY School.	MHB.
	22/4/17		Routine same as for previous day. 2/Lt. C.R.THORPE and 1 R.S. Section proceeded to Divl. Bombing School MERICOURT. 2/Lt. G. JESSOP & Bombing Section returned from Same School. 2/Lt. J.C. CHATTERTON returned from 42nd Divl. Gas School. MERICOURT. Instructions for Special Training for Coming week issued in orders. Lovely fine day. Revd E.C. HOSKYNS & 21 O.R. proceeded England on Special Leave.	MHB.
	23/4/17		Instructions for training cancelled Monthly Janker activities. All ranks arrayed 7.30 am no punishments. 2/Lt. H.MCKAY and 76 O.R. proceeded to England on Leave.	MHB.
	24/4/17		Whole Batt: roadmaking. 2/Lt. J. BAKER returned from Leave.	MHB.
	25/4/17		Routine same as for previous day. 30 O.R. allowed for 12 hours 48 min to Kosher hour.	MHB.
	26/4/17		Pte J. GIBSON of C Coy accidentally killed whilst working near BIACHES. 150 O.R. returned from leave. Routine same as for previous day. 2/Lt. J. Batto again allowed Leave for 2 hours. Funeral of Pte GIBSON at 11-30 at I.21.d.5.1. Advance Party of Movement to the Line received. The Commanding Officer Lt. Col. A.E. CRONSHAW went forward to reconnoitre the line portion of it to be occupied by the Batt.	MHB
	27/4/17		The Batt: moved up from FLAMICOURT to VILLERS FAUCON by route march via LONGAVESNES. Head of column moved off at 9.30am and arrived at destination 1.10 p.m. where billets were occupied. Capt. TINKER. Lt. MARSHALL. 2/Lt. T. BAKER. and 2/Lt. G. JESSOP and 4 Signallers went up to the line - leaving at 6.45 p.m. to join at guides of the 4th Seaforth Regt at EPEHY. In this area the Batt: is under the administration of the 126th Brigade. The M.T. Line Transport accompanied the Batt: on the march, and brought up to authorised loads in addition 2 M.T. Lorries and 2 G.S. wagons were allotted. These brought up Blankets. Officers Kits + Spare Baggage.	MHB

1875 Wt. W593/825 1,000,000 4/15 J.B.C. & A.   A.D.S.S./Forms/C. 2118.

MAPS. FRANCE. 1:20000
62 C

WAR DIARY of 1/7th Battalion MANCHESTER REGT.
INTELLIGENCE SUMMARY

Army Form C. 2118.

Place	Date	Hour	Summary of Events and Information	Remarks and references to Appendices
VILLERS FAUCON	27/4/17		Capt G. O'CONNELL (RAMC) 1140 R proceeded to England on leave. 3 NCO² proceeded to England on instructions from War Office to take Commissions. They are struck off the strength. A temporary dump was left at FLAMICOURT in charge of a NCO and 3 men, spare baggage & S.A.A. left behind. The late Purkins. Capt HANNIGAN (RAMC) reported to relieve Capt CONNELL and accompanied the Batta forward. Weather fine.	
	28/4/17 Day		The day was spent in preparing for going up to the Line. The Batt⁰ marched out by platoons at 50 y distance. at 7.30 pm enroute for EPEHY to the H.Q. of the 4th Seaforths Regt to carry out relief. Order of march A.C. B.C. D. ready to take up posts in Red area. Guides for platoons picked at EPEHY and corp taken to B Coys and thence to the posts. Disposition — A Co Left Outpost Coy. C Co Right Outpost Coy B Co in support at 13 Coys. D Co in reserve at EPEHY.	
	28/29 Night		Rear H.Q₁s left behind at VILLERS FAUCON. Forward H.Q₁s at EPEHY. Relief completed and everything taken over by 1 am. Night work to be consolidation and general extension and improvement of the trenches. Day work. Practically impossible. It was found that extra tools were wanted for the work. The following forts were in telephonic communication with forward H.Q. A C⁰. B C⁰. and C C⁰. and though an HQs to the Bgde. An ammunition stores dump was taken over and also similar small dumps in the trenches. Weather – fine. Between 2 and 4 am the enemy shelled EPEHY heavily, but otherwise there was nothing of note. at 4 am Situation NORMAL arrived from the posts in the line. Map indicating the posts taken over is marked and attached.	Appendix II M.8

MAPS.
1:20000.
62 C. NE
57 C. SE

FRANCE

Army Form C. 2118.

WAR DIARY of 1/7th Battalion
of MANCHESTER REGT.
INTELLIGENCE SUMMARY.
(Erase heading not required.)

Instructions regarding War Diaries and Intelligence Summaries are contained in F. S. Regs., Part II. and the Staff Manual respectively. Title pages will be prepared in manuscript.

Place	Date	Hour	Summary of Events and Information	Remarks and references to Appendices
EPEHY.	29/4/17		The Enemy shelled the road from EPEHY to ST EMILIE regularly between 8.30 am and 11 am; also EPEHY with heavy guns, probably 5.9in. Map Reference F.1.C.&.B. During ━━━ to night Rations & bombs were sent up to 13 Copse & at 9 pm for distribution. Commencing at 9 pm the following reliefs were carried out in 17th Batt. - B Co. relieved A. at CATELET COPSE. A relieved D in reserve. C relieved B at 12 and 9 Copse. D relieved C at LITTLE PRIEL FARM. Relief completed at midnight and everything quiet. Weather fine. 4 pm Shrapnel NORMAL. In the early morning there was a burst of shelling over the Brigade front, which lasted only a short time. Enemy aerial activity very considerable up to noon. Aircraft apparently attempting to locate a 60p. Battery. Heavy guns commenced shelling to find the battery in the afternoon but without success. Arrangements made for a relief by the 15th MANCHESTERS to commence at 9 pm. Guides provided at 13 Copse at 9 pm, and all troops in their new quarters. Relief completed arriving two days in the line. 2 killed, 2 wounded. Strength of Batt: on going up to the line - Officers 38 OR. 979	MTB
	30/4/17		There was a considerable difficulty in getting and good and coprious supply of water for cooking & drinking. 6 villages were visited and not one could supply enough for 6 carts for them. There is a great demand on the water resources of the district. Operations whilst in the line - NIL MOR. - Consolidation and improvement - principally in sanitary arrangement. MTB.	MTB

A. Cronshaw
LIEUT.-COLONEL
COMMANDING 7TH BATTN MANCHESTER REGT.

Appendix I. April 1917

To. H.Q.
    127th Brigade.

1.   Re Divisional and Brigade Orders for organising working parties in Groups, the engineer requirements of the work need not interfere with the Group organisation.

2.   If parties have to be worked in twos and threes one group can comprise several such small parties. On the other hand if 20 or 30 men have to work together on a job where no sub-division is possible, e.g. extracting a heavy piece of wreckage, the requisite number of Groups can be combined for the job.

3.   It is suggested that where, say, a platoon provides 10. 12, or 14, men, it is preferable to divide it into two groups of less than 8 each, rather than keep it in one Group exceeding 8.

    This seems the spirit of the Group System, viz. the delegation of authority to as many junior N.C.Os and senior soldiers as possible.

                              (sgd)   E.M.Mozley
                                       Lt.Col. R.E.
                                  C.R.E. 42nd. Division.

50th.Div.No.G.X.3406/19.

149th.Inf.Brigade.
150th.Inf.Brigade.
151st.Inf.Brigade.
C.R.E.

Appendix I April 1917

In future all working parties will be detailed as so many groups.

Each group will consist of one N.C.O. or senior soldier and 8 men.

Multiples of three groups will be accompanied by one Officer or senior N.C.O., who will be in charge of the whole party.

e.g. 3 groups- 1 officer or senior N.C.O.,3 N.C.O's,24 men.

9 groups- 3 officers or senior N.C.O's,9 N.C.Os,72 men.

Before leaving billets, groups will be numbered off so that on arrival the officer organising the work can call upon groups by number and put them on their work at once.

Multiples of 12 groups will have one additional officer or senior N.C.O.

e.g. 12 groups- 5 officers,12 N.C.Os,96 men.

C.R.E. and Brigades will please report in due course if this system is an assistance in the organisation of work.

Any other suggestions should be submitted at the same time.

(sd) H.KARSLAKE.
Lt.Col. G.S.
50th.Division.

24th.Feb.1917.

APPENDIX ii.

April 1917

SPECIAL TRAINING

SIGNALLERS:- Under 2/Lt.M.BATEMAN as for Saturday last, all Headquarters and Company Signallers for duty and training of new men.

BAYONET
FIGHTING. :- Two N.C.O's per Company will parade outside Orderly Room at 9-15 a.m. to carry on training under the Bayonet Fighting Officer. *For instructional purposes*

RIFLE
GRENADE :- The Section Commanders of Rifle Grenade Sections will parade for training under the Rifle Grenade Officer.

BOMBERS :- The same instructions apply here as for Rifle Grenadiers.

GAS :- The first hour will be devoted to Gas instructions, demonstration and training in such duties. *for all these Classes.*

The following Instructors will parade outside Orderly Room at 9-15 a.m. tomorrow.

Bayonet Fighting Officer.   2/Lt. A. HODGE.
N.C.O. Instructor.   Sergt. A. BAINES. (277052)
Rifle Grenade N.C.O. Instructor.   L/Sgt. J. STOTT (275534)
Bombing N.C.O. Instructor   Corpl. E. REYNOLDS (276041)
Gas N.C.O. Instructor   Sergt. W. STAINSBY (275500)
Assistant Instructor   Corpl. J. BASNETT (275067)

14/4/17

W. H. Barratt Lieut
ADJUTANT. 7TH. BATTN. MANCHESTER REGT

Appendix III   April 1917

PERMANENT REGIMENTAL EMPLOY.

	Numbers		Remarks.
	Sergt.	O.R.	
Transport.	1	43.	Includes 6 grooms.
Cooks.	1	10	4 Companies & Headqrs.
Battn.Q.M.Stores.)		4	Asst.R.Q.M.S. & Q.M's Clerk.
R.Q.M.S.)	1		
Coy.Q.M.S.	4.		
Butchers.		1.	
Shoemakers	1	3	
Tailors		3	
Sanitary Squad.		10	Necessary in so large an area.
Pioneers	1	10	Includes 2 Cold shoers.
R.A.M.C.	1	4	
Battn.Orderly Room Clerk.	1	2	
Runners		4	
Provost Sergt.)	1		
Police)		7	
Armourer Sergt.		1	
P.R.I.		3	Chiefly for canteen.
Signal Office	1	6	
Post man		1	
Officers Mess		6.	
Batmen		6.	
M.O's Orderly		1	
Battn.Guard		5.	
Battn.Orderly Sergt	1		
" " Corpl.	1		
Company Storemen		4	
Mess Sergt.	1		
Gas Instructor)	1		When classes
Bombing Sergt)	1		
Lewis Gun Sergt)	1		are held.
Coy.Orderly Sergt.or Corpl.	4.		
Company Clerks.		4.	

(Regimental Institute -1 man-
when such Institute is
available)

| Total. | 21. | 142. |

19/4/17.

Lieut.Colonel.
Commanding 1/7th.Manchester Regt.

Appendix IV
April 1917.

FRANCE.

Map 1:20000.
57C.SE.
62C.NE

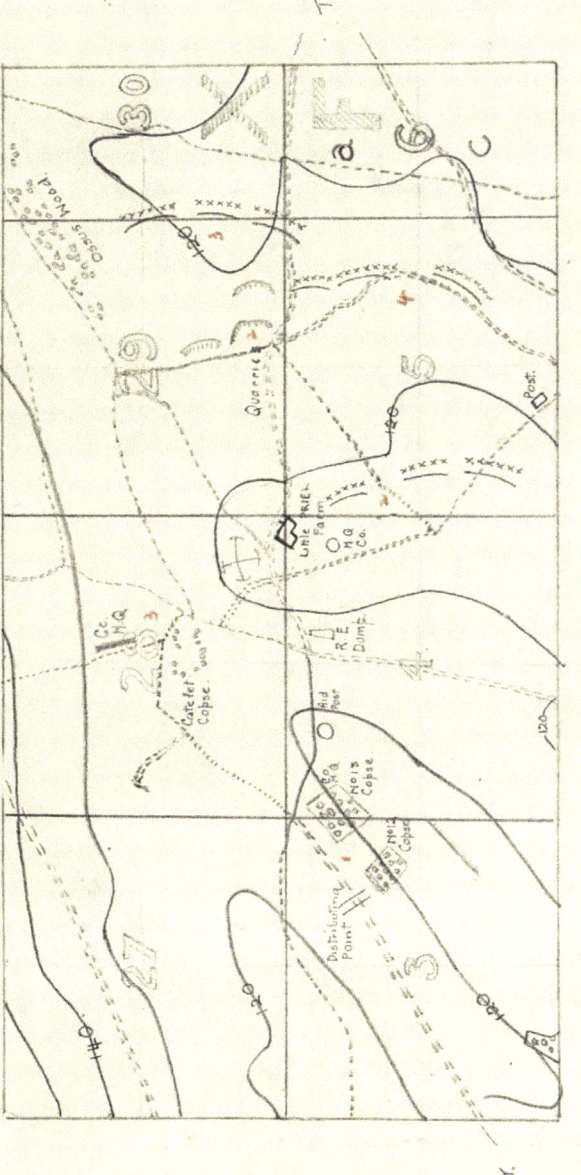

No 1 Support Post
  2   Right Outpost
  3   Left   "
  4   Forward Trenches under construction.

CONFIDENTIAL

WAR DIARY

OF

1/7th Bn. MANCHESTER RGT.

FOR

MAY - 1917.

VOLUMNE

V.

MAPS. FRANCE.
1:20,000. 62C. NE
57C. SE

Instructions regarding War Diaries and Intelligence
Summaries are contained in F. S. Regs., Part II.
and the Staff Manual respectively. Title pages
will be prepared in manuscript.

WAR DIARY of 1/7th Battalion
MANCHESTER REGT
(Erase heading not required.)

Army Form C. 2118.

INTELLIGENCE SUMMARY

Place	Date	Hour	Summary of Events and Information	Remarks and references to Appendices
EPEHY & IN TRENCHES	1/5/17		Strength of Battalion Officers 38 O.R. 975. The Battn. having been relieved in the trenches, came into Reserve and spent the day immediately after relief was great with practically no shelling or rifle fire. The enemy however still continued to make use of gas shells. About 9 am enemy heavy guns commenced shelling EPEHY and completely destroyed the HQrs of a Battn there. Shelling continued at 11 am. The trench was directed at a 60 pr Battery in position at F.1.c.4.5. Remainder of the day was quiet. Aerial activity was not so great as on the previous day. There is police considerable difficulty in getting men properly 2/Lt C.S. WOOD and 16 O.R. proceeded to Sylvand on leave. Capt H.H. WOD returned from leave and joined his Coy. Sgts BURGESS and O'CALLAGHAN proceeded to new HQrs for interview by the G.O.C. prior to being to England as Cadets for Commissions. At night 3 Coys went forward with all tools to commence work on the GREEN LINE WORK was from LITTLE PRIEL FARM to cruciform post at X.28.d.7.3. and then N.W. towards CATELET COPSE. Hours of work 9.30 p.m. to 1.30 a.m. and 360 men engaged. Progress 200 x of new trench made practically complete to 3 ft 6 in deep. 1 Coy as carrying party. R.E. materiel. During a tour of inspection of the front line posts at about 11:30 pm Brig Genl V.A. ORMSBY, C.B. the G.O.C. 127 Bde was wounded in the neck with shrapnel and expired in about 5 minutes.	
	2/5/17		The day was spent in refitting and preparing for relief of 1/5 MANCHESTERS in the front line at night. Special instructions as contained in Appendix I were issued in the form of Operation Order No 1. with some additions. Extra tools for carrying in the construction work in trenches were drawn. Many more fields than were being prepared. The intelligence officer completed the O.C. D211 How Battery at F.7 & 6.8 regarding a target on the road to TENDWILLE and in front of our left outpost Coy at (F.6 was a (Road defences) also the presence of minnenwerfer German trenches situated in X.30.c. It was intended and arranged to engage these targets.	Appendix I

* if opportunity presented itself. Transport had been
fired on the road the previous night.

MAPS. FRANCE.
1:20,000 62c NE
        57c SE

Instructions regarding War Diaries and Intelligence Summaries are contained in F.S. Regs., Part II. and the Staff Manual respectively. Title pages will be prepared in manuscript.

Army Form C. 2118.

WAR DIARY of 1/7 Battalion
MANCHESTER REGT.
or INTELLIGENCE SUMMARY.
(Erase heading not required.)

Place	Date	Hour	Summary of Events and Information	Remarks and references to Appendices
EPEHY & IN TRENCHES	2/5/17		Battn commenced relief of the MANCHESTERS at 9.0 p.m. and completed same at 1 a.m. The situation at 4 a.m. was NORMAL. Work during the night of relief was consolidation and sinking of trenches. MOR on the GREEN LINE was also continued. Casualties. 1 wounded. Weather fine & warm.	M/13
	3/5/17		Battalion holding the line. Situation NORMAL. Enemy shelling very slight. For the most part the day was quiet and nothing of note occurred. At 9.15 our guns in front of the Corps area opened a very heavy bombardment and kept it up until 11.20 pm. The enemy then commenced a counter bombardment which gradually died out towards 1 am. There was nothing abnormal on our front and no heavy shelling. Capt E. TOWNSON and 16 O.R. proceeded to England on leave. Weather fine in morning, frost at night for a few hours.	M/18
	4/5/17		Enemy Aircraft very active during the morning between 9 and 10 am. The 175th Bge. FA. one of our right rear left outpost got into touch with our right at TOMBOYS FARM, Report Battalion at dusk. Forenoon quiet. Preparation made and orders issued completed for Coy. relief which takes place at night. During the early morning the enemy shelled PILLERS FAUCON and put round 4 (Rounds) in the village. Time 1-20 am. Afterwards the night was quiet. Operations NIL. Casualties 2 killed in PILLERS FAUCON. Wounded in the arm. Brigade fair.	M/18
	5/5/17		The Battn holding the line and working at night on the support line as known as Porride in accordance with orders as issued in Appendix I. Very good progress being made and good posts being prepared for occupation. The day passed quietly and there was nothing of note. On the left of the Corps boundary a heavy bombardment began at 11-20 pm and continued for 2 hours. Both our and enemy artillery taking part. There was nothing else of importance. There being practically no reply.	M/18
	6/5/17		Operations NIL. Casualties NIL. Weather fine in day & frost at 6.30 pm 8.12. midnight M/18 Battn holding the line. The morning was fine and quiet again. Our patrols do not come in actual contact with the enemy. He seems to be holding his outpost line very thinly and does not appear very confident.	

(A7909). Wt. W12859/M1293 750,000. 1/17. D. D. & L., Ltd. Forms/C.2118.14.

MAPS. FRANCE
1:20.000 62C.NE
57C.SE

WAR DIARY of 17th Battalion
of MANCHESTER REGT

INTELLIGENCE SUMMARY.
(Erase heading not required.)

Army Form C. 2118.

Place	Date	Hour	Summary of Events and Information	Remarks and references to Appendices
EPEHY & IN TRENCHES	6/5/17		4 NCOs proceeded to England for temp: commissions. 1 NCO on leave to proceed to 38 Parliament St. London for the same purpose. These 5 are latter of the Batty.K According to Bus: Res. 1. The Hon. A.M. HENLEY. DSO. assumed command of the 127 Bgde. The enemy dropped 6 shots close to the Bn's Battery at F.1.C.35 – between 9 and 9-30 p.m. Bn HQrs (London) moved from F.1.C.45 to F.1.d.79 (under instructions from the GOC of 127 Bgde. Move complete at 10 p.m. Also F.1.c.61. The Bn's were relieved by 15th MANCH Regt. Relief commenced at 11/35 am situation NORMAL. Operations NIL. Casualties 3 killed. Weather fine.	Appendix II NIL.
	7/5/17		Bn's given time for rest and cleaning during the morning and afternoon. 3 Corp sent out wiring parties under the R.E. at 13.45 pm at 9 p.m. The day time quiet and fine. Night neb and dull. Went dangerous. Casualties NIL.	NIL.
	8/5/17		Under Bde orders No. 10, the Battn's was ordered to move out. 2 Corp to VILLERS FAUCON and 2 Corp to VILLERS FAUCON Move complete by 11 pm Casualties NIL. Weather fine but cloudy.	Appendix III NIL.
VILLERS FAUCON & IN TRENCHES	9/5/17		2 Corp of the Bn at VILLERS FAUCON proceeded to the Right sector to relieve 2 corps of 17th Lancs Fusiliers. Relief complete by 2 p.m. Remaining 2 corp returns the BROWN LINE in the left sector. They were relieved at 9 p.m. by 2 corps of the 18th MANCH. Regt. Capt C.E. HIGHAM and 2/Lt H.N.KAY returned from leave. 2/Lt J.C. MORTEN ret'd from hospital as Town Major at FLAUCOURT. CASUALTIES. NIL. Weather fine and warm. 2 Corp HQ situated the Brown Line (Right sector) & in reserve at VILLERS FAUCON. Orders received at a Conference of C.Os at Bgde. HQ that the remaining 2 Corp in reserve are to move up to Quarries in F.27. All army operators have ceased. Report situation at 9-30 am Quiet day fine. Week of relief minor 11pm. Casualties NIL.	Appendix III NIL.
	10/5/17			NIL.

4

MAPS, FRANCE
1:20000
62cNE. 57C.SE.

WAR DIARY of 1/7th Battalion MANCHESTER REGT

INTELLIGENCE SUMMARY.

Army Form C. 2118.

(Erase heading not required.)

Instructions regarding War Diaries and Intelligence Summaries are contained in F.S. Regs., Part II. and the Staff Manual respectively. Title pages will be prepared in manuscript.

Place	Date	Hour	Summary of Events and Information	Remarks and references to Appendices
VILLERS FAUCON & IN TRENCHES	11/5/17		2 Coys still in reserve on the BROWN LINE. The other 2 Coys moved up to new quarters in the Quarries in F.27. at 9-30 a.m. to be near the work being done under the R.E. Move complete at 11-30 a.m. The 4 Coys worked on night work under R.E. digging and wiring at 9 pm. worked until 3 a.m. The enemy shelled VILLERS FAUCON heavily with heavy guns from 11-30 am. to 1 pm. Enemy aircraft very active, apparently attempting to bring down our Kite Observation Balloon. 1 NCO proceeded to England to Scots Cadet School for commission. Casualties NIL. Operations NIL. Twenty Brie. MTB.	MTB.
BROWN LINE & F.27.c.a.d.d.	12/5/17		4 Coys still in same location; Forward Batt. HQ.ars moved up to the Quarries in F.27.C.A. at 7-30 pm. Much more convenient locality to be in touch with the Battn at work. 2/Lt CRITHORPE & 2/Lt O.R. Kent to be attached to 429 Field Co R.E. for the plenty spent a month previously. Capt. CONNELL RAMC R.A.P. from Leave. 2 Reinforcement Officers arrived from England MAJOR RIDGE and Capt. J. RICHARDSON and takes on the strength. Casualties NIL Operations NIL all 4 Coys out on night work under R.E.	
	13/5/17		The R.E. made a change in the system of work. 2/Lt R V R BAKER & 2/Lt. MATKILTRICK worked during the day from 3 pm to 6 pm. The 2 Coys at LEMPIRE and TOME WOOD Place and the attempt at day work proved successful. No unusual occurrence took were up at the Twine. Other 2 Coys carried on with night work. Several Germans Aero before working the same hours. The R.E. favour the Tank system and it has worked very much so far. Capt. J. R. CREAGH arrived from Leave 2/Lt R V R BAKER and 2/Lt O.R. returned on relief from 429 F. R.E. Archie activity took our men and of the enemy countered and a lot of hostile A.A. shelling. Casualties NIL. Operations NIL. Day bit fine night. Very stormy and wet.	MTB.

(A7092). Wt. W12839/M12935 750,000. 1/17. D.D. & L., Ltd. Forms/C.2118/24.

MAPS. FRANCE.
1:40000 ---- 57C.
1:20000 ---- 57C. SE
             62C. NE

Instructions regarding War Diaries and Intelligence
Summaries are contained in F. S. Regs., Part II.
and the Staff Manual respectively. Title pages
will be prepared in manuscript.

5
1/7th Battalion
of
MANCHESTER REGT.

Army Form C. 2118.

WAR DIARY of INTELLIGENCE SUMMARY.
(Erase heading not required.)

Place	Date	Hour	Summary of Events and Information	Remarks and references to Appendices
BROWN LINE & F.27.Cent'd	14/5/17		2 coys still on the BROWN LINE. By Kerner arrangement they worked during the day from 8.30 am to 5 pm without disturbance. Instructions received and arrangements referee verify by the 15th MARCH. for 2 coys on BROWN LINE and 2 in the Quarries. See Appendix II 2 coys went out to carry on night work at the same times as before. Operations NIL Casualties NIL Weather fine and warm.	Appendix II NIL MB
	15/5/17		2 coys on BROWN LINE relieved by 2 coys of 1st MARCH. Relief complete at 6.50 am. Very late on account of 15th MARCH sending their 2 coys about 2½ hours later than time arranged. The 2 coys in the Quarries were relieved at 11 am. The Batt'n concentrated in the new area at K.11.a. and by coy proceeded to MILLERS FAUCON for a bath, except 1 coy, which was sent out at 6 am to work on a crate on the St EMILIE road. 2/Lt J.C. MORTEN proceeded to take over the post of Town Major at EPEHY. 2/Lt C.S. WOOD ret'd from leave. Batt HQ at K.11.a.7.7 Operations NIL Casualties NIL Weather fine but showery at times of thunder rain.	NIL MB
K.11.a.7.7.	16/5/17		The day was spent in cleaning up clothing & equipment generally and making things ready for a move out of the II Corps area to the XI Corps area at YTRES. During the morning the Rear HQ personnel joined the baths and made it complete. The separation of the Batt's HQ. has too many disadvantages for it to be a point system. There is too much room for both of time and Energy in keeping up communication. Hon'd A.E.CRONSHAW and 15 O.R. Proceeded to England on leave. Operations NIL Casualties NIL Weather very wet all day and night. Orders received for move.	NIL MB Appendix II
P.32.t. (57C S.E.)	17/5/17		The Batt'n moved out at 3.50 am by route march to VAUXHART WOOD. P.32.f. and arrived at destination at 9.40 am. 2 men only failed to arrive accompanied with good and well hidden from observation. 2/Lt C.S. WOOD left for England. Convoi at QUESNOY CHA'E at 10.30 pm after demonstration of the Gas Cloud attack Alarm Rocket was fired throughout the 20 t. Div. in whose area we are at present. Operations NIL Casualties NIL Weather NIL	NIL MB

MAP 57c N.E. 1 / S.E. 3 c, 30,000

WAR DIARY of 1/7 Manchester Regt.

INTELLIGENCE SUMMARY.

Army Form C. 2118.

(Erase heading not required.)

Instructions regarding War Diaries and Intelligence Summaries are contained in F.S. Regs., Part II. and the Staff Manual respectively. Title pages will be prepared in manuscript.

Place	Date	Hour	Summary of Events and Information	Remarks and references to Appendices
VALLULART WOOD	19/5/17		Quiet day. Ancillary of Lunch. Receive orders to move tomorrow and occupy Intermediate Line in HAVRINCOURT WOOD. 7th & 3rd Bns will be in the Line and supports & we will be in Brigade Reserve.	gw
P.18.b.2.7 [Batt H.K.]	14K		Batt. commences moving up at 5 p.m. Move relief complete 9.30 p.m. 7th D.C.L.I. 61st Brigade. 7th Bn. we occupy area N.W. along to back from 6.9.c.1.0 to 6.1.c.5.9 and due N. from there to 6.1.a.5.6. A Coy being right sector 6.9.c.1.0 to P.I.B.a.0.5 to J.36.c.0.7 C. " " centre " 6.g.a.1.6. to 6.1.c.5.9.6. Not occupied: D Coy hold from 6.2.c.5.9 to 6.1.a.5.6. B Coy hold detached trench from P.6.a to J.36.c. See APPENDIX sketch 6th Manchester hold right sector of Brigade frontage, 5th hold centre sector and 5th the left.	APPENDIX II
	20th		Weather fine. Situation normal. B Coy trench shelled morning & afternoon for about 10 minutes each time; 1 casualty. Lewis guns of all 4 Coys fired on a little plane which came down in to British lines.	gw
	21st		No change. Mustin Showery. All Parties & Guards returned to Camp.	gw
	22		No change. Good deal of rain during day.	gw
	23		Sector of trench held by D Coy heavily shelled with H.E. During morning; 2 mm killed & 1 wounded. a gas alarm was raised at 7.30 p.m.; at 10 p.m. "all clear"; turned out a false alarm sector of trench held by LT. HEATHCOTE HACKER. Proceeds home on leave.	gw

MAPS France
57c N.E. } 1:20,000
S.E.

WAR DIARY of 1/7 Manchester Regt

Army Form C. 2118.

INTELLIGENCE SUMMARY
(Erase heading not required.)

Instructions regarding War Diaries and Intelligence Summaries are contained in F.S. Regs, Part II. and the Staff Manual respectively. Title pages will be prepared in manuscript.

Place	Date	Hour	Summary of Events and Information	Remarks and references to Appendices
P.15.b.2.7	24/5/17		No change. Weather fine.	gue
	25/5/17		2/Lt JESSOP rejoins from Bombing Course. 2/Lt GRESTY rejoins from Leave. Relieve 2 Bedfords & relieve 5th Manchesters in left sector of Brigade front on night of 27th/28th.	gue
	26th		2/Lt J.C. CHATTERTON rejoins from Hospital. In charge	gue
	27th		Batt. relieved 5th Manchesters in the line in left sector of Brigade front. See attached Appendix Nos VII and VIII. Relief completed 12.50 am on 28th	Appendix VII & VIII
	28th		Situation normal. Posts & working parties can only be approached after dark except by single men. Transport not permitted to approach Batt. H.Q. during daylight. Transport to the Trenches of water, R.E. Materials & to Rot. Head Front creates difficulties. All Carrying parties concentrated in digging a New Reserve line by night. 2/Lt S.J. WILSON returns from leave. Large of Working Operations on our Brigade Front. Inspired to take some German posts about 4th June but by a New Line East H.900 yds from Hindenburg line	gue gue
	29th 30th		Patrols ask of operation observed herewith from 125 June. Situation normal. Enemy very quiet Maj. Lt. L Q.M. H. ROSE 11th Army vacated	gue gue
	31st		2/Lt BELL ILDERTON to England on leave. Appendix IX. Lt. Col. A.E. CRONSHAW rejoins from leave & resumes Command of Batt. 2/Lt F.G. BURN to England on leave. Work on widening Trenches proceeds each day	Appendix IX. Appendix X which

A.E. Cronshaw

Appendix I May. 1917

Map. 1,20,000
62 c.N.E.
57 c.S.E.

OPERATION ORDERS   NO. 1   Copy No.

HG. Brigade.
-@-

(1) INFORMATION.
  The present Picquet Line(i.e.the line of resistance of the outposts running approximately through F.5.c.central--through PRIEL FARM to X.15.d.central) will shortly become the main line of defence. Every effort will be made to make this line continuous and improve it as quickly as possible. This line will in future be known as the GREEN LINE.
  Outposts to cover this line will eventually include GUILLEMONT FARM - THE KNOLL. The Quarries E.of Little PRIEL FARM and the posts on the high ground E.of those Quarries in X.29 d.- Spur in X.16 d. This line will be called the BLACK LINE.

(2) WORK:- During moonlight nights advantage will be taken to:-
 (a) Strengthen and extend the advanced posts we already hold in or near the BLACK LINE E.of Little PRIEL FARM and on the two spurs N.of this point,making them,up to 6th.May the advanced posts of the line of resistance of the outposts and to be held at all costs. After that date they will become the line of resistance to the Outposts.
 (b) Work on the GREEN LINE to prepare it as a main line of resistance for the Brigade- including cover in trenches for the garrison from fire and weather. O.P's and machine gun emplacements.
 (c) The Forward trenches in X.29 d.must be extended and improved and communications made between them.
 (d) The hedges round LITTLE PRIEL FARM must be wired,and wire continued round the flanks.

(3) RELIEFS:- Attention is again called to 48th.Division Standing Orders No.1
  The work in hand and all orders,trench stores,etc.must be most carefully taken and handed over even though the relieving unit knows the ground and has occupied the trenches before.

(4) INTERVALS:- East of the BROWN LINE Sections will keep at an interval of 10 to 20 yards according to the darkness.

(5) STAND TO:- "Stand To" will be for the present from 8 p.m.to 9 p.m.and from 3-45 a.m.to 5 a.m.or until such time as visibility is good.

(5) RELIEF:- The Lewis Gun Magazines handed over to A, will be taken over again. Lewis Guns will be man handled to the posts.
  Platoon guides from A will be at 13 Copse to take troops of "D"Coy.to their posts to relieve present garrison at Catelet Copse and Cruciform Post.
  The Water carts will be sent up to 13 Copse after the Battn. has left EPEHY and Companies must make their own arrangements on arrival for filling of spare Petrol Tins.
  Rations will be carried up on the man or in Section sandbags. These will be ready for distribution at 7-30 p.m. to Companies at) A.& D.Area)On completion of relief,Companies will wire
) B.& C. Area. through to H.Q.the message O.K.

  Disposition of Companies to various posts and positions as detailed in Battn.Orders to-day. Coy.Tools will be taken on the Tool Limbers, Companies will have their limber in their area. Each Coy.should send a representative to look after the tools in transit.

W.H.Barrett
2/Lieut.
a/Adjutant.

2/5/17

Appendix I   May 1917

SECRET.   BATTALION ORDERS
                    by
LIEUT.COLONEL A.E.CRONSHAW.   COMMANDING.
    In the Field.   2/5/17.

(1) MOVE:- The Battalion will relieve A. to-night, for two nights.

(2) DISPOSITION:-

POST.	GARRISON.	COY.H.Q.	NIGHT OF May 2nd. COY.	May 3rd. COY.
Advanced Trenches. Quarry.	3 Platoons. 1 Platoon.		C.	D.
Preparation of New Trenches by night. Reserve in EPEHY by day.	4 Platoons.	EPEHY.	B.	C.
Trenches South of PRIEL FARM.	4 Platoons.		A.	B.
Cruciform Post. Catelet Copse. 12 Copse. 13 Copse.	1 Platoon 1 Platoon, 1 Platoon. 1 Platoon.	13 COPSE.	D.	A.

(3) HOUR OF MOVE:- The Battalion will move by Platoons at 50 yards interval
    with ¼ hour between Companies in the following order:-
        D. B. C. A.
    The head Companies will pass MALASSLEE Farm at the time stated.
    "D" 9 p.m.   "B" 9-15 p.m.   "C" 9-30 p.m.   "A" 9-45 p.m.
(4) DETAILS:-
    (a) The advanced trenches must be held at all costs. Only 50% of
        garrison to work at one time. The rest must be on guard.
         In new trenches at this post only three men must be sent out to
         dig at one time, then relieved at intervals.
    (b) Strong covering party must protect the Troops digging on new
        trenches South of the Quarry. It must be ascertained if a covering
        party is found by A.
    (c) Every Officer and N.C.O. must learn the trenches and positions
        thoroughly.
(5) PATROLS:- Patrols must go out warily and never return by the same route.
(6) REPORTS:- All Clear(or otherwise) reports **must** be sent to Battn.H.Q.
        to reach that office at 3-30 a.m. and 3-30 p.m.
            Casualty Reports) by
            Progress   "   ) 12 noon.
         Intelligence report ready to hand to Intelligence Officer or
         one of his Staff by 6-0 a.m.

                                        W.H.Barratt
                                                        2/Lieut.
                a/Adjutant.

Appendix II   May 1917

BATTALION ORDERS
by

Lt.Col.A.E.CRONSHAW   Commanding 1/7th.Manchester Rgt.
    In the Field   6/5/17.
          :-:-:-:-:-:-:-:-:

(1) MOVE:- The Battalion will be relieved to-night in the line by
    A & The first Company of this unit will leave EPEHY
    at 9 p.m.and reliefs will be carried out as follows.

         A Battalion.   C. Battalion.

    A Coy.will relieve   D. Company.
    B   "   "   "   B   "
    D   "   "   "   A   "
    C   "   "   "   C   "

    The following guides will be found by C .
4 guides from C. at 13 Copse at 9-30 p.m.to take 4
platoons of A Coy. A to Quarry X.29 a.2.3.and hand
over to D.Company C.
    4 guides of D.Coy.to put A.Coy. A into their posts
when handed over at Quarry.
    4 guides from B.Coy.at 13 Copse at 9-45 p.m.for B.
Coy. A.
    4 guides from A.Coy.at 13 Copse at 10 p.m.for D.Coy.
A.
    2 guides from C.Coy.at 13 Copse at 10-15 p.m.for C.
Coy. A.
                On completion of duty all guides will,
return at once to the Battalion H.Qrs.if their Coys.
have already moved off.
    The following will be handed over to A on relief.
Lewis Gun Magazines,Spare petrol tins,except those
belonging to this Battalion and they must be brought
back) Rockets etc.and a list given to A. and one kept
by C. Trench log books if they have already been
commenced.
        Rations will be kept at Battalion Forward H.Qrs.
for distribution on relief and relief of Companies.
       Water will also be at Battalion H.Qrs.
Each Company will be responsible for its own tools and

.Contd.

Lewis Guns which will be brought back by the men.

    On return to EPEHY Companies will be billeted as follows.
        C Coy. as before.
        B ."   as before.
        A.Coy.in German stables by H.Qrs.
        D.Coy.in railway cutting.

WORK. Work will be carried on with all speed until the actual time of relief. It is of the greatest importance that rapid progress be made.
    Officers must see that this done.

                                              2/Lieut.
                    a/Adjutant. C.

appendix II may 1917

Appendix III May 1917

BATTALION ORDERS

Lt.Col.A.E.CRONSHAW. by COMMANDING.
In the Field 8/5/17.

MAPS. 1:20,000 57c. S.E. & 62c. N.E

(1) The Brigade will be relieved on the nights 8/9 and 9/10 May by the 125th.Brigade.

(2) The following move will take place to-day.

On relief by 1/6th.L.F's about 8 p.m. B.& C.Companies will move out of their billets by route march to VILLERS FAUCON. They will parade fully equipped and report all clear to the C.O. by messenger on moving off.

Spare kit, Officers kit, Company tools will be placed on a dump close to C.Coy's.H.Qrs. on the road ready for loading.

Lewis Guns and equipment will be loaded on to the limbers when they arrive, at the same place. Loading in each case under Company arrangements.

Spare Lewis Gun magazines will be loaded at old H.Qrs under the supervision of Sergt.Harrison and distributed to Companies later.

Evening meal will be at 4-30 p.m. and the Cookers ready for removal at 5 p.m. They will proceed to VILLERS FAUCON and prepare a late meal for the incoming Companies.

An Officer from each Coy. and a platoon representative from each platoon of B.& C.Companies will be sent beforehand to report to Major ALLAN at Rear H.Qrs. to have billets allotted and will guide their Companies in on arrival at VILLERS FAUCON.

Forward Battalion H.Qrs. will be packed and prepared to move down to VILLERS FAUCON after dinner at about 8 p.m.

A.& D.coys. will relieve two Companies of the 1/8th.L.F's.in the BROWN LINE(Left Sector Divisional Area). Relief to be complete by 9 p.m. O.C.these Companies will make arrangemnets to see the positions they will occupy during to-day and make their dispositions.accordingly. Coy.tools will be taken.

Contd.

Arrangements are in hand with the 1/5th. Manchesters to have the Lewis Gun magazines handed back to-day to make up the corresponding amount handed over on relief on night 6/7 May. Further details as to drawing these will be announced later by circular.

One water cart will be left full in the hollow at the New Battn. H Qrs. for the use of D.Coy. during their occupation of the BROWN LINE.

A.Coy. cookers will also be brought up during the evening and put in a place arrange for by O.C. A.Coy.

The water cart will proceed there after supplying D.Coy.

One water cart will remain at Rear H.Qrs. to be used by B.& C. Companies on arrival and during their stay there.

All Companies will see that all petrol tins are taken along with them and not dumped. These are on charge and must at any time be accounted for.

Relief complete will be sent down to Orderly Room at this H.Qrs. immediately.

W.H.B.
a/Adjutant.   C.   2/Lieut.

Appendix III May 1917

Appendix IV

BATTALION ORDERS
by

LT. Col. A.E. CRONSHAW. COMMANDING. 1/7th. MANCHESTER RGT.
   In the Field. 14/5/17.

(1) RELIEF:- The following relief will take place and will be completed by 12 noon on the morning of the 15th. inst
    The 5th. Manchesters will relieve the 7th. Manch. in the Right Brigade Sector of the BROWN LINE and will take over all their duties and working parties and hand over any duties or permanent working parties they themselves provide.

(2) DISPOSITIONS after relief will be as under.
    5th. Manchesters.:-
    H.Qrs & 2 Companies in Quarries F.27.
    2 Companies (minimum garrison) in vicinity of BROWN LINE Right Brigade Sector.
    7th. Manchesters.:-
    Reserve in K.11 a.

(3) The relief of Companies in the BROWN LINE will be completed by 6 a.m. on 15th. inst.

(4) Exchange of duties etc. will take effect from daylight on 15th. inst.

(5) List of current duties and working parties will be handed over on relief by each Battalion.
    Each Coy. in the BROWN LINE will hand over a map of the positions occupied and the amount of work done.
    Also a list in duplicate of trench stores etc. will be prepare ready for handing over. The duplicate copy to be handed in to Orderly Room on relief.
    Messages of Relief Complete will be sent to Forward H.Qts as soon as possible.

(6) The following tools will be handed over on relief (Picks & Shovels)
    A. Coy. All tools on charge as per List handed in.
    B " All tools on loan from R.E. Park sent up 4 days ago.
    C. " " " " " " " " " " " " "
    D. " Same as for A. Coy.
    The corresponding quantity of tools handed over by A. & D. Companies will be taken over from the 5th. Manch.

Appendix IV May 1917

Appendix V May 1917

BATTALION ORDERS
by

Major J.H.ALLAN.   Commanding
In the Field.   16/5/17.

ROUTINE. The Battalion will move with the Brigade tomorrow 17th. from this area to the YTRES area.

Reveille 2 a.m.   Tea 2-30 a.m.

3-45 a.m. Battalion will fall in ready to move off in file facing N. on the road behind H.Q. in order A.B.C.D. Coys.

400 yards distance will be kept between Battalions, 10 yards between Companies, platoons will be closed up, 100 yards between each Unit,s Transport.

Order of march of Brigade as below :-
127th. Bde. H.Q. and Signal Coy.
8th. Battalion Manchester Regt.
6th.   "   "   "   "   "
5th.   "   "   "   "   "
7th.   "   "   "   "   "
127th. T.M.B. and M.G.Coy.
427th. Field Coy. R.E.
Brigade Transport.
Field Ambulance.
431st. Coy.Divisional Train.

L.G.Limbers and Cookers will march in rear of their Companies. The remaining transport will rendezvous in order of march on the LIERMONT - VILLERS FAUCON Rd. Head of transport column will pass cross roads E.14.b.9.2. at 5-40 a.m.

Halts will be made at the clock hours for 10 minutes. Packs will be removed, mounted men will dismount, and men will fall out on the right hand side and clear of the road during Halts. There will be a halt of 1 hour and 10 minutes from 8 a.m. to 9-10 a.m. when breakfast will be partaken of.

O.C."D"Coy.will detail 1 platoon under an Officer to march in rear of the transport to collect stragglers and to take the names of any men who have fallen out, without written permission from their unit. The 2nd.East Lancs.F.A.will detail a Medical Officer to accompany this party. He will decide if men who have fallen out are fit to march or whether they should be carried in the ambulance wagons.

Rations for the 18th.will be taken to units billeting areas after arrival, under supply arrangements.

DRESS:- Full Marching Order. Overcoats in pack with oil sheet showing underneath flap of pack so that it can be easily extracted to wear over shoulder should the order for it be given.

Marching out states to be rendered to 5 p.m. to-day. Marching in states to be rendered to H.Q. within half an hour of arrival at destination.

Water Carts will travel full, Companies making their own arrangements to refill the boilers of their Cookers after meal at 2-30 a.m. Breakfast to be eaten at 8 a.m. should be prepared en route.

Between Reveille and Breakfast blankets must be rolled tightly in bundles of 10 and piled on Coy.Dumps along side the road in rear of camp. Companies will arrange their own loading parties to load at 3 a.m.

All Battalion ammunition, grenades, and tools must be loaded and ready to-night: the R.S.M.will detail a fatigue party for this purpose at 7 p.m. Company Lewis Gun limbers will be brought alongside their Cookers to-day and they must also be loaded up and ready before dark. Everything possible must be made ready for moving before dark to-day.

Signallers, Shoemakers and Tailors equipment must be cut down as much as po
s

Appendix V. May 1917

Contd.

as much as possible and also dumped alongside the road: each must report to the Transport Sergt. where their dump is and be responsible that it is not overlooked.

The motor lorry attached for use to the Battalion will return to PERONNE on night of 17th.

A Divisional dump will be formed at VILLERS FAUCON: Corpl. Binks will be in charge of the Battalion baggage there.

The Battalion camp area must be thoroughly cleaned up this afternoon and will be inspected at 7 p.m. by the 2nd. in Command.

O.C. Companies will be responsible that their areas are left as clean as possible before moving off in the morning.

Strict march discipline must be enforced.

McCough
a/Adjutant.   Capt.

Sketch from Sketch 54. S.E. N.E.

APPENDIX VI
May 1917.

APPENDIX VI
May 1917 BHQ - IORB.

Appendix XIII

S.E.C.R.E.T.   BATTALION ORDER   No. 5
                         by
MAJOR J.H.ALLAN   COMMANDING.
        In the Field.   26/5/17.
                :-:-:-:-:-:-:-:-:
              MAP 57c. S.E. 1:20,000.

(1) In continuation of this morning's order re Move on night
         27/28th.inst.
    A.Company will move to Firing Line via road leading N.E.from
    Place St.HUBERT through Q.1.d. and Q.2.a.central.to reach
    there not earlier than 10-30 p.m. Guides will meet them
    about 200 yards from the Firing Line.

    C.Company will be at 5th.Manchesters H.Qrs.at 10 p.m.where
    they will be met by guides.

    D.Company will be at 5th.Manchesters H.Qrs at 10-15 p.m.and
    pick up guides there.

    B.Company will report at 5th.Manchesters H.Qrs.at 10-30 p.m.

    Battalion H.Qrs advance party will parade at 9-30 p.m.
    The remainder at 10.p.m. Details of these will ne notified
    later.

    Each Company will place all the Trench Stores it hands over
    in one pile and leave a senior N.C.O.behind to hand over and
    get a receipt for it.
         This N.C.O. should also be able to point out to the
    incoming Company the trench and dug-outs to be occupied.

[margin note: X with 2 men]

(2) The use of water tomorrow must be restricted and each man
    should take up with him to the trenches a full waterbottle.
         A water cart will only reach Companies and H.Qrs ,once
    tomorrow in daylight. Companies must take up with them
    every possible receptacle for holding water. Both water
    carts will report full at 5th.Manchesters H.Qrs.at 10 p.m.
         Transport Officer will arrange for a fatigue party of
    6 men to be at RUYAULCOURT each evening to fill the carts.
         It is hoped to let Companies have 20 petrol tins of

Contd:- 2.

water each night for 24 hours use. They will always return empty tins in exchange for full. Water bottles should be refilled as soon as possible on arrival of fresh supply.

A number of tins are being taken over as trench stores. O.C.Companies should arrange to mark all their own petrol tins before they move up.

(3) A ½ limber will report to A. C.& D.Companies at 9 p.m.and B.Company at 9-30 p.m.to carry Lewis Gun Equipment and Officers Mess Stores.

The Maltese Cart, Mess Cart and 2 limbers will report to Battalion H.Qrs.about 10-15 p.m.

The trench rations for A.C.& D.Companies will be loaded on Pack Mules, per Company, at the Dump. Rations for B.Coy., H.Qrs. Officers and Details, and the cooker rations for A. C. & D. Companies will be loaded on two limbers. They should all report at 5th.Manchesters H.Qrs.at 9-45 p.m.accompanied by CQMS's and Sergt.Harrison for H.Qrs.

Transport Officer will arrange to move all Company Cookers to 5th.Manchesters H.Qrs.at the same time as Company moves.

(4) O.C."B"Coy.will detail every night,one Officer and 3 parties of 1 N.C.O. and 10 men each to be at H.Qrs.at 9-30 p.m.:
Tomorrow night 10 p.m. These parties are for carrying water,tea and R.E.material to the forward trenches.

The Officer detailed should get in touch tomorrow with the Officer of the 5th.Manchesters: who has been working this fatigue and learn details of it.

(5) Work to be done tomorrow night will be detailed later.

(6) All trenches and areas vacated,must be left perfectly clean and latrines & in a sanitary condition.

(7) Companies will report immediately reliefs are completed.
The usual cypher O.K. will be used.

(8) All Officers are reminded that nothing of tactical interest must be sent "in clear"on the wires,and the very greatest care must be exercised in the same respect to speaking over the telephone.

Contd.   3.

As Battalion H.Qrs. is reasonably near, runners will probably be found the speediest method of communication.

(9) Fires are not allowed in any of the trenches.
During hours of daylight great care must be taken by all ranks to keep out of view of the enemy, and men are forbidden to leave their trenches except on duty.
The O.C. Company in the Left Support Trench should not allow orderlies to enter his trench at his H.Qrs. and so give away to the enemy its location.

10. All tools in possession of Coys will be taken with them.
11. Standing Trench Orders as handed over by 5th Manchesters will be strictly adhered to.
No patrols will be sent out except by order of Battn H.Q.
From down to dusk all ranks must use Communication trenches.

                                    J.R. Creagh
                                        Capt.
            a/Adjutant.

issued by orderly, at .... to.

No.1 O.C. A Coy.
No.2 O.C. B Coy.
No.3 O.C. C Coy.
No.4 O.C. D. Coy.
No.5 Hdqrs. & File.
No.6 Transport Officer & Q.M.
No.7 5th Manchesters
No.8 File

Appendix VII
May 1917

H.Q. Officers

Commanding Officer.
2nd in Command.
Medical Officer
Chaplain
Signalling Officer
Intelligence Officer
Asst Adjt.

Appendix VII

S.E.C.R.E.T. BATTALION ORDERS
by
Major.J.H.ALLAN.   COMMANDING   1/7th.Manchester Rgt
     In the Field.   26/5/17,

(1) MOVE. The Battalion will relieve 5th.Manchesters in the left
    sub sector of Brigade Front on night of 27/28th.May.

   DISTRIBUTION.
      A.Coy.will relieve D.Coy.of 5th.Manchesters on right
                sector of Battalion front.
      C.Coy.will relieve B.Coy.of 5th.Manchesters on left
                sector of Battalion front.
      D.Coy.will relieve C.Coy.of 5th.Manchesters in the
                Support line.
      B.Coy.will relieve A.Coy of 5th.Manchesters in Reserve.

      O.C.Companies accompanied by an orderly will report
   at 5th.Manchesters H.Qrs. J.36.d.8.1. in sunken road at
   3 p.m.to-day. They will be guided from there to the
   sectors they will take over and will make themselves
   acquainted with all necessary details,tactical and
   administrative. Careful note should be made of patrols,
   work being carried on,number of sentries on duty etc.,as
   we shall take over their system as it stands,for the
   present.
      Note should also be made as to watering and rationing
   arrangements.

                                              Capt.
                        a/Adjutant.1/7th.Manch.Regt.

Appendix VII
May 1917

Appendix IX

OPERATION ORDERS No. 4.
by
LIEUT COLONEL. A.E.CRENSHAW.   COMMANDING.
In the Field.   31/5/17.

(1). Previous orders re moves of Companies are cancelled.

(2) Companies will occupy the following frontage to-night 31st.May/1st.Jun each Company finding its own supports.

		In support.
A.Coy.	from the Battalion boundary to road at K.32.a.8.2 d.0.7.	2 Platoons.
D.Coy.	from A.Company's left to Cinder track K.32.a.8.5.	2 Platoons.
B.Coy.	from D.Company's left to Canal.	1 Platoon.

C.Coy.will be in Battalion Reserve in the New Reserve Line: right boundary Q.2.a.9.6.

O.C.Companies will reconnoitre this afternoon the trenches they are going to occupy and arrange among themselves the details of relief.

Care should be taken that a note is made of all work in progress.

Reliefs should be commenced as soon as it is dark enough, and every endeavour must be made to interfere as little as possible with the work detailed in para.3.for the Battalion.

(3) WORK TO-NIGHT. Every possible available man of all the Companies will be employed on improving, widening, deepening (where necessary) the Fire and Support trenches and strengthening the wire entanglements all along our front. Completion of dug-outs can also be proceeded with.

All shelters must be cleared at once from Fire and Support trenches. None of the concertina barbed wire now being made must be used until completion of the 50 coils on the Dump at point arranged: these 50 coils must not be used.

(4) Completion of reliefs will be notified to H.Qrs.by wiring the cypher, HUG.

PART ii ORDERS.

POSTING:- Lt.Colonel A.E.Crenshaw having returned from leave resumes Command of the Battalion, Dated 31/5/17.
Major J.H.Allan takes over the duties of 2nd.in Command. Dated 31/5/17.
Capt.C.E.Higham resumes Command of D.Company. Dated 31/5/17.

                                                Capt.
                            a/Adjutant. 1SLS.

Copy.No.1 A.Coy.
       2   B "
       3   C "
       4   D "
       5   H.Qrs.& File.
       6   T.O. & Q.M.
       7   War Diary.

Appendix IX
May 1917

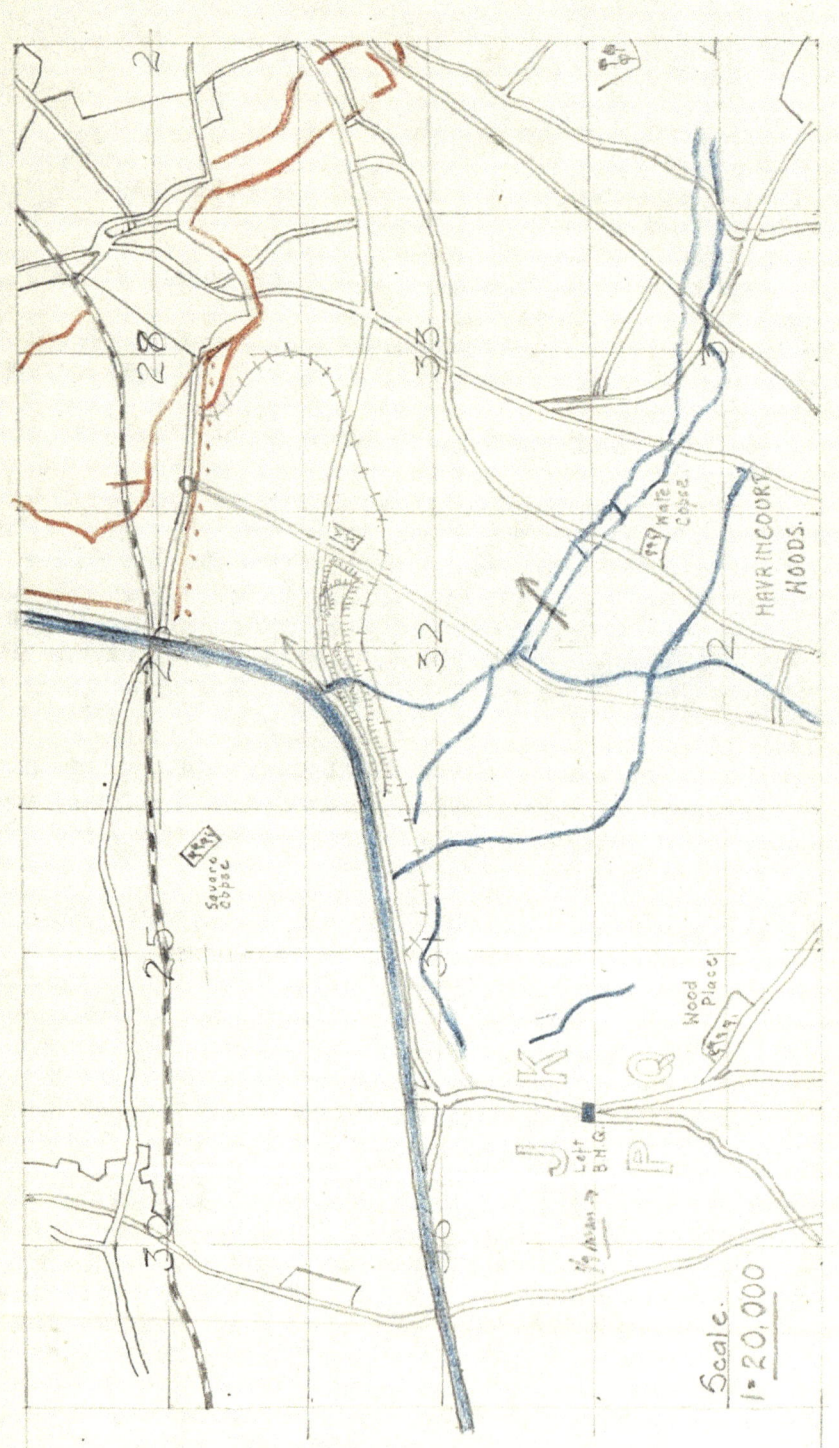

Vol 5

CONFIDENTIAL

WAR DIARY.

OF

1/7th Bn. MANCHESTER REGT.

FROM. June 1st 1917   TO. June 30th 1917.

VOLUME
VI.

WAR DIARY

Army Form C. 2118.

INTELLIGENCE SUMMARY.

(Erase heading not required.)

Summary of Events and Information

Place: France — 57C SW and NE 20,000 — 1/7th Manchester Regt.

Place	Date	Hour	Summary of Events and Information	Remarks and references to Appendices
I.36.d.9.1.	1/6/17		Casualties during day — KILLED Other Ranks 2 O.R. Wounded 11 O.R. with B.M.G. 26 Officers & O.R. Other Ranks. Strength of Batt. Officers 40 Other Ranks 946.	
			Enemy sent up two S.O.S. signals about 10.20 p.m. & commenced a barrage. It did not last long. Daily practice in working & fitting of new Lewisite gun to a dump to bring front to future use. Information of Zareska fires a good deal. Running very withering & deepening & straining: occupation for every party. Recovery situation normal. Weather remains fine. 126 S Bde: at our right in either a small advanced Post.	gas gas
	2/6/17	3.30 4.5	Situation quiet. 5.30 a.m. Alarm taken 11.15 p.m. turned out a gas alarm. 5th Manchesters relieved us in the line.	gas gas
		5.30 6.5	At Brigade reserve. At our D Coys (from L right) occupy left section of intermediate line, B & C Coys left sector of Reserve Line Coy. arrive H.Qrs. J.36.c. Batt. H.Q. see hot sheet.	gas gas
			No change.	
		9.30 8.20	B⁵ Orders of 3/7/17 th Brigade: Orders to dig a two firing line 200/300 yds in advance of present one, each Batt. digging & wiring a sector & giving back of operations is not enticipated but preparations are being in case of necessity for artillery, etc. officers recce (two timed trebled Rails) has been issued & circulated in divn's & brigade's orders of our line.	gas gas
		9.30 8.20	See Appendix I for arrangements for tomorrow's digging. No digit work tonight. Situation as per Appendix I was carried out without hitch. See Appendix II for situation report. Weight favourable. Cloudy. Moon rose about 12.30 am (9⁵). No opposition from enemy on our front. Obviously having lost the inkling of our operations. No casualties. Capt. A.H. TINKER returned from Home Leave on 6th instant and 2/Lt J.W. SIVEWRIGHT on 7⁵	APPENDIX I APPENDIX II gas

MAPS FRANCE
57c. NE & SE. 1:20,000

Army Form C. 2118.

WAR DIARY
or
INTELLIGENCE SUMMARY.
(Erase heading not required.)

of 1/7th Manchester Regt.

Place	Date	Hour	Summary of Events and Information	Remarks and references to Appendices
J.36.d.9.1	9th		Consolidation of new line was continued & rapid progress made. A communication trench back to the Young Line was commenced & dug to an average of 4 ft wide & 2 deep. A minenwerfer was fired at intervals on our new line and killed 1 man & wounded 3 others. Enemy aeroplanes to other of position. An offensive III sketch of new line a day.	APPENDIX III / p.c. / p.c.
	10th		Consolidation of our line & deepening new communication was continued with all available men during hours of darkness & good progress was made. 2 men were wounded. Enemy fired M.G's. French Mortars and occasionally dropped an H.E. shell through the night & we were fortunate to have such light casualties. Their fire was very scattered. Aeroplanes, those few being active. Work continued same on 10th.	p.c. / p.c.
	11th		Communication trench dug to average 5 feet. Firing line to average of 4 feet. Double rows of barbed wire complete on whole front. No consultation wire.	p.c.
	12th		"C" Coy on orders took over from Reserves to Intermediate Line in accordance with new Brigade disposition viz 2 Bn(?) front up held by 2 Coys each in depth (each Coy 2 platoons in line & 2 in support) each Bn(?) with 1 Coy in support attack line (old support line) & 1 Coy in Reserve line. The 3rd Bn will hold Intermediate Line at 4.5. & took to RUYAULCOURT in Brigade Reserve. Took 3 Coys further orders & deepened our forward communication trench. To relieve 5th Manch in the trenches. Relieved 5th Manchester in left sector of Bde front are Appendix IV for dispositions & Appendix VI for attacks. 5th Manchester on our right. 5th Lancs on our left. Trenches on the relief by 5th Manch began at 8.20 p.m. 9.30 p.m. to avoid enemy shellfire. Relief completed 1.25 a.m. 2 men wounded.	p.c. / for Appendix IV / p.c.
	13th			

MAP FRANCE
57/C N.E. & S.E.
1/9 Manchester Regt.

Army Form C. 2118.

WAR DIARY
or
INTELLIGENCE SUMMARY.
(Erase heading not required.)

Place	Date	Hour	Summary of Events and Information	Remarks and references to Appendices
T.36.d.9.1.	14		Situation unchanged. See Defence Orders APPENDIX VI	See APPENDIX VI
	15		No change. Two Stay officers patrols went out after dark to Eastern end of Flag Heap; no opposition.	
	16		2/Lt. F.G. BURN returned from leave. Weather very warm & fine. No change.	
	17		2/Lt. T.C. CHATTERTON returned from and 2/Lt. C.B. DOUGLAS proceeded to Divisional bombing course. B boy relieved D boy in left sector. C boy relieved A boy in right sector of line. A boy goes into Suppt. and D boy into Reserve. Lines. Patrols go out each night into "No Man's Land" to find out enemy movements.	
	18		End of Flag Heap and WIGAN COPSE Chief objectives. Weather very warm. Thunder storm at 5 pm. A patrol under 2/Lt W.T. THORPE going to 6 Eastern end of Flag Heap got heavily fired on: 2 Men wounded. Both continued on their firing from & new Observation Trenches.	See
	19		Rain & bumbled weather. No change.	See
	20		5 Minenwerfers observed in front Line and Batts. Coy. three trench mortars. Reserve Coy. at RUYAULCOURT. C Coy moves to garrison 2nd Line in Sunken Rd.	See
P.15.d.8.7 RUYAULCOURT			Trenches T.36.C. Relief and new dispositions complete 4:30 am, 21st. Drops. taken.	
	21st		to RUYAULCOURT by DECAUVILLE Railway.	See
	22nd		Men get complete rest for 24 hours. A Batte. parade of commanders at Brigade Baths.	See
	23rd		All available men on working parties.	See
	24th		O/L. Batt. are being inoculated with T.A.B.	See
			A few Batt. shells dropped into village, some not far from our H.Q.	See

MAP FRANCE,
57c N.E and S.E.

Army Form C. 2118.

WAR DIARY
of
INTELLIGENCE SUMMARY
1/7th Manchester Regt.

(Erase heading not required.)

Place	Date	Hour	Summary of Events and Information	Remarks and references to Appendices
MAP FRANCE 57c N.E and S.E. P.15.6.8.7. RUYAULCOURT	25th		Revolver practice by Officers & Lewis Gunners. Regt. 1 & 2. No Change	p.c.
	26th		ditto. broken parties lever	
			Coy of 100 to 200 men informing villages and Group for 2 Battalion 2 hours training daily in the morning of all available men.	gre
	27th		90 change. Bn Hqts in Ytterman	gre
	28th		On relief 5th Manchesters in left sub sector of Line, Morning down by Decauville Railway. Dispositions D Coy on right, 2 Platoons up + 1 in Support. C Coy in left, 2 Platoons up + 2 in Support. A Coy in support 1.40 p.m. Coys counter attack Coy. B Coy in Reserve. Reliefs completed 1.40 p.m. Coy boundaries are the same as previously held by 2s battalion formed gre	
J.36.d.9.5	29th		A Raid on WIGAN COPSE is decided on 2 No 9 Platoon is to do it under 2/Lt HODGE in command on night of 31st/1st July. Situation quiet.	gre
	30th		Learn that German have been raiding trenches South of us. Coy warned to be alert. A reconnaissance toward WIGAN COPSE found it occupied at night.	gre

A. C. Graham
LIEUT COLONEL,
COMMANDING 1/7th Br MANCHESTER REGT.

APPENDIX I June

S.E.C.R.E.T.   OPERATION ORDER No.10   Copy. No. 9
                              by
LIEUT COLONEL A.R.CRONSHAW.   COMMANDING   J.R.
         In the Field.   7/6/17.   Maps. 57c.S.E. & N.E.
         :-:-:-:-:-:-:-:-:-:

(1) On the night of the 8th/9th June the Brigade will establish a line on
    approximately Post "F" K.33.c.70, to K.32.b.21, K.32.b.17, K.52.a.99.

(2) This Battalion will be responsible for digging and wiring a line from
    K.32.d.7.8. to K.32.b.1.3., approximately 420 yards. The right flank
    will be the strand of old German barbed wire, and the left about 50 yds.
N.W. from fork in St.HUBERTS Rd.

(3) This line will be wired its own length with a single row of barbed
    French wire coils doubled in front of tactical points and throughout
    if time permits.

(4) The Brigade Line will be dug continuous with the exceptions of the
    portion between K.32 b.13 to Southern edge of YORKSHIRE BANK, if possible
    at a distance of not less than 40 yds. behind the wire, so as to show a
    continuous parapet to the Germans.
        Points which are suitable Lewis Gun positions will be dug to a
    depth of at least 4 feet and made occupiable for small garrisons of
    riflemen and Lewis Gunners.

(5) The 5th.Manchesters will be digging on our right left and the 8th
    Manchesters on our right.

(6) The 5th.Manchesters will provide covering parties in front of their own
    and our Battalion. Covering parties will be in position by 10-30 p.m.
    Wirers and diggers will commence work at 11 p.m.
        Punctuality in starting is essential and everyone must work their
    hardest. Strength of covering parties will only be such as to ensure
    that the whole front is under observation, and that warning will be
    given to working parties of the approach of hostile infantry.

(7) The line will be taped out by the R.E's. A tape flash being put every
    14 yards. Firing bays will be 9 yards and traverse 5 yards.

(8) The 5th.Manchesters are providing a garrison of 1 Coy. to hold their
    present sector of front line.

(9) The whole of "A" Coy. will be employed in wiring and carrying parties.
    2/LT.A.HODGE will be in charge of the wiring.
        The remaining 3 Companies will dig the line. "D"Coy. on the right -
    "C"Coy. in the centre.--"B"Coy. on the left.-- One third part each.
        Each Company will employ 3 Platoons on digging its frontage and
    concentrate the fourth to help on the best tactical sector of their
    front in which they will leave a small garrison on the 9th.

(10) B. C. & D, Companies will each detail 2 junior N.C.O's to proceed in
     advance as Company Markers. They will be met by 2 Officers detailed
     by O.C."D"Coy. at 10 p.m. tomorrow on the St.HUBERT Rd., where it
     crosses the Firing Line. The party will meet there 2/Lt.WATKINSON R.E.
     and proceed forward with him.
         The 2 flank Company's inward markers will step 170 paces along
     the line which should about equally divide the frontage.
         One Officer will superintend at each end of the line. Markers
     will look out for the approach of and direct their own Companies.

(11) Companies will parade in their own time so as to start work
     punctually at 11 p.m. "B"Coy. will proceed via the Cinder Track.

No.11.Contd.

"C"Coy.will go through the wire at the gap just on the right of St.HUBERT Rd.
"D"Coy.will go through a gap 100 yards or so further to the right.
O.C."D"Coy.should find out tomorrow definite location of this gap.

(12) Every man will carry a shovel and every third man a pick.

(13) Each Coy.will supply a garrison of 3 Lewis Gunners&(1 Gun.), 6 Riflemen and a N.C.O.to occupy the constructed Strong Post during the 9th. Further details will be made known tomorrow.

(14) Co-operation of the Artillery has been arranged for if needed.

(15) COMMUNICATIONS. A joint advanced Battalion H.Qrs.for 5th.& 7th. Manchesters will be in the cutting in Canal Bank K.32.a.0.4. and Advanced Brigade H.Qrs.at Q.1.a.3.7. The Battalion advanced Aid Post will also be in the Canal Cutting.
The Signalling Officer will send a watch to advanced Brigade H.Qrs.at 7 p.m.tomorrow to be synchronised and will then notify H&Qrs and all Companies.

(16) Work will cease at 3 a.m.at which hour troops not detailed for the defence of the new line will be withdrawn to their trenches and bivouacs.

(17) One Battalion from Reserve Brigade will move into the following positions at 10 p.m.on the 8th.inst,and will be available for counter attack under the orders of the G.O.C.Brigade.

```
1 Coy. Sunken Road.   J.36 a.15.
1  "   In Post. C.1.  Q. 1.d.30.  )
                C.2.  Q. 1.c.67.  ) Intermediate.
                C.3.  Q. 1.a.61.  )    Line.
                C.4.  Q. 1.a.67.  )
1 Coy.in Reserve Line Right  Sub Sector.
1  "      "     "      Left.   "     "
```

McCuagh
a/Adjutant.   J.R.   Capt.

Copy.No.1 to A.Coy.
    2   B. "
    3   C "
    4   D "
    5   T.O. & Q.M.
    6   H.Qrs. & File.
    7   2nd.In Command.
  8.& 9 War Diary.

Appendix I

S.E.C.R.E.T. OPERATION ORDER No.10   Copy.No. 8
by
Lieut.Colonel A.E.CRONSHAW.   Commanding J.R.
    In the Field   8/6/17.
:-:-:-:-:-:-:-:-:

(1) Reference para 2.:- The right flank of the Battalion will be at a point 100 yards West of CAULIFLOWER TREE.
    The R.E.Officer referred to in next para will fix this point.
(2) Reference para 10:- The 2 Officers and Company Markers will meet 2/Lt. WATKINSON at appointed place at 9-30 p.m. to-night instead of 10 p.m.
(3) Officers will not take forward with them to-night any maps or papers that would be of use to the enemy.

                                            Capt.
                        a/Adjutant.   J.R.

Copy.No.1 To A.Coy.
       2   B
       3   C   CAULIFLOWER TREE is just West
       4   D   of old German barbed wire fence.
       5   T.O.& Q.M.
       6   H.Qrs. & File.
       7   2nd.in Command.
   8 & 9   War Diary.

APPENDIX I

O.C.   Company.   Addenda No.2 Operation Order.10

　　Companies will go out to-night with two Officers each.

    A.Coy.   2 Subalterns. (Senior and one other)
    B "   Capt.H.H.NIDD. and one Subaltern.
    C. "   Senior Subaltern and one other.
    D. "   Capt.C.E.HIGHAM and one Subaltern.

The other Officers will remain in their present dug-outs.

　　Please arrange accordingly the work, especially tactical point, and who is in charge, and report to me at once.

　　Senior Sergeants will take the place of the other Officers.
　　The St.HUBERT Rd.will not be used should there be heavy shelling - but troops must go by the communication Trench.

　　Reports <u>must</u> be sent in to me via Major J.H.ALLAN at every clock hour.

                        signed A.E.C.
                                        Lieut.Colonel
8/6/17.   Commanding   J.R.

"A" Form.
MESSAGES AND SIGNALS.
Army Form C.2121 (in pads of 100).

APPENDIX IV

TO: O.S. (127th Bde)

Sender's Number: J.R.C. 307.
Day of Month: 9 June.

AAA

Single wire complete along whole front in touch with 8th and 5th. Manchesters wire. aaa. Double wire complete in front of 3 Strong Posts. aaa. Trench dug complete along front to average depth of 3 to 3½ feet aaa. Trenches at Strong Posts about 4 feet deep aaa All Companies clear behind line aaa.

From: J.R.
Time: 3-2 a.m.

Capt.

Appendix IV

S.E.C.R.E.T.   OPERATION ORDERS No.12 .   Copy No. 9
            :-:-:-:-:-:-:-:-:-:

1. The Battalion will relieve "A" Battalion to-night 13/14th.in the left sector of the Brigade Front.

2. Dispositions of Companies will be :-
   "A" Coy. in right sub sector. 2 Platoons in Firing Line and 1 Platoon in Support Line.
      Their right boundary is the road running S.W. from K.32.c.7.10.and their left, the bottom of the Slag Heap. Company H.Qrs.in Slag Heap cutting.
   "D" Coy. in left sub sector. 2 Platoons in New Firing Line and 2 Posts between Slag Heap and Canal,and 2 Platoons in Old Firing Line on Slag Heap.
      Company H.Qrs. at advanced Regtl. Aid Post.
   "B" Coy's 3 Platoons will occupy remainder of Support Line i.e. from K.32.a.4.1. to Slag Heap.
      Company H.Qrs.at K.32.a.1.3.
      This Company will be held available for counter attack
   "C" Coy. will occupy the left Battalion sector of the Reserve Line.

3. "A" Battalion's present dispositions are.:-
   "C" Coy. right sub sector.
   "A" "   left "   "
   "D" & "B" Companies in the Reserve Line.

4. Company Commanders will arrange details of reliefs with the Companies of "A" Battalion they take over from. Reliefs should commence as soon as it is dark enough.
   Companies will take over the trench stores,ammunition etc of the Companies and Platoons in the trenches they will occupy sending duplicate receipts to H.Qrs.for what they take over, and also for what they hand over, by 11 a.m.tomorrow.
   An adjustment will then be made as soon as possible.
   As at present there is only the establishment of S.A.A., Grenades etc.of 2 Companies in the front system of trenches, A. B. & D. Companies must each make themselves acquainted with the location of these two Company dumps.
   Latrine seats and buckets will be handed over as trench Stores, tools and petrol tins will not be handed over.

5. "D"Coy. will pick up Platoon guides of "A"Battalion at the Company H.Qrs. in Slag Heap cutting.
   Each Company will send a guide to report to R.S.M. at H.Qrs. at 9-30 p.m. for their ration mules.

6. The Strong Posts garrisons in the Brown Line will be relieved by "A"Battalion about 7 P.M. The R.S.M.W will arrange a N.C.O. guide for the relieving garrison, who will report to him at about 6 p.m. This N.C.O. will take receipts for stores handed over.

7. The Medical Officer will arrange to send a Waterman up to take over the Pump and Water Tanks in the Cutting in the Slag Heap and medicate the water as required.
   All Companies can refill their petrol tins from these Tanks.

8. Work in progress should be carefully noted by O's C.Comapnies on taking over.

9. The tunnelling fatigue found by "C"Coy. will be relieved by "A"Battalion at mid-night to-night, & if possible before.

10. "C"Coy. will find any carrying parties required to-night.

11. Trench areas must be left perfectly clean.

12. Immediately on completion of relief the cypher "DUG" will be wired to H.Qrs. Battalion H.Qrs. will remain in its present location.

13/6/17.

a/Adjutant. Capt. J.R.

Copy No. 1 to A. Coy.
     2   B
     3   C
     4   D.
     5   T.O. & Q.M.
     6   H.Qrs & File.
     7   5th. Manchesters.
     8   Right Battan of 145th. Bde.
   9-10   War Diary.

Appendix VI

S.E.C.R.E.T.   1/7th. Bn. MANCHESTER REGIMENT.   Copy No. 9
Maps. 1:20,000. ---- D E F E N C E - O R D E R. --- No. 2.
57c.N.E.& 57c.S.E.   14/6/17.

1. **INFORMATION:-** The 1/7th. Bn. Manchester Regt. holds the left Sub Sector of the 127th. Brigade Sector. (Named X).
   The 1/8th. Bn. Manchester Regt. holds the Right Sub Sector. (Named W.)
   The 1/5th. Bn. Manchester Regt. hold the Intermediary Line. (Named Y.)
   The 1/6th. Bn. Manchester Regt. are out of the Line in Rest at RUYAULCOURT (with one Company in the Brown Line) (Named Z.)

2. **FRONTAGE:-** The Battalion Boundaries are as under:-
   NORTHERN BOUNDARY
   K.27.a.45.20., K.26.d.18.30. (copse included), K.32.a.70.85. K.31.b.9.4. thence along Canal. (
   SOUTHERN BOUNDARY.
   K.27 Central to point on road K.32.b.4.3. to junction of roads K.32.a.85.15. to K.32.c.0.0.

3. **DISPOSITIONS:-** Disposition of the Battalion:-

Right Company.	K.32.c.7.8. to K.32.c.6.4.	2 Platoons Firing Line. 1 Platoon Support.
Left Company.	K.32.c.6.4. to Canal.	2 Platoons Firing Line & 2 Posts. +2 Platoons in Support
Counter Attacking Company.	K.32.c.4.9. to Cinder Track.	1 Company in Support Line.
Battalion Reserve.	K.31.d.	1 Company in Reserve Line.
Battalion H.Qrs.	J.36.b.9.0.	

4. **ACTION:-** (i) The front line will on no account be vacated. All portion of trench will be held even though the flanks are turned.
   (ii) In event of the front line being penetrated by the enemy, he will be immediately counter attacked by the Counter Attacking Company under orders of the local Commander.
   Supporting troops will not reinforce the front in driblets but will be used for counter attacks.
   (iii) The Company in Reserve is Battalion Reserve in the hands of the Battalion Commander.
   (iv) If front line on the Slag Heap is taken - the Platoons in Support will hold the enemy to the captured trench to prevent his escape. The guns will be called upon and a counter attack arranged from behind.

5. **MACHINE GUNS & STOKES MORTAR.** :- (i) Machine Guns are placed as follows:-

Guns.	Disposition.	Direction of fire.
1	Q.2.b.8.9.	N.N.W.
1	K.32.c.5.7.	N E.
1	K.32.a.4.5.	S.E.
1	K.32.c.4.6.	N.E.
1	Q.1.b.8.5.	N.E.
1	K.31.d.1.6.	E.

   (ii) Stokes Gun Defence positions are as follows:-
   1 Gun. K.32.c.6.4.
   1 Gun. K.32.a.3.4.

6. **PATROLS:-** Reconnaissance patrols will be arranged by the Scout Officer in consultation with the O.C.Battalion and Company Commanders. Listening Posts will be established.

Both the above should not go out by, or be established in, the same route or position every night.

Patrols want to keep in mind that they are the "HUNTERS" not the "HUNTED".

7. **AIRCRAFT:-** Signal for hostile aircraft is 3 blasts on the whistle. "All Clear" is one blast.

The Company in Reserve will mount one Anti-aircraft Lewis Gun by DAY only. This gun will only be fired by order of an Officer.

8. **AMMUNITION:-** The following is the new scale of Ammunition etc. to be kept up by Platoons, Companies etc. in the Line.

	Boxes S.A.A.	Grenades No.5	Boxes. No.20	No.23	Pistol Webley. Boxes.	Very Light Boxes. 1"	1½"
Platoon each.	6	-	-	-	-	-	-
Company each.	12	12	2	2	1 @	1	1
B.H.Qrs.Dump.	40	64	2	5	1 @	4	4

@ 250 Rounds.

9. **DEFENCE SCHEMES:-** Company Commanders will:-
   (i) Call for Platoon Defence Schemes in writing.
   (ii) Prepare their own scheme for action in writing and submit to Battn.H.Qrs., with sketch of their trenches showing map squares.
   (iii) Ensure that each Section Commander has a scheme for action.

10. **S.O.S.** The S.O.S.Signal is a rifle Grenade bursting into 4 green lights. It is only to be fired when the enemy can be seen advancing towards our own trenches or can be seen massing opposite to them.

11. **WORK:-.** The Garrisons of the Firing Line do not work on the trenches at night, but are responsible for the safety of the line.(2 Platoons on Left sub sector & 2 Platoons on Right sub sector)

The 2 Platoons in support on the Slag Heap do not leave their own trenches to work at night but remain and improve their own trench.

No covering party on Slag Heap but a strong system of sentries in the trench.

[signature] Capt.
a/Adjutant. J.R.

By orderly distribution.
Copy.No.1 to O.C. "A"Coy.
    2   B
    3   C
    4   D
    5   H.Qrs. "A"Mess.
    6   H.Qrs. "B"Mess.
    7   2nd.in Command.
    8   File.
  9 & 10   War Diary.

Appendix VI.

S.E.C.R.E.T.   1/7th.Bn.Manchester Regt.   Copy.No. 9
       — D E F E N C E   O R D E R —   No 2 a.
       :-:-:-:-:-:-:-:-:-:-:-:-:-:   14/6/17.

Proposed Defence Scheme in the event of the
Battalion on our Left being driven back.

1. It will be necessary to form a line facing northerly.

2. It is proposed to take up the following line approximately.
        (probably by a Reserve Battalion.)

3. Reserve Trench - parapet of Communication trench in K.31 c.
   to White Slag Heap (200 yds N.W. of Battalion H.Qrs.)
   inclusive.

   Note.:- The Communication trench should be made if possible
          into a fire trench facing northerly.

                                                    Capt.
                              2/Adjutant.   J.R.

By orderly
   distribution.

Copy.No.1 to O.C. "A" Coy.
       2   B
       3   C
       4   D
       5   H.Qrs. "A" Mess.
       6   H.Qrs "B" ans.
       7   2nd. in Command.
       8   File.
    9 & 10   War Diary.

CONFIDENTIAL

WAR - DIARY.

FOR

1st July to 31st July

1917

1/7th Bn. MANCHESTER REGT.

VOL. VII

WAR DIARY
INTELLIGENCE SUMMARY

Army Form C. 2118.

Place: France
57C N.E. and S.E.
1: 20,000

of 1/9th Manchester Regt.

Place	Date 1917 July	Hour	Summary of Events and Information	Remarks and references to Appendices
T.3.6.d.9.5.	1		Bn. trench strength 40 officers 913 O.R.; Ration strength 29 officers 677 O.R. Bns. raiding Battle casualties during June O.R. 2 killed, 2 died of wounds, 14 wounded. Situation normal.	
	2		Arm. Bomb Shells were dropped on Front, Support & Reserve Lines. Final preparations completed for raid at 1.8 a.m. tomorrow on WIGAN COPSE. 2/Lt. Pitton in command of 2/Lt. A. HODGE Made a successful raid on WIGAN COPSE. Zero 1.5 a.m. Ours and hostile artillery started simultaneously at Zero and both terminated at 1.23 a.m. when all our men had begun.	
	3		Surprise was complete. 3 prisoners brought in. 1 wounded. Estimates at least 6 of enemy were killed. Our Casualties 2 officers [...] wounded. Several enemy dug-outs bombed. Part of 1 platoon of 8th Manchester on [...] Zero in DEAN COPSE was spoiled by M.G. fire. They had 2 killed & 10 wounded & did not reach copse. Quiet. No change. 2/Lt M. BATEMAN returned from R.F.C. Grows gustatory.	Appendix I
	4		2/Lt. W. T. THORPE returned from Musketry School PONT REMY. New artillery [...]	
	5		Lieut. 2/Lt Bivins M.Gs. back to BAPAUME Area about S/9 5 July. 2/Lt C.S. WOOD arrived from [...] Artillery and T.M.s Put Barrier on DEAN COPSE. Situation normal.	

WAR DIARY / INTELLIGENCE SUMMARY

Army Form of 1/7th Bn. Manchester Regt.

MAP. FRANCE 57c 1/40,000

Place	Date	Hour	Summary of Events and Information	Remarks and references to Appendices
J.36.d.9.5	6		The 5th Manchesters take over the line from us relieving our 2 front Coys and Coy in support line with 1 of their Coys according to the new disposition. B Coy remains where it is in Reserve and is under tactical orders of C.O. 5th Manchesters. C Coy goes back to Sunken Rd Trenches in 2nd line J.36.c.5.0.3. A and D Coys to Intermediate line R.31.c. and J.36.b.5.5.2. The 42nd Div: moved back from this area: our Brigade is relieved by 175 Bde on 5/9/5 July.	ge
	7		Situation quiet. Preparations made for pushing over to 2/11th London Regt.	ge
	8		Battalion relieved by 2/11th London Regt of 175th Bde. see APPENDIX II 7th APPENDIX II Relief of 42nd Div: by 58th Div: Completed night 8/9th except for Artillery & Engineers and other gunners. Battalion relief completed 1.35 a.m. & troops move by train to YPRES when they billet for the night.	
	9		13m. marched to camp at BARASTRE starting 2.30 a.m. arriving 3.30 a.m.	ge
BARASTRE	10		Bn. marched as part of the Brigade to camp at ACHIET LE PETIT starting 8 a.m. and arriving 12.55 p.m. 1 casualty. Cool day, men did very well, march discipline fair.	ge
ACHIET LE PETIT	11		Cleaning up & reinstating of men. A Guards Regt. instructor lent to Bn. for N.C.Os. Class & the Drill Training.	ge
	12			ge
	13		History of July 1918 to be an ordinary working day. 2/Lt. RICHARDSON and 1 Platoon of "A" Coteven from march with R.E. Line to AMIENS open to officers and other ranks	ge

Army Form C. 2118

57C / No. 000

3 WAR DIARY of 1/7 Manchester Regt.
or
INTELLIGENCE SUMMARY

(Erase heading not required.)

Instructions regarding War Diaries and Intelligence Summaries are contained in F. S. Regs., Part II. and the Staff Manual respectively. Title Pages will be prepared in manuscript.

Place	Date 1917	Hour	Summary of Events and Information	Remarks and references to Appendices
Camp at ACHIET LE PETIT	July 14		Training as per Programme of Training attached APPENDIX III is carried on.	APPENDIX III
	15		No change. 2/Lt. A. HODGE awarded Military Cross per WIGAN COPSE Raid on 2/3rd July.	gre
	16		Training as usual	gre
	17		No change. Lt. D. NORBURY accepted Capt. dated 12/2/17.	gre
	18		Brigade schemes for 6th and 7th Manchesters. Attack a trench & open warfare. see APPENDIX IV. 2/Lt. R.J.R. BAKER to England on leave.	gre
	19		Training. No change.	gre
	20		Training. 2/Lt. C.T. BRYAN to England on leave.	gre
	21		Training.	gre
	22		Training. 1/Lt. R.J.R. BAKER to England on leave.	gre
	23		Training. Also Battalion sports	gre
	24		Training	gre
	25		Training. 2/Lt. J. BAKER proceeds on months Course to VII Army School.	gre
	26		Training. Brigade Sports.	gre
	27		Training. Capt. D. NORBURY proceeds on leave to England.	gre

FRANCE
51 40,000

WAR DIARY of 1/7th Manchester Regt.

INTELLIGENCE SUMMARY.

Army Form C. 2118.

(Erase heading not required.)

Instructions regarding War Diaries and Intelligence Summaries are contained in F.S. Regs., Part II. and the Staff Manual respectively. Title pages will be prepared in manuscript.

Place	Date	Hour	Summary of Events and Information	Remarks and references to Appendices
ACHIET LE PETIT	July 28		Training – 2/Lt. W.T. THORPE to England on leave.	
	29		Training. 2/Lt. W.H. BARRATT to England on leave. 127th Brigade Sports	
	30		Training. 42nd Divisional Sports.	
	31		Training. Heavy rain at night.	

A.J. Graham
LIEUT-COLONEL,
COMMANDING 1/7th BN. MANCHESTER REGT.

Report on Raid 2nd/3rd July, 1917.

On the night of the 2nd/3rd July, 1917, near HAVRINCOURT, 2nd Lieut. HODGE, 1/7th Manchester Regiment led his platoon against an enemy party who were working in WIGAN COPSE, protected by a covering party and entanglements. In spite of the stillness of the night and the entanglements, 2nd Lieut. HODGE successfully led his party to within 50 yards of the enemy before being discovered. He then rushed the party with his platoon, killed several Germans with the bayonet and point blank rifle fire, and brought back two unwounded and one wounded prisoner. The raiding party suffered no casualties.

The preparations for this operation were skilfully made by 2nd Lieut. HODGE, and its success was due to his leadership and determination.

The strength of the raiding party was one officer and 37 other ranks.

I consider 2nd Lieut. HODGE showed courage and conspicuous skill in organisation and leadership.

* * * *

1/7 Manchester

APPENDIX I (a)

SECRET.   Copy.No.3.
           127th.BRIGADE OPERATION ORDER NO. 31.

Ref. Map. 57c. N.E. & S.E. 1:20,000.   1/7/17.

1. Enemy working parties are employed nightly at :-

    (a) DEAN COPSE   (K.32.b.85.70.)

    (b) WIGAN COPSE. (K.26.d.20.45.)

2. An enterprise will be undertaken on the morning of the 3rd.July
   to obtain identifications and to kill or capture the garrisons
   of WIGAN COPSE & DEAN COPSE.

3. (a) Artillery. (See appendix A. Attached).

    (b) Trench Mortars.
        (i) One 9.45" will fire on VESUVIUS from Zero to Zero
            + 15. Rate of fire maximum.

        (ii) 127th.Stokes Mortar Battery will fire on
             (a) S.E.corner of DEAN COPSE (K.32.b.87.63.)
             (b) Northern edge of DEAN COPSE.
             (c) N.E.corner of DEAN COPSE to cross roads (K.32.b.
                 88.)
        From Zero to Zero + 1 Minute 45 seconds. Rate of fire
        maximum.

    (c) Machine Guns.
             3 Vickers Machine Guns will fire on top of
        Eastern edge of YORKSHIRE BANK from positions near K.32.b.48.00
        and K.32.d.05.75. from Zero to Zero + 20.

    (d) Infantry.
        (i) One Platoon from 1/8th.Bn.Manchester Regt.will
        take up position under S.E.end of YORKSHIRE BANK before Zero.
          At Zero + 2 it will advance on DEAN COPSE capture 2
        prisoners and kill the remainder of the garrison.

        (ii) One Platoon from 1/7th.Bn.Manchester Regt.will
        at Zero advance upon WIGAN COPSE capture 2 prisoners and kill
        the remainder of the garrison.

4. Zero will be 1-8 a.m.July 3rd.

5. Watches will be synchronised at 127th.Infantry Brigade Headquarters
   at 6-30 p.m. 2nd.July.

6. ACKNOWLEDGE on attached slip.

                                   Signed. W.T.Woods.   Capt.
                                        a/Brigade Major.
                                        127th.Inf.Brigade.

APPENDIX I (a)

APPENDIX "A".

ARTILLERY PROGRAMNE.

Zero to Zero + 15 minutes.

A.210.

   3 Guns Trench K.26.d.7.9. to K.26.d.9.8.
   3 "   "   K.27.c.0.3. to K.27.c.3.2.

C.210.

    Trench.   K.26.d.9.8. to K.27.c.3½. 7½.

D.211.

   1 How. VESUVIUS - K.27.c.2.8.
   1 " Cinder Track. - K.33.a.4.5. (Rt.Sec.)

Zero to Zero + 20 minutes

D.211.

Lt.Sec. 2 Hows. ETNA. - K.26.d.9.1.

The Divisional Artillery on our left will fire as under:

8 - 18 pdrs. Trench K.26.b.½.0. to K.26.d.7.9.

   1 How. suspected M.G. K.26.d.6.8½.
   1 "   "   "   K.26.d.9.8.
   1 "   "   "   K.26.b.7.5.
   1 "   "   "   K.27.a.1.3½.

APPENDIX I (6)

OPERATION ORDERS by 2/Lt. A. HODGE.
Commanding No. 9. Platoon.

1. ASSEMBLY POINT.
   The raiding party will assemble on the left of Old Firing Line in correct order.
2. They will leave the trench at   before Zero and proceed along Canal Bank to "X" Post, then up the Canal Bank, through gap in new wire and crawl into position (see plan)
3. TASKS. 1 N.C.O. and 6 men with L.G. & Nos 1 & 2 as a screen and take up a position stretching from Canal Bank protecting the left flank of the attacking party. The L.G. will take up a position to fire on new trench North of Copse.
   1 N.C.O and 5 men with Lewis Gun will take up a position South of Copse commanding the East of Copse.
   The raiding party will consist of, 1 N.C.O. & 4 Bombers on the left -- 1 N.C.O. and 10 Riflemen centre and 1 N.C.O. & 5 Bombers on the right. This line will be followed by the Commander and 6 men.
4. The whole party will leave the trench in the order, the two covering parties slightly in advance. After leaving our front wire they will crawl to their position and await ZERO.
5. WITHDRAWAL. On a prearranged signal the whole party will retire by sections. The two sections in the left going straight to Canal Bank and back to Old Firing Line.
   The two sections on the right will go straight to the gap in front wire and into Old Firing Line.
6. In the attack it is the duty of the bombers to take any dug-outs in rear of Copse and the trench in front of Copse, and the Riflemen to clear the centre of the Copse. The 4 men with Commander will if necessary act as S.B's. or any other purpose

Plan is attached to report on Raid
X. 1 Very light sent up from Old Firing Line at 1.13 am., 2 at 1.18 am and 3 at 1.22

APPENDIX I (c)

RAID on WIGAN COPSE.

July 3rd, 1917.

COMPOSITION :-   1 Officer.
                     1 Sergeant.

		N.C.O.	O.Rs.
1 Section Bombers.		2	10
1 " Lewis Gunners.		1	4.
1 " Rifle Grenadiers.			8.
1 " Riflemen.		1	11.

Additional Lewis Gun with No,s 1 & 2.

OBJECT OF RAID. To raid WIGAN COPSE, take two prisoners and kill remainder of garrison.

PROCEDURE. (see accompanying plan).

The party left our front wire at point Q. 12-40 am in the following order in single file:-

1. Screen of Rifle Grenadiers with Lewis Gun and No,s. 1 & 2.
2. Five Bombers and one N.C.O.
3. Officer.
4. 1 N.C.O. and 11 Riflemen.
5. Sergeant.
6. 1 N.C.O. and 5 Bombers.
7. 1 N.C.O. and 4 men with Lewis Gun.

On leaving the gap in wire the screen (1) extended to left with left flank on Canal Bank and moved in direction of Canal to position "Y".

The remainder crawled until position "A" was formed with the exception of No.7.who crawled out to position "X" commanding East side of Copse.

The party in "A" position then crawled forward to "B" position and were not challenged or fired upon.

Here they lay about 20 seconds until artillery barrage commenced, upon which they got up and rushed towards the Copse. Zero hour was 1-8 a.m.

ENCOUNTER. The Copse was entered for about

ENCOUNTER. The Copse was entered for about a distance of 10 to 15 yards, and three prisoners were immediately taken. Wire was then encountered consisting of loose concertina and irregular single strands fastened to trees and shrubs, some face high.

A number of enemy rose from centre of Copse, and rapid fire was opened on them and bombs thrown. Our men started to cut the wire. Bombers on the left penetrated wire and entered Copse for about 20 yards. Some of enemy were seen to drop in Copse as result of our fire.

ACTION OF LEWIS GUNS.
(a) The gun in "Y" position fired six drums along new trench position North of Copse, commencing at Zero.
(b) The gun in "X" position, on seeing a body of enemy leave Copse at point "a" on east side, after raid commenced, opened fire. The enemy had run to "b" but immediately doubled back. Subsequently they ran out again towards "c" and were again fired upon.

At 1-23 a.m. the signal for withdrawal went up, and party withdrew with 3 prisoners, one of whom was wounded, to gap Q, by sections.

OPPOSITION. On the first rush the raiding party was met by erratic fire and one bomb thrown. There was no further opposition.

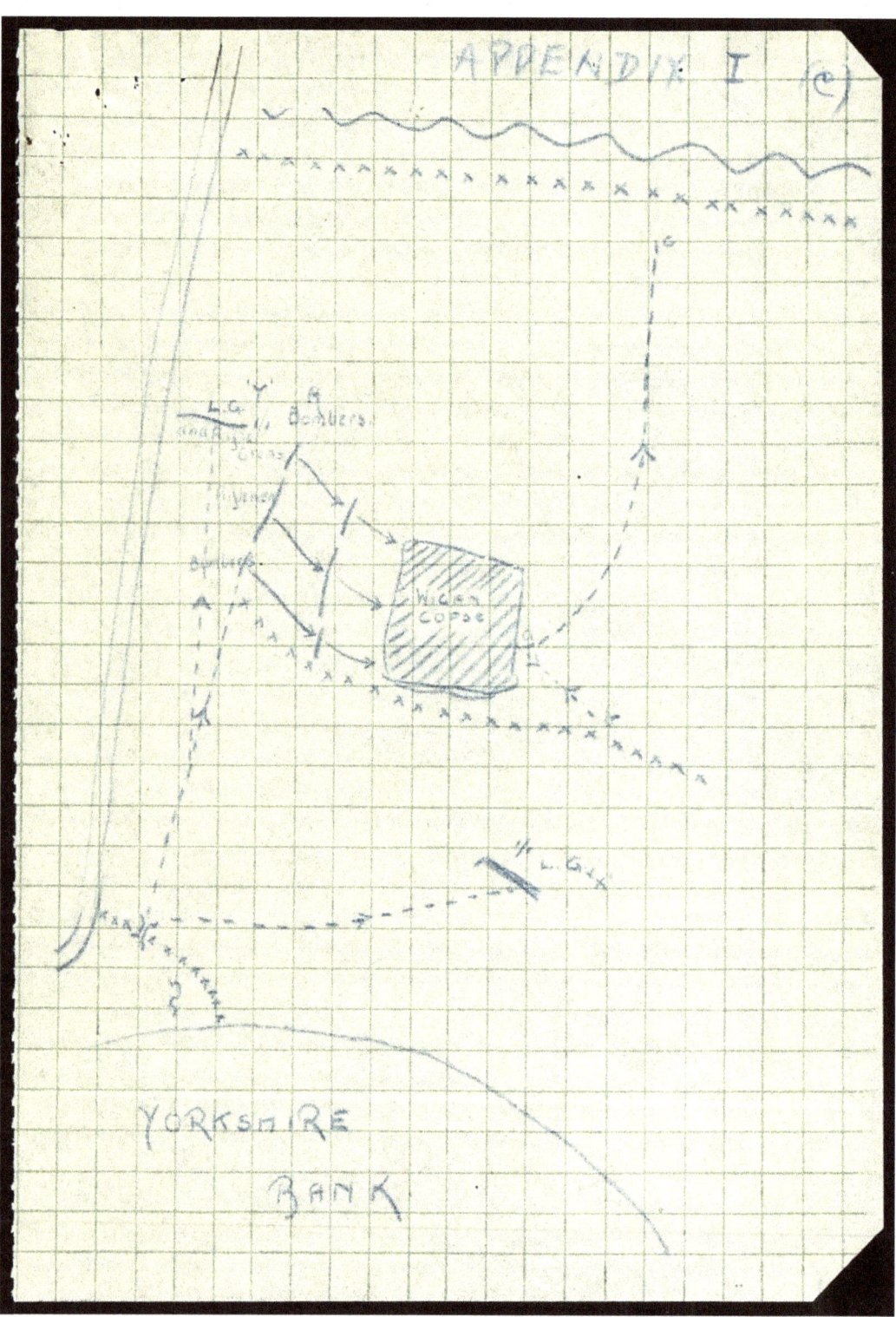

APPENDIX I (2)

Copy of ROUTINE ORDER No.380. by
MAJOR GENERAL B.R.MITFORD C.B., C.M.G., D.S.O.

HONOURS AND REWARDS --- IMMEDIATE.
Under authority delegated by His Majesty the King, the Corps Commander has been pleased to award the

MILITARY MEDAL
to
No.275355 Sergt. PATRICK SAMUEL McHUGH.
No.276418 Pte. THOMAS BRAITHWAITE.
No.275933 Pte. THOMAS McLEAN.
For the following actions.

Sergt.McHugh. " Near HAVRINCOURT on the 3rd.July 1917, Sergt McHugh was Platoon Sergeant of No.9.Platoon which under 2/Lt Hodge successfully raided a German working party. Sergt. McHugh lead the first line. The success of the enterprise was largely due to his leading and example.

Pte.BRAITHWAITE. "Near HAVRINCOURT on the 3rd.July.1917 during a successful raid by No.9.platoon, Pte.BRAITHWAITE singly attacked three Germans of whom he killed two with the bayonet and captured one.

Pte.McLean. " Near HAVRINCOURT on the 3rd.July 1917 during a successful raid by No.9.Platoon, Pte.McLean captured a German and subsequently killed at least one other with the bayonet, after which he went to the assistance of Pte. BRAITHWAITE.

Capt.
a/Adjutant, 1/7th.Manchester Regt.

APPENDIX II

SECRET.   O P E R A T I O N   O R D E R   No.19.   Copy.No. 9

:-:-:-:-:-:-:-:-:-:-:-:-:-:-:-:-

1. The Battalion will be relieved tomorrow night 8/9th.July, by 3 Companies of 2/11th.London Regt.
   "C"Coy. 2/11th.London Regt.will relieve "A"Coy.
   "B"Coy.   "   "   "   "B"Coy.
   "D"Coy.   "   "   "   "D"Coy.
   "C"Coy.will evacuate its trench as detailed below.

2. Guides will be sent as under by A. B. & D.Companies and Hdqrs. to be at a point where Artillery Road meets Havrincourt Wood. P.12.b.4.0. at 9-45 tomorrow.
   1 Pre.Battalion Hdqrs.
   1 " Company   "
   1 " Platoon.
   R.S.M.will detail guide for Battalion Hdqrs.
   Each party of guides should know the title of,and keep a look out for the Coy. it has to guide.

3. Immediately reliefs are complete Companies will send the cypher "TOK" to Hdqrs.

4. Five trains(each of 7 trucks) will be at J.36.d.8.6.,i.e. nearly opposite Battalion Hdqrs.at mid-night tomorrow.
   Companies will entrain in following order:-
   "C" - "D" - "A" - "B". Each truck to hold 25 men.
   2/Lt.S.J.WILSON will act as entraining Officer.
   "C"Coy.will evacuate their trench in time to entrain at mid-night.
   2/Lt.J.BAKER will travel on the first train and act ac detraining Officer for all Battalion trains at the other end.

5. <u>Movement of Kit etc.from the Line.</u>
   The Transport Officer will arrange to send up tomorrow evening as early as practicable the 4 Lewis Gun Limbers,the 2 Tool Limbers(all empty) the Mess Cart,the Maltese Cart,and teams for 4 Cookers.
   1 Lewis Gun Limber and 1 Cooker team will go direct to "C" Coy.in Sunken Road and the remainder report to Hdqrs.
   "A" "B" & "D"Companies will have their Lewis Guns and magazines at Hdqrs.by 9-45 pm.,with loading parties.

2.

All Lewis Guns and Equipment must be packed in front half of Limber, each Coy, in a separate one. The rear half limber will be available for Officers Kits, Stores, Orderly Room boxes etc. which must be ready stacked outside Orderly Room by 10 pm.

R.S.M. Will arrange for loading party.

All transport must move back as soon as possible, each Coy. sending a Lewis Gunners with its own Guns.

On arrival at YTRES the limbers will be unloaded at the Battalion Dump and repacked with their authorised loads as per Mobile Establishment.

6. Coys. will render to Orderly Room by noon on 9th. all receipts for Ammunition, Trench Stores etc. No petrol tins will be handed over. All shelter sheets will be handed over except 2 per Coy. which will be brought along.

Advance Parties are being sent by incoming unit to take over Trench Stores etc.

7. Each Coy. will send down 4 Lewis Gunners to the Dump tomorrow afternoon to sort out their magazines tins, Lewis Gun boxes and Reserve S.A.A. so that it will be ready for immediate loading on return of the Lewis Gun Limbers.

8. ADVANCE PARTY :(a) 2/Lt. J.C. CHATTERTON and 1 N.C.O. from each Coy. will report to Staff Capt. outside E.F. Canteen YTRES at 10 a.m tomorrow 8th., to be shown Battalion Billets on night of 8/9th and the day of the 9th. This party will assemble outside Orderly Room at 8 am. tomorrow.

(b). 2/Lt. F.G. BURN & 2/Lt. J.C. CHATTERTON and 2 N.C.O's from each Coy. will assemble outside the Town Major's office BUS at 7 a.m. on the 9th. to proceed under the Staff Capt. by motor lorry to the new area. They will take two days rations

This party will take over the camp allotted to Battalion and thoroughly clean it up prior to arrival of main body on 10th.

Guides from it will be posted to conduct the Battalion to its own camp immediately on arrival.

9. All Coys. must leave their trenches in a clean and sanitary condition. Each Coy. must obtain a signed certificate to this effect from relieving Coy.

10. If the Battalion is billeted at BUS on night 8/9th. the Transport loaded according to Mobile Establishment will move there too, independently.

3.

The Transport Officer will arrange to draw 2nd.Line baggage Wagons from O.C.431st.Coy.A.S.C. at YTRES at 8pm.tomorrow or before. These will carry Battalion Rations for 9th.and Officers kits.

11. The Battalion will move from YTRES or BUS to a camp about O.16 on the 9th.and on the 10th.from there to ACHIET-LE-PETIT.

12. Rations will be delivered at the New Camp.O.16.about 5pm.on 9th.inst.for the 10th. Rations for the 11th.will be brought by Supply Column from Railhead ROCQUIGNY to the New area.

13. The Battalion Dump will be moved tomorrow by the Transport to a suitable site near the Light Railway at P.20.c.4.6. The Present guard at the Dump will remain in charge of all Battalion kit there,on the train and at its destination.

The train timings are:-

	Ready to load.	Loacation.	Depart.	Destination.
9th.July.	8 a.m.	P.20.c.4.6.	8-15 a.m.	G.14.a.
10th. "	8 a.m.	"	"	"

Trains will consist of 8 trucks,each capable of taking 9 tons.

The Battalion is allotted 1 truck on 9th.and 2 trucks on 10th.

2/Lt.S.J.WILSON will be in charge of the Brigade Train on the 10th.

"C"Coy.will detail 5 Other Ranks to act as loading party both days. This party will march down to Q.M.Stores YTRES, tomorrow after evening meal and report to Q.M.

14. Q.M.Personnel and Drummers will join Battalion at YTRES or BUS on morning of 9th.

Capt.
a/Adjutant. 1/7th.Manch.Rgt.

7/7/17.

Copy.No.1 to A.Coy.
      2   B "
      3   C "
      4   D "
      5   T.O.& Q.M.
      6   Hdqrs.& File.
      7

War Diary

SECRET. ADDENDUM to OPERATION ORDER No. 19. Copy.No. 9
:-:-:-:-:-:-:-:-:-:-:-:-:- 8:7:17.

1. Battalion will be billeted at YPRES to-night 8/9th. July.

2. All Tools in possessions of Companies and Hdqrs. will be handed over to incoming Unit and receipts taken.

3. Entraining Point to-night will be in P.12.b. and not as stated in para 4 of O.O.No.19.
   Companies will move there on relief.
   Hdqrs. personnel will parade at 11-45pm. and proceed under command of 2/Lt.M.BATEMAN.

4. "C" Coy. by 11 pm. to-night will send to Hdqrs., all shelter sheets and other moveable property in their charge and hand them over to R.S.M. These will be included in Stores handed over by Hdqrs. to incoming Coy.

5. GUIDES:- Reference para 2. O.O.No.19. Relieving unit will xxx arrive by train and is expected to detrain about Artillery Rd. P.12.b. at 11 p.m. Guide parties must look out for these trains and follow them if necessary.

6. Reference para 3.O.O.No.19. O.C. "B" Coy. on relief will also wire "A" Battalion the cypher " NO INOCULATIONS".

7. Companies will collect their overcoats on arrival at YPRES to-night. They are being arranged in Coy. Dumps in locality of Battalion Billets. & At 3 a.m. on 10th., 1 Lorry will be available to carry Battalion Greatcoats on to ACHIET LE PETIT.

8. When Companies have taken over their Billets to-night they will immediately report to this effect to Battalion Hdqrs.

Copy.No.1 to A.Coy.
       2   B "
       3   C "
       4   D "
       5   T.O. & Q.M.
       6   Hdqrs. & File.
       7   Qm
       8   Asst Adjt   9-10 War Diary

a/Adjutant. 1/7th. R.Wch.Rgt.

Appendix III

1/7th. MANCHESTER REGT.

Programme of Training for:
(Sections and Platoons.)

	A.	B.	C.	D.
Early morning. 6-30 – 7-0.	Officers' Roll call – Reading orders.			
Morning. 8-30 – 9-0.	Inspection of Company – Rifles etc.			
9-0 – 10-0.	Range.	Close order drill.	Assault C'se.	Musketry.
10-0 – 11-0.	Close order Drill.	Range.	Close order Drill.	Assault C'se.
11-0 – 12-0.	Musketry.	Assault C'se.	Range.	Close order Drill.
12-0 – 12-30.	Ceremonial.	Ceremonial.	Ceremonial.	Ceremonial.
Afternoon. 2-0 – 3-0.	Assault C'se.	Musketry.	Musketry.	Range.
3-0 – 4-0.	Close order Drill.	Close order Drill.	Close order Drill.	Close order Drill.
30 – 7-0.	Recreational Training.			
	Conference.			

NOTE:- Physical Training – Saluting Drill will be carried out at times allotted to Close order drill.

A.R. Anshaw
Lieut. Col.
Commanding : 1/7th. Manchester Regt.

13/7/17.

Appendix IV

EXERCISE No. 1.

Ref. Map BUCQUOY scale 1:20,000. FIFTH ARMY (B).

GENERAL IDEA.

1. Z day – the day of the exercise.

2. The trench running from L.6.a.09. – the ACHIET-le-PETIT – BUCQUOY Road at L.11.b.7.5. will be called LOGEAST TRENCH.

3. For several days the Germans have been retiring from West to East, from one trench system to another, leaving small rear guards to delay the advance of the pursuing British.

4. At Z – 180 on Z day British Troops ('X' Battalion of 'W' Brigade, not those included in the exercise) occupied the trenches E. of BUCQUOY in L.4.a.& C. without opposition except for a few 77 mm shells thought to have been fired from E. of LOGEAST WOOD.

5. At Zero – 70 on Z day troops of 'K' Brigade are assembled in Column of route in BUCQUOY as follows:-
    Head of 'R' Battalion L.3.b.55.00.
    Head of 'S' Battalion at L.4.a.0.5. tail about L.3.b.5.0.
    Machine Gun Coy. in BUCQUOY on BUCQUOY – ESSARTS Road (just W. of map.)

SPECIAL IDEA:

First Stage.

At Zero – 60 the following message is received by Os.C., 'R' 'S' and Machine Gun Company :-

B.M. 176 – Zero – 85.

Patrols from 'X' Battalion of 'W' Brigade on approx. line L.11.a.00. – L.5.a.05. were fired at by few rifles from LOGEAST TRENCH aaa. 'R' & 'S' Battalions will seize and consolidate LOGEAST TRENCH aaa. 'R' Battalion between L.11.b.75.66. and L.5.d.90.82. aaa. 'S' Battalion between latter point and L.6.a.09. aaa. Machine Gun Coy. will detail two sections to put Machine Guns in action to give covering fire to advancing infantry aaa. Liaison Officers from Divisional Artillery will report to 'R' & 'S' Battalions shortly aaa. Head of main body of Battalions will cross Railway in L.4.a.& c. at Zero aaa. similar and simultaneous advance will be made by infantry on both flanks of 'K' Brigade aaa. Reports to BUCQUOY Church L.3.b.45.10. aaa. Addressed 'R' Battalion 'S' Battalion, Machine Gun Coy. repeated Division and Flank Brigades.

Required.

Action by Os.C. 'R' 'S' and Machine Gun Company.
(This will be discussed at evening conference on Y day.)

17/7/17.

Capt.
a/Adjutant. 1/7th. Manch. Rgt.

Vol 7

CONFIDENTIAL

WAR DIARY

of

1/7th Bn. MANCHESTER RGT.

From:- 1st Aug. 1917.   To:- 31st Aug. 1917.

VOLUME.

VIII.

FRANCE
MAP
1/40,000

Army Form C. 2118.

WAR DIARY
of 1/7th Bn. Manchester Regt.
INTELLIGENCE SUMMARY.

(Erase heading not required.)

Instructions regarding War Diaries and Intelligence Summaries are contained in F.S. Regs., Part II. and the Staff Manual respectively. Title pages will be prepared in manuscript.

Place	Date 1917	Hour	Summary of Events and Information	Remarks and references to Appendices
ACHIET LE PETIT	August 1st		Return strength of Battalion 'tday officers 27 O.R. 725.	
			Casualties during July. Killed NIL Wounded 12.	
			Training	
	2		Training. 2/Lt. J.C. MORTEN and E.B. TAYLOR returned from leave	gre
	3		Training. 2/Lt. C.J. BRYAN returned from leave. Capt A.H. TINKER returned from course	gre
	4		Training. 2/Lt. G. JESSOP to England on leave.	gre
	5		Training.	gre
	6		Training.	gre
	7		Training.	gre
	8		Training. Lieut D. NORBURY returned from leave.	gre
	9		Training. 2/Lt. W.T. THORPE ————— Major J.H. ALLAN to England on leave.	gre
			Brigade School. Rued to Trench attack. 2/Lt. W.H. BARRATT returned from leave.	gre
	10		Training.	gre
	11		Training.	gre
	12		Training.	gre
	13		Training. 2/Lt. J.C. MORTEN to England on leave	gre
	14		Training. 2/Lt. C.R. O'R. TAAFE joined Battalion.	gre
	15		Training. 2/Lt. G. JESSOP returns from leave. Capt. C.H.G. PHILP M.O. attached to duty with Bn.	gre
	16		Training. 1/Lt. G. JESSOP proceeds to England for transfer to R.E.	gre
			2/Lt. F. WEBSTER joined Bn.	gre

FRANCE
57/C
40,000

Army Form C. 2118.

WAR DIARY
INTELLIGENCE SUMMARY
(Erase heading not required.)

of 1/7th Bn. Manchester Regt.

Place	Date 1917 August	Hour	Summary of Events and Information	Remarks and references to Appendices
ACHIET LE PETIT	17		Training. Bn. has recently received re-inforcements of 31, 36, 8 and 2 other ranks. All have acquired a good deal of polishing up & have received special instruction. Type & quality quite fair. With 3 or 4 exceptions.	
	18		Training. Big Ads. held big tournament. Received warning order that Bn. would probably move by road to AVELUY – BOUZINCOURT area on Tuesday 21st. 2/Lt. G. NORBURY to England on leave.	
	20		Training & preparing to move tomorrow.	
BOUZINCOURT	21		Bn. moves and with the Brigade to camp near BOUZINCOURT. Lee APPENDIX I. Start marching 7.50 am. Arch "Midland Huts" at noon. Heavy casualties en route, due to hot day & heavy packs. Breakfasts chiefly army biscuits.	APPENDIX I
	22		Bn. entrains for HOPOUTRE (W. of YPRES) tomorrow night. Bn. (less D Coy under Capt. HIGHAM) entrain 10.11 pm for HOPOUTRE just W. of POPERINGE. See APPENDIX II. Lt. J.W. SIVEWRIGHT to England on leave.	APPENDIX II
HOPOUTRE L.15.d.9.1	23		Arrived about 10 am. 1½ mile march to camp, arrival about 11.20 am. Encampation in tents short.	
	24 25		Training in the morning. 2/Lt. W. GRESTY to hospital. Training. Lt. J. BAKE returns from France. Learn that we shall shortly relieve 15th Div. in the line E. of YPRES.	
	26		Major J.H. ALLAN returns from leave.	

WAR DIARY
— or —
INTELLIGENCE SUMMARY

Army Form C. 2118.

FRANCE
BELGIUM and FRANCE
Mar 27 to...

of 1/7th Manchester Regt.

Place	Date	Hour	Summary of Events and Information	Remarks and references to Appendices
HOPOUTRE L.15.6.9.-1	27		Entrained	
	28		Training Lewis Gun Bayonet fighting (Shut-28) 3rd & final extract Q.11 & L.G.B.	
	29		Training (very wet)	
	30		Training and preparing to move forward tomorrow.	
BRAND HOEK G.18.a.2.6	31		2/Lt. G. NORBURY and J.C. MORTE return from leave. 2/Lt. G. NORBURY attached to Division for Traffic Control work. Bn. arrived into K Bde. at 6 am see APPENDIX II. Bn. arrived in Camp about 9.30 am. Camp very dirty. No casualties on route. Find the 13th Bn. Royal Scots in Camp (1st Division). This is the Division the 42nd relieves in the line. Our Division Bn. bivouaced in this area has come into the XIX Corps, Commander Lt. General WATTS, but the V Army, Commander General GOUGH. 12.5 P.M. Moved into the line that night. Our Bde is in Divisional Reserve.	APPENDIX II

A.E. Mahon
LIEUT. COLONEL
COMMANDING 2/7th BN. MANCHESTER REGT

Map 57C. 1:40000   APPENDIX I

BATTALION ORDERS
by
Lieut Col. A.E. CRONSHAW., T.D.   Commanding: 1/7th. Manchester Regiment

In the Field.   -:-:-:-:-:-:-:-   20/8/17.

(1) **DUTIES:-** Officer of the day tomorrow: 2/Lt. R. Heathcote HACKER.
         Next for Duty   : 2/Lt. C.S. WOOD.
         Company for Duty   : "C" Coy.
         Next for Duty   : "D" Coy.

(2) **ROUTINE:-** Reveille 5-0 am.   Breakfast 6-0 am.
        Parade on Battalion ground in Mass ready to move off at 7-45 am.
        with Band and 1st. Line Transport complete.

(3) **MOVE:-.** The Battalion will move by route march from this area tomorrow
        and pass the starting point (G.19.b.3.7.) at 8-23 am. en route
        for AVELUY. Halts will be made for 10 minutes at 9-0 am.,
        9-55 am., 10-55 am., etc.
          Transport will move in rear of the Battalion and the distance
        between units will be 400 yards. The Battalion will march
        closed up.

(4) **BAGGAGE:-.** All baggage proceeding with the 1st. Line Transport e.g.
        Officers Kits, Orderly Room boxes etc. will be ready for loading
        at the Q.M. Stores at 6-45 am. The R.S.M. will arrange the
        necessary loading party.

(5) ~~XXXXXXXXXXXXX~~
    REAR PARTY:-. 2/Lt. S.J. WILSON and 8 Scouts will remain behind as a
        Rear party to hand over the camp and all tents etc. standing, to
        the Town Major at 8-30 am. They will proceed after the Battalion
        under orders issued separately.
        2/Lt W Gresty will report to the asst. Staff Capt. at Brigade H.Q.
        at 5-30 am. tomorrow and proceed to AVELUY to be allotted billets.
        He will take a bicycle with him and the day's rations.

(6) **CLEANLINESS OF CAMP.** It is strongly impressed on all ranks that the Camp
        area must be left in a clean condition and no efforts are to be
        spared to bring this about.
          The tentage and shelters will be left standing, unless fresh
        orders are issued, and all tent flies will be neatly rolled and
        the floor boards raised and placed against the tent poles.
          The 2nd. in Command and the Medical Officer will inspect the
        whole camp before the Battalion marches out.

(7) **HEAVY BAGGAGE:-.** All baggage surplus to 1st. Line Transport will be
        loaded on motor lorries at 5pm. this afternoon and sent by road
        to AVELUY. A loading party and guard to proceed with this
        baggage will be detailed by the R.S.M. Men unable to march
        will have the preference. This party will take the unexpired
        portion of the day's rations and 3 extra days rations.

(8) **BOMBERS:-.** The following qualified for the Red Grenade Badge during
        Course Aug. 6th. - 17th. inclusive.
           276199 Pte. G. Turner.   "C" Coy.
           276753   "   H. Mudd.   "
           276294   "   J. Warburton.   "

                                     W H Barratt
                                                  2/Lieut.
                             asst/Adjutant. 1/7th. Manchester Regt.

APPENDIX II

OPERATION ORDER No.19   22/8/17.

1. The Battalion, less "D"Coy. and 1 Cooker will entrain to-day at AVELUY Station, the train leaving at 10-11 pm.
2. For the purpose of this move there will only be 4 Companies, Hdqrs. personnel will be attached to their own Companies.
3. ROUTINE:-.

    5 pm (punctual) Evening Meal.
    6 pm. All Transport will be ready completely loaded to move to the Station. R.S.M. will detail necessary loading parties for Officers Kits, Mess Stores, and supply wagons for loading at 5-30 pm.
    8 pm. Battalion less "D"Coy. will parade ready to move, in full marching order.

Rations for the 23rd. will be carried on the man except tea, sugar and milk which will be taken in bulk by Platoons, in case an opportunity is given for making tea en route.

    Full water bottles will be carried.

Companies must leave their huts and surroundings perfectly clean, O&C. Coys reporting to this effect to the Commanding Officer before Battalion moves off.

4. Marching out States will be handed into B.O.R. by 2 pm.

5. ENTRAINING:-. (a) Once in the train no troops will leave their trucks without permission.

    (b) Composition of Train.

1 Officers carriage.   For 30 Officers.
30 Trucks.   Each holds 40 Other Ranks, or 8 light Draught or 6 heavy Draught animals.
17 Flats.   Nominally 4 axles on a Flat but owing to varying sizes 1 G.S. Wagon and ½ Limber only can be relied on.

Companies will entrain in order A.B.C. Coys. commencing from the front truck allotted. 1 Officer and 60 Other Ranks from 1/3rd. Field Ambulance will also be on the train.

    (c) Entraining must be completed ½ hour before train is timed to start.

    (d) No man to go near Canteen until entrainment is finished and Canteen to be cleared 1 hour before departure of train.

6. DETAILS OF DUTIES:-. (i) 2/Lt. C.J. BRYAN will be Battalion entraining Officer. He will report on the Station at 7 pm. to Lt. A.S. PARKER the Brigade entraining Officer and assist him.

    (ii) 2/Lt. S.J. WILSON will be Battalion detraining Officer and will report immediately on arrival to Lt. J. MARSHALL the Brigade detraining Officer and assist him.

    (iii) O.C. "A"Coy. will detail off 1 Officer and 6 men to picquet the forward end of the train and O.C. "C"Coy. likewise a similar picquet at the rear end of the train. Their duty will be to prevent men leaving the train without orders at the various stops, and to prevent men leaving the station when leave to quit train has been granted.

    (iv) 2/Lt. W.T. THORP with 5 men of "B"Coy. will report to the R.T.O. on arrival of Battalion at AVELUY station and act under his orders as a picquet until the train moves.

    (v) O.C. "D"Coy. will detail a working party of 1 Officer and 30 other ranks to load heavy baggage. This party will report to the Station at 7 pm. to-day. The Quartermaster will generally supervise the loading and care of baggage and report what baggage guards he considers necessary en route.

APPENDIX III

BATTALION ORDERS
by
LIEUT.COLONEL A.E.CRONSHAW T.D. COMMANDING 1/7th.MANCHESTER REGT.
IN THE FIELD.   AUG. 30th. 1917.
:-:-:-:-:-:-:-:-:-:

(1) DUTIES:-. Officer of the day tomorrow. 2/Lt.T.P.WILKINSON.
              Next for duty.   2/Lt.W.T.THORP.
              Company for duty.   "A"Coy.
              Next for duty.   "B"Coy.

(2) ROUTINE:- Reveille 3-45 am. Breakfast 4-30 am.

(3) MOVE:-.   The Battalion with the Band will parade in Mass on the
              Battalion parade ground at 5-55 am. ready to move off at 6 am.
              prompt by route march to the new area. *order of Coys* B C D A
              The head of the column will pass the starting point
              L.11.b.2.5. at 6-30 am.
                   The following distances will be maintained
                   200 yds. between Companies.
                   200 yds. between rear of Infantry Column & Transport.
                   25 yds. between each section of 6 vehicles.
              Halts will be made:-
                   5 mins. at 6-20 am. - 7-20 am. - 8-20 am. - 9-20 am.
                   10 mins. at 6-45 am. - 7-45 am. - 8-45 am. - 9-45 am.
              The Battalion will occupy TORONTO Camp at G.18.a.2.6.
                   A Platoon of the 5th.Manchesters will march in rear of
              the Infantry Column to collect stragglers and to take names of
              all men who have fallen out without written permission.

(4) TRANSPORT:-. The Transport will be Brigaded under Lieut.YOCKNEY, Bde.
              Transport Officer.
                   All 1st.Line Transport is to be loaded this evening by
              7-30 pm. with its recognised stores and equipment, in addition
              the following articles will be carried.
                   Surplus pack saddles on the near animals of limbered vehicles.
              All YUKON packs and any special crates issued for pack
              saddles.
                   The R.S.M. will detail the necessary loading party, except
              for Coy.L.G.Equipment and Medical Stores.

(5) BAGGAGE:-. One motor lorry is available for the carriage of all extra
              baggage. This extra baggage must be packed and dumped ready
              for loading this evening by 5-0 pm. The dump will be made
              close to the entrance N.W.of Camp.
                   The R.S.M. will detail the necessary loading parties.
                   A small section of men, to be detailed later, will accompany the
              motor lorry as guard and loading party at the new camp.

(6) REAR PARTY:-. 2/Lt.S.J.WILSON and 6 Scouts will remain behind to hand
              over the Camp to the Area Commandant and receive from him the
              necessary "CLEAN CERTIFICATE".
                   It is brought to the notice of all ranks that as much
              cleaning up of the camp will be done this evening on account of
              the early start tomorrow.
                   If necessary Coy.Sanitary Men will assist with the inciner-
              ating of all rubbish to avoid leaving an accumulation behind.

(7) TRENCH STORES:-. Trench Stores, Tents, Bivouac Shelters, SA.A.Grenades,
              Flares etc., in Dumps will be taken over from 15th.Division.
                   Complete lists of all stores and ammunition taken over
              to be sent to Orderly Room, as soon as possible after relief.

(8) WATER:-. Drinking water for all Camps can be obtained from Tank No.32
              at G.12.c.60.

(9) OFFICERS KIT ETC.,
Officers Kits and Coy. Mess Stores must be packed and dumped close to the N.W. entrance of Camp ready for loading at 5-9 am. prompt. Thr R.S.M. will arrange the necessary loading party.

(10) MARCHING OUT STATES:-. Marching Out States will be rendered to Orderly Room by 5-30 am. tomorrow.

PART II ORDERS.

PROFICIENCY PAY. 275976 Sergt. J. Hamnett "C" Coy. granted Proficiency Pay Class 1 with effect from 11/1/17.

(signed) Capt.
a/Adjutant. 1/7th. Manchester Regt.

(vi) O.C."A"Coy.will be prepared to supply ~~the loading~~ an unloading party of 1 Officer and 50 other ranks on arrival at destination. (Officers detailed in (i) & (ii) will report at B.O.R. for fuller instructions.)

7. "D"Coy.under command of Capt C.E.HIGHAM and their Cooker and team, will entrain at 2-11 pm.tomorrow 23rd.in train No.23, under command of Major LINGS 8th.Manchesters.

   The Cooker must be at the Station for entraining by 11-15 am.and the Company by 12-40 pm. Stores and Kits that cannot be carried on the Cooker must be man-handled to the station.

   Rations for 23rd.& 24th for this Coy.have been drawn and will be taken over by CQMS of "D"Coy. Rations will be carried under similar arrangements as detailed for Battalion.

   Watering arrangements will be notified separately.

   O.C."D"Coy.will render complete marching out state to the R.T.O.,4 hours before the train is due to move.

   O.C."D"Coy.will send 1 N.C.O.from each Platoon to proceed ahead with the Battalion to-day as billeting party.

   They will meet "D"Coy.on the station on arrival.

[signature]
Capt.
a/Adjutant.1/7th.Manchester Regt,

CONFIDENTIAL.

WAR DIARY.

1/7th Bn. MANCHESTER REGT.

From 1st. Sept. 1917.

To. 30th Sept. 1917.

VOLUME.

IX.

BELGIUM + FRANCE
Sheet 28 NW   40,000
Sheet 28 NE

Instructions regarding War Diaries and Intelligence Summaries are contained in F. S. Regs., Part II. and the Staff Manual respectively. Title pages will be prepared in manuscript.

Army Form C. 2118.

WAR DIARY
of 1/5 Bn: Manchester Regt.

INTELLIGENCE SUMMARY.
(Erase heading not required.)

Place	1917. Date	Hour	Summary of Events and Information	Remarks and references to Appendices
BRANDHOEK 6·18·a·2·6	Sept. 1		Strength of Bn. officers 41. O.R. 962. Strength with Bn:—officers 27. O.R. 800. Training & cleaning up. 4 Coys of 65 Manchesters moved forward in support tonight of 125th Bde tonight.	gre
	2		Sunday. No training.	gre
	3		Bn. training hours 6.15 – 6.45 a.m. 8.20 a.m. to noon. Weather warm. 2/Lts C. S. WOOD and R.N.C. HEATHCOTE HACKER appointed local temp. Company Commandants	gre
	4		Lt. C. J. BRYAN to I.O.O. to I.B.D. ETAPLES for 2 months to train troops to trenches	gre
	5		Training. A demonstration given at Ples. of a Flammenwerfer in action.	gre
	6		Training & watching preparations for moving into front Area tomorrow	gre
1.11.b.15.6 Aon. N.E.	7	7.30 p.m.	Bn: (less Battle Surplus & Administration personnel) evacuates Camp & moved forward by Rail & March to relieve 1/5 Bn: Lanc: Fusiliers in support of right Batt. sector, see APPENDIX I. Bn: strength in Line 16 officers and 500 O.R. (2/Lt HACKER & WOOD will report Bn: tomorrow). Coldy!	APPENDIX I
	8		Casualty during relief. Pte. Empleton 1.20 a.m. O.S. Orders received that we relieve 5th Manchesters in the line tomorrow night: Town Major Millar and 7 carpenters in A and D Coys to H.E. Phillo. See APPENDIX II. Sketch Artillery fire not excessive. Gas shells used frequently.	gre APPENDIX II

WAR DIARY
INTELLIGENCE SUMMARY

Army Form C. 2118.

Place: FREZENBERG

Date	Hour	Summary of Events and Information	Remarks and references to Appendices
9		Bn. relieved by 1/5 Manchesters	
		Bn relieved by 1/5 Manchesters 9.30 to 11.30 p.m. E 11.30 p.m. Bn. relieved 5th Manchesters in front line 11.30 p.m. to 1st. Bn. over D.25.a.d.N. See APPENDIX III for dispositions. Being reported on him to be relief	APPENDIX III
10		Enemy attack on FREZENBERG — BECK and BERRY FARMS which Germans further failed to hold after attack at 4.5. 5.15 when 7th & 6th on 11/25 had drove them attack on 108 — Pte WOOD and gth HACKER repair Bn + are posted — D & B Coys	
11		Shelling pretty intense art & grenade bombardment for 9½/05. 5 O.R. wounded. A and D Coys dug in German jumping off trench said to be enemy depth. D.31 on line D.25.6.30 — 6.1.12 — 6.1.16 & 6.0.07 just disturbed by the enemy or occupation Pt. 10/11 - Officers wounded 9/11 2/Lt J.G. CHATTERTON (duty) & C.B. DOUGLAS (very slight – at duty), Other ranks killed 1 wounded 15. Enemy fairly quiet Very shelly A and D Coy improve new jumping off trench.	
12		Enemy of 6½ Div on left to establish themselves on Hill 35 K. Attack of 5th and 2th Div to pc to probably 13th 6 casualties for 11/12 other ranks wounded 1. Appendix 19. Bn R.E. (Concrete Pill Box) were subjects & occupant identity in person, but were able to use cart & alerting was part of front	

MAP FRENZENBERG
1/5

Army Form C. 2118.

WAR DIARY
of 1/5 Gloucester Regt
INTELLIGENCE SUMMARY.
(Erase heading not required.)

Instructions regarding War Diaries and Intelligence Summaries are contained in F.S. Regs., Part II. and the Staff Manual respectively. Title pages will be prepared in manuscript.

Place	Date	Hour	Summary of Events and Information	Remarks and references to Appendices
T.11.8.15.c	12 Aug		Remained stationary in the line. 5 Shropshires relieved 1st Rifle Bde in that sector. Bn. made trip to support trenches up the same position (from 1/5 Worcester) which they vacated on 9/10 August. See on APPENDIX I.	
	13		Relief completed 1.40 am. 10.13 August Intervening quietness of 5th and 5th Worcesters in line. Cancelled. Group T.H. ALLAN took command of 1/5 Worcesters on 9 August. Quiet day. B, C & D Coys in at day. Six guns known by Worcesters in front of Appt but in their direction. L.O.B. 5 T.C. Worcesters in reserve. Bgm. T.H. ALLAN reported from F.D. The Bgm. very quiet winter all day. Men & men & baggage. St Farm. Nothing added in any way to the TORONTO camp. Gas Mask aware to YPRES but from farmers to BRANDHOEK. Relief completed at 2 am. 24th by Worcesters received in Sheet 28E 1/40,000 Band no 61 new 4.40 am to 17t the Sheet.	gre gre gre gre
TORONTO CAMP	15 16		Quiet day. The weather had prevailed the past 10 days. All our bottles & the moves tomorrow to relieve 26 Bde in BRANDHOEK No. 3 Area about 2/3 miles further West.	gre
G.11.4.1.5	17		a.m. Moved to Camp G.11.4.1.5. Vacated by 7 Seaforth Highlanders (9th Bde). All our supplies 4.25 pm. March ? by 3 miles to Croupettes.	gre

(A 7590) Wt. W1839/M1293 750,000. 1/17. D. D. & L., Ltd. Forms/C.2118-14.

Army Form C. 2118.

WAR DIARY
or
INTELLIGENCE SUMMARY.
(Erase heading not required.)

1/7th Manchester Regt.

Place	Date	Hour	Summary of Events and Information	Remarks and references to Appendices
BELLE ALLIANCE SHEET 27 40.050	1917 Nov 18		Training. Receive orders to move tomorrow into the line to arrive Camp L.15.6.9.4.	
L.15.6.6.4 SHEET 27	19		Bn. moves to Camp at L.15.6.6.4 starting at 11.30 am, arriving 1.25 pm. Move in by Coys. 3 pm. Receive orders to proceed early tomorrow to WINNEZEELE hut. 2 mls. W. of POPERINGHE	
J.4.6.7.6.	20		The Bn. in Coys. left the Camp. Moved at 6.40 am to WINNEZEELE h.2. area. Bn. Camp about a mile of tomiles. 3 or Casualties en route; kills were made to our Camp about the half hour loop day. One aircraft struck in reality, and the other down just the half hour loop day. In the B. Bde A.E. CRENSHAW in command of the Bn. to command on B[?] to the reinforcing tanks training Regt. (US Eng.) but he stood of his Regt to be in command but has Bn. This is part of a new scheme. Lt. Worthington (5/4 dr) was exchanged	
	21		Lt. Col. H.A. CARR 3/7th. B.G. TAYLOR to England on leave	
COXYDE	22		Training & preparing to move tomorrow. 1st line transport less 2 cookers & 1 Sukr lorry by Rd. to Coxy D.E. on tanks to Camp at 7 am — entrains about 3 miles away and arrives at COXYDE about 5 mile. W of NIEUPORT. Men all settled in L'Est. by 2.15 pm. 1st Line Transport arrives about mid-day.	
	23		Receive orders to relieve 2/6 Manchester. Dispo. accommodates trenches ty. 199 Bde. 6.E. Bur. tomorrow.	
	24		The 2/4 Manchester relieves 2/6 Manchester in fillets and relieves 2/6 Manchester in duffart	

BELGIUM
SOST - DUNKERKE Sheet 11 ᴮ

WAR DIARY
or
INTELLIGENCE SUMMARY.

Army Form C. 2118.

1/7th Manchester Regt

(Erase heading not required.)

Place	Date	Hour	Summary of Events and Information	Remarks and references to Appendices
R.19.C.33	24		In different sectors of Bn. front. Relief complete at 4 p.m. Bn. H.Q. incomplete in Northern H.Q. for Bn.	G.R.O.
	25		Training and working parties. Some large working parties engaged on shelling of our area.	G.R.O. G.R.O.
	26		Training and working parties.	
	27		Training & working parties. 10 men of "C" Coy were wounded by an H.E. shell.	G.R.O.
			3 returned remained on duty.	
	28		Training & working parties. Lt. C.J. BRYAN rejoins Bn from ETAPLES.	G.R.O.
	29		Training & working parties. Capt. C.E. HIGHAM rejoins Bn from "E" Lewis Fusiliers. 2nd/Lt. H.H. NIDD to England on leave. Had an shelled intermittently but no casualties.	G.R.O.
	30		D Coy is detached from Bn to find working parties and takes up its quarters in the Reserve Trench of Grenier brie. Numerous H.E. shells. The Bn less "D" Co. "C" moves up to support the trenches. All platoon Commanders go up to inspect the trenches.	G.R.O.

Hatton
LIEUT.-COLONEL,
COMMANDING 1/7th BN. MANCHESTER REGT.

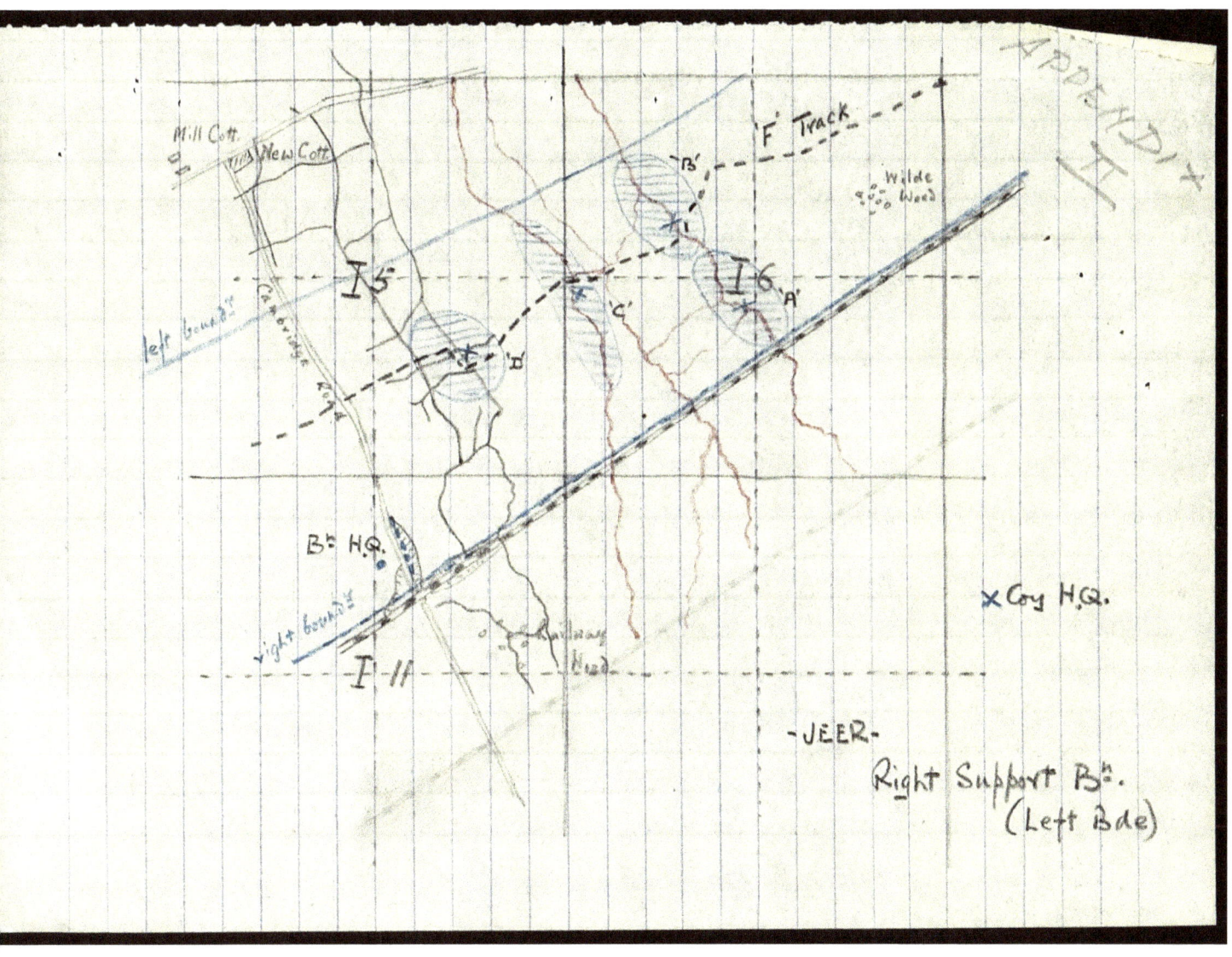

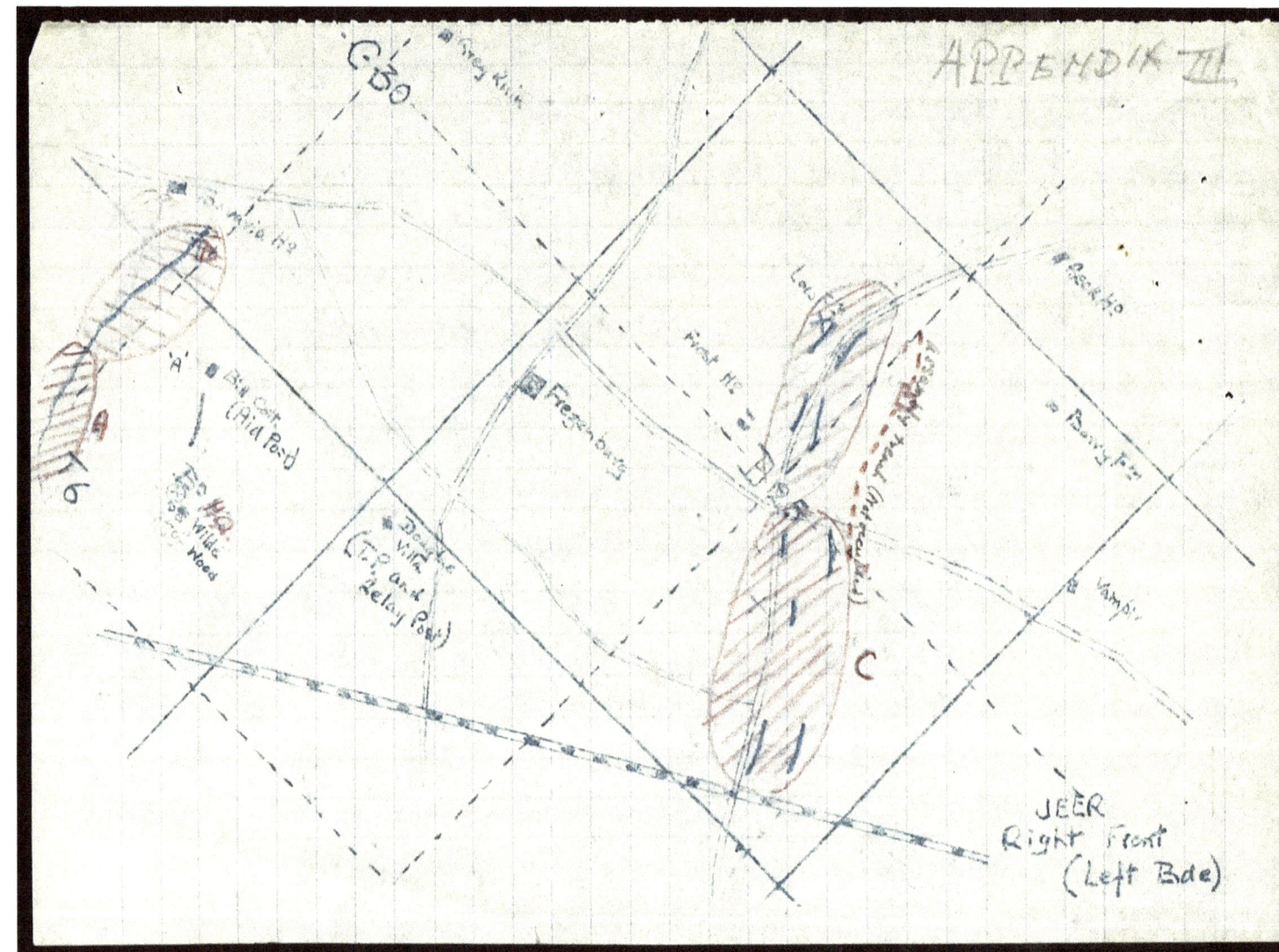

File   APPENDIX I

BATTALION ORDERS No. 23.   7.8.17.
Ref.Map.Sheet 28 N.W.
:-:

1. The Battalion will move to the forward area this evening to relieve 1/7th.Lancs.Fus. in the Support area of Right Sub Sector I.5.d, - I.6.c. I.11.b.

2. The Battalion(less Battle surplus and Administrative personnel already detailed) will entrain at 9-30 pm. at No.3 Crossing G.11.a.9.9.
   The Brigade Hdqrs, 127th.T.M.B. & Hdqrs.of 6th.Manchesters will also be on the train.
   The Battalion will fall in, in Close Column, ready to move at 8 pm in order:- Hdqrs. "A", "B", "C", "D"Coys.
   Greatcoats & Haversacks will not be taken. Entrenching Tools will be carried. Water bottles will be filled.
   2 days rations and the Iron Ration will be carried in the pack.
   On the march after detraining, 200 yds will be kept between Platoons, touch being maintained by connecting files.
   Box Respirators will be worn at the "Alert" position and a look out for gas shells must be kept on the march forward from YPRES.
   Guides are being provided on the following scale and will be met at 10 pm. at the MENIN GATE.
       2 per Battalion Hdqrs.
       1 per Company.
       1 per Platoon.
   Companies are relieving opposite numbers and must look out for and pick up their own guides.

3. Companies will take over those sections of the Support Line which their representative Officer reconnoitred on the 5th.
   Order of Companies will therefore be commencing from the Right Front "A", "B", "C" "D" Coys.
   A full list of all Trench and Area Stores, Maps, Photographs, Sketches Bombs etc., taken over will be sent to Battalion Hdqrs. as early as possible.

4. Battalion Hdqrs. and Aid Post will be at I.11.b.2.7.

5. 1 N.C.O.(Sergt.Stott) and 8 men(Bombers) will report to Brigade Ammunition Officer at the Advance Brigade.Hdqrs. MILL COTT - I.5.a.3.7. at 1 am.tomorrow 8th.to take over Brigade Dump.
   2 Bombers per Company will therefore fall in with Battalion Hdqrs to-night and Sergt.Stott will move out with this party from Battalion Hdqrs.in the Line, at about midnight.

                    NORBURY
6. Major ALLAN, Capt. TOWNSEND, Lieut.SIVEWRIGHT, C.S.M's Joyce & Borland will remain behind with the Battle Surplus.

7. WATER & RATION ARRANGEMENTS IN THE LINE:- As many petrol tins as possible will be taken up and it is hoped to take over more in trench stores. Each Company should have 16 and Hdqrs 8. These will be sent down empty each evening by 10 pm. and refilled from water carts at Battalion Hdqrs.While in Support it may be found possible to arrange earlier hours. To-night when Coys. have settled in their positions, they will will send down a water carrying party to Battalion Hdqrs.- 16 tins per Coy. is a days water supply.
   2 days rations will be sent up every other day under a C.Q.M.S. who will remain until relieved and be responsible for carrying distribution of rations.

Ⓒ and a party for Officers Mess Stores.

5. The 126th Brigade will be on the Right of our Brigade and the 182nd Infantry Brigade on our left.

6. Immediately on completion of relief each Coy. will wire or send the cypher "HEAD" to Battalion.Hdqrs.

McHugh Capt.
c/Adjutant. 1/7th.Manchester Regt.

War Diary

Confidential

of

1/7th. Manchester Regt.

Period

Oct. 1st to Oct. 31st.

1917

Vol II

WAR DIARY
INTELLIGENCE SUMMARY

1/7th Bn: Manchester Regt

Place	Date	Hour	Summary of Events and Information	Remarks and references to Appendices
MAP BELGIUM Sheets 11 and 12 S.W.	1917 Oct			
R.33.c.2.9 MIDDLESEX Camp	1		Casualties during Sept:—	
			Officers — Killed —, Wounded 2	
			Other Ranks — Killed 12, Wounded 57	
			Strength of Bn. on 30 Sept. Officers 39 – other Ranks 912	
			Details with Bn. " " 24 " " 752	W.E.
M.19.B.1.9 Infantry Barracks at back of NIEUPORT BAINS sur	2		Further preparations made to relieve 1/5 Manchesters in L left sub-sector of Lombartzyde Sector on night 2/3. All Lewis Gun teams go up into line in advance of Bn.	APPENDIX I
			The Bn. relieved the 1/5 Manchesters in the left sub-sector of the Line vide Appendix I. Relief completed without casualty at 11.50 p.m. B Coy still detached on Tunnelling work. Sector is almost unique in that front L.T.s are all subways or tunnels and these are accommodated mostly in underground shelters.	
	3		Front Line held during the day with Lewis Gun Posts. 2/Lt E.R. THORPE to hospital. Situation quiet. All Coys busy cleaning & repairing trenches, siting L.G. Positions and generally organizing.	W.E.

WAR DIARY
INTELLIGENCE SUMMARY of 1/7th Bn. Manchester Regt.

Army Form C. 2118.

Place	Date	Hour	Summary of Events and Information	Remarks and references to Appendices
MAP BELGIUM Sheets 11 and 12	Oct.			
M.19.a.1.9	4		Quiet day except that 3.15 to 4.15 pm Enemy heavily shell area & trenches round & in rear of LAITERIE. Learn that 41st Bde. relieving 42nd Bde in the sector a 6/7th instant. 1/2-3rd Bdes to relieve 127th Bde. Work continued on trenches. MAJOR G.B. HURST reports for duty to Bn. See APPENDIX II for sketch of Bn. dispositions. One Lewis gun platoon & gunner to be held by A Coy 1. Ystra area by C Coy. next area by D Coy. The Reserve Line is garrisoned by B Coy. 1/5th Manchester Battn. referring APPENDIX III.	APPENDIX II WM APPENDIX III WM
	5		2/Lt. E.B. TAYLOR rejoins from leave. Weather changed to wet, stormy & cold. Situation normal. 20th Durham L.I. relieve us in the line tomorrow night Oct 6th inst.	
	6		Arrive back to Camp at ST. IDESBALDE. Bn. relieved by the 20th Durham L.I. (41st Bde). Relief line 10 p.m. Last midnight. See Appendix IV. Dusk when both move to St Idesbalde Camp, arriving about 1.45 am. Remainder of Bn. to private billets. Bn. cookers to St Idesbalde during relief.	APPENDIX IV WM

BELGIUM.
Sheet 11 S.E 1/40,000

Army Form C. 2118.

WAR DIARY
of
INTELLIGENCE SUMMARY. 1/7th Bn Manchester Regt.
(Erase heading not required.)

Instructions regarding War Diaries and Intelligence Summaries are contained in F. S. Regs., Part II. and the Staff Manual respectively. Title pages will be prepared in manuscript.

Place	Date	Hour	Summary of Events and Information	Remarks and references to Appendices
LA PANNE.	1917 Oct 7		Bn Arrived from Camp at St IDESBALDE to billets at LA PANNE.	
	8		Accomodation very good. Weather hot & stormy.	nil
			Lt. J. BAKER to England on leave	nil
	9		General overhauling of men clothing. Interior economy.	
	10		Training as as so on. Coord. Coys Coy and trade for study Gas training. C Coy detached for duty with Tunnelling Coy.	nil
	11		Training and rifle shooting on the range.	nil
			Capt V. HEATHCOTE HARPER and 2/Lt H. CHAMP from Bn to England and posts to reinforcements to A any C Coys.	nil
	12		Route march in morning. Night operations 6 to 9 pm.	nil
	13		Training Capt NIDD (from France) and Lt SIVEWRIGHT (from a course) rejoin Bn.	nil
			Inspection of "Box-tin top kit" by I.O. Weather very wet.	nil
	14		2/Lt RICHARDSON to England on leave.	nil
	15		Church parade as training. A Coy attached for 3 days to CANADA Camp sand-bagging etc.	nil
	16		2/Lt W.H. BARRATT proc in 10 days leave, home.	nil
	17		Training. 2/Lt G. WARD joins the Bn.	nil

BELGIUM
Sheet II S.E. 1 / 20,000

Army Form C. 2118.

WAR DIARY
of 1/7th Bn: Manchester Regt.
INTELLIGENCE SUMMARY.
(Erase heading not required.)

Instructions regarding War Diaries and Intelligence Summaries are contained in F. S. Regs., Part II. and the Staff Manual respectively. Title pages will be prepared in manuscript.

Place	Date 1917 Oct.	Hour	Summary of Events and Information	Remarks and references to Appendices
LA PANNE	18		Training.	nil
	19		All ranks just back from "Lunar fet". Preparing to move to Lui tomorrow (1 days advance) to relieve 1/5 Lanc Fusiliers in Bgde support NIEUPORT SECTOR. "C" Coy will be left behind on Divisional duty.	nil
SHEET 12. S.W. 1/20,000 NIEUPORT M.28.c.8.8	20		Bn: moved to COXYDE 10 a.m., had meal there and moved forward to Lui. 3.50 pm. see APPENDIX V. Relief of 1/5 Lanc Fusiliers in Nuyport completed without casualty by 10.50 pm. Relief necessarily slow on account of crossing YSER by one floating Bridge [PUTNEY]. Situation apparent, shelling very quiet.	APPENDIX V nil
	21		The Bn: finds Large R.E. working parties daily. usually (1 Bridge Guard Lui) About 225 men Before & after. The 5th M.G. Coy & Lt S.E. Manchesters in the left front	nil
	22		Achieve tonight. The Bn: is now in the line for 16 days.	
	23		Situation normal. See dispositions on sketch APPENDIX VI.	APPENDIX VI nil nil
	24		Situation unchanged. Bridges broken at intervals during the day. No change.	
M.28.6.5.2.	25		Bn: relieved 5th Manchester in right sub-sector of Lobe front. See situation	nil

WAR DIARY
or
INTELLIGENCE SUMMARY.
(Erase heading not required)

Army Form C. 2118.

BELGIUM
Sheet 12 S.W. 20,000

1/9th Bn. Manchester Regt.

Place	Date	Hour	Summary of Events and Information	Remarks and references to Appendices
M.28.c.5.2	Oct 1917 25 Continued		A quiet and woth. D Coy left subsector, both finding files from supports. 1 Platoon of B and 4 Lewis Guns held HASAR WALK i.e. reserve Trench. Remainder of B Coy in REDAN used for carrying parties sent to re-inforce front line if required. See APPENDIX VII for defence scheme and detail showing dispositions.	APPENDIX VII
	26		Situation quiet. 2/Lt WILSON and troops broke into a future; they find a enemy moved depot in L Gun Maxim. A good distribution quiet. Makes some alteration.	
	27		deal of work being done improving Posts & communications. Enemy arm. Little activity except with guns & T.M.S. Westein fine & cold	
	28		No change. An enemy feature which the many sent down got seen NoSE Post & thence came barely about 4.30am. 2 man killed & 1 wounded. A patrol sent out to reconn. for enemy but they had got away.	
REDAN (NIEUPORT)	29		The 5th Manchesters relieved us in the line and gave their to Dyffryn the Consolation. Relief complete about 8.30 a.m. B many NASAL PARADE. A many Pots & PETIT REDAN. D Coy are in Reserve.	
	30		A matters quiet. 2/Lts W.H. BRADSHAW, J.H. MILNE and H.M. EVANS joined Bn. 2/Lt BRADSAW is posted to B and to Coy A & D Coy	

BELGIUM
Sheet 12 S.W.
2y 300

WAR DIARY
or
INTELLIGENCE SUMMARY. of 1/7th Bn Manchester Regt.
(Erase heading not required.)

Army Form C. 2118.

Place	Date	Hour	Summary of Events and Information	Remarks and references to Appendices
REDAN (NIEUPORT)	31		No change. Learn that R.S.M. HARTNETT wounded YPRES about 12th Septr died of wounds 19/10/17.	wef

J W Lun
LIEUT.-COLONEL
COMMANDING 1/7th BN. MANCHESTER REGT.

APPENDIX I

OPERATION ORDERS No.39.   2/10/17.

Ref.Map. Sheet. 11 & 12.

:-

1. In continuation of yesterday's Warning Order, the Battalion will move in order "A" - "C" Coys. and Battalion Hdqrs., the head of "A"Coy. leaving Camp at 7-45 pm.

    200 yds distance will be maintained on the march between bodies not larger than 25/30 strong.

2. "A"Coy. will take over the Right Sector. "C"Coy. the Left Sector and "D"Coy. the Support Line.

3. The wire track or the road will be used at the discretion of Platoon Commanders in accordance with the situation at the time.

4. Before they move Companies will detail off their Platoons into the Posts they will occupy, the right of each Coy. leading.

5. Guides of 1/5th. Manchesters will be picked up at the Cross Roads in OOST DUNKERKE BAINS on the scale of 1 per Coy. Hdqrs., and 2 per Platoon.

6. "D"Coy. in the Reserve Line will arrange details of relief with the Company Commander of the Support Line. If possible this relief should be completed by 9 pm.

    O.C. "D"Coy. will hand over to the O.C.Coy. he relieves all details of the working parties he has been finding.

7. The Section of "C"Coy. attached to "D"Coy. will rejoin their own Company to-night, as they pass BODMIN ALLEY off BATH AVENUE, about 9 pm. The Section Commander will report himself at once to his Coy.Commander.

8. Trench Maps, Photos, Trench and Area Stores will be taken over on relief and receipts given. A copy of these receipts will be forwarded to Battalion Hdqrs. by 8 am. on 3rd. inst.

9. All Standing Working Parties and schemes for work in progress will be taken over on relief.

10. The necessary number of limbers will be on the road by Battalion Hdqrs. at 7-15 pm., and rations, Officers kits, mess stores, dixies and petrol tins will be ready dumped alongside the road by 7 pm.

    The R.S.M. will detail the necessary guard and loading party.

11. Coy.Officers will report to the Commanding Officer at 7-15 pm. that their areas have been left perfectly clean.

    The whole area will be thoroughly cleaned up in daylight this afternoon.

12. O.C. "D"Coy. will send 8 carrying parties of 1 N.C.O. and 12 men each, to Battalion Hdqrs. at 9 pm. to-night. They must know their way to the front Coy.Hdqrs. These parties will be found daily by "D"Coy. except that after to-day the parties will be 11 strong instead of 13.

13. Rations for cooking will be carried in bulk by Companies.

14. The Transport Lines and the Q.M.Stores will remain in their present location

15. Companies will report relief complete by the cypher "PHEASANT".

                                                        Capt.
                                    Adjutant.   ROOT.

APPENDIX I

MARCHING ORDER.

1. The Battalion will relieve the 1/5th. Bn. Manchester Regt. in the left sub-sector of the line tomorrow night, 2nd./3rd. Oct.

2. Advance Parties as detailed verbally will proceed ahead tomorrow morning.

3. Dress will be full marching order except for the light entrenching tool which will be handed in to the Quarter Master Stores by Coy. Q.M.Ss. tomorrow morning.

4. Companies and Battalion Head Quarters will take up with them 15 AA Rifles and 16 petrol tins each. *This will be carried on limbers*

5. Water is drawn from pump near Battalion Head Quarters. Coys. will send parties down to draw water during the day.

1/10/17.

Adjutant "XXX" Captain

APPENDIX III   Copy No. 5.

DEFENCE ORDERS.

Left Subsector, --- N I E U P O R T - B A I N S - Sector.
Ref.Maps.sheet 11 S.E. } 1/20000 & Attached Maps.
             12 S.W.

:-

1. The following general principles will serve as guides in all defensive tasks allotted to the Battalion holding the Left Sub sector.
   (a) Every commander and every soldier must know whether he and his command are to fight as garrison or as counter-attackers.

   (b) Every soldier forming one of the garrison must know exactly where he is to fight.

   (c) In face of hostile infantry attack garrison troops will continue to fight in the positions allotted by their commander till every man is killed or disabled.

   (d) In face of hostile bombardment, garrison troops may be withdrawn from fire positions on the authority of the Battalion Commander. This authority is delegated to Company Commanders.
       Any Officer who orders such a withdrawal will immediately inform his commander and will be personally responsible that the garrison return to their fire positions as soon as the situation admits and before there is a possibility of German infantry forestalling them.

   (e) No soldier or party detailed as garrison of a fire position will abandon it because the enemy have captured any other position, whatever may be the relative situation of such positions.

   (f) Every soldier who forms part of the counter attack troops must know his new alarm post.

   (g) The success of local counter attacks depends largely on the promptitude with which they are delivered.
       This entails careful preliminary reconnaisance.

   (h) If the enemy succeed in establishing themselves in any part of our trenches they will be counter attacked not only by the troops specially detailed, but by garrison troops on the flanks who are not themselves engaged in repelling an infantry assault.

2. FRONTAGE & BOUNDARIES:-.
   The 127th. Infantry Brigade holds the 42nd. Division front, called the NIEUPORT BAINS or Left Sector of the XV Corps front.
   The 1/7th. Bn. Manchester Regt. holds the Left Sub sector of the above front which extends from M.14.d.75.40.(BEACON STREET exclusive) to R.28.b.3.9. inclusive, where it joins the OOST DUNKERKE BAINS Coast defence Sector.
   The Battalion Front is bounded on the North by the sea as far as M.14.a.7.5. and then extends along the Left bank of the YSER Canal to M.14.d.75.40., where it joins the Right subsector of the 127th. Brigade Front.

3. DEFENCES:-. These consist of-
   (a) Fire trenches with close support trenches, except in coastal area.
   (b) Support Line from M.14.c.60.35. to M.14.c.1.7. BEACH SUPPORT & BATH SUPPORT.
   (c) Reserve Line from M.20.a.5.7. to M.13.d.7.2.
   (d) Communication Trenches are -
       BLIGHTY AVENUE & BENT LANE - XXXXXXXXXXXX
       BATH LANE, BEACH AVENUE & BRIDGE STREET.
       BRISTOL TUNNEL (Under construction).
       BEDFORD TUNNEL. --- BATH AVENUE.

Sheet 2.

4. **DISTRIBUTION:-.** The Line is held by 2 Companies in front line and 1 Coy. in Support. *These Coys. will act as Garrison to their respective trenches*

1 Coy.Left Support Battalion is stationed in dug-outs at M.13.b.85.85 as reserve to the left subsector.

Right front Coy. with H.Q. in dug-outs under Railway Station holds from Right of Subsector to M.14.d.05.90.

Left front Coy. with H.Q. at M.14.c.55.65. holds from M.14.d.05.90. to junction with Coastal Defence at R.23.b.5.9.

Support Coy. is in dug-outs at M.14.c.45.35. and M.14.c.20.65. in rear of BEACH SUPPORT TRENCH.

Battalion Hdqrs. at M.19.b.1.9.

For distribution of garrisons of Front & Support Lines see sketches attached.

5. **DEFENSIVE ACTION:-.** By day the garrison of the Front Line system is withdrawn to dug-outs in rear, the front line trenches being occupied only by L.G.Posts, Snipers, Observers also M.G's. ✱

IN CASE OF ATTACK the front line system will be maintained at all costs. Should the enemy succeed in penetrating any portion, he will be at once counter attacked by the troops on each flank and with reserves.

The Support Company will be in readiness in BATH SUPPORT & BEACH Support, and will move forward to counter attack, as the situation demands.

The garrison of the SUPPORT Line will consist of 2 reserve L.G's in BATH SUPPORT and 2 L.G's of SUPPORT Coy. in BEACH SUPPORT.

All details will be held in readiness under the Asst.Adjutant at Battalion Hdqrs. to act as a Battalion Reserve.

The action of all units will be strictly governed by the principles of para 1.

No.5 Section 2nd.Australian Tunnelling Coy. and attached Infantry. (about 50 Other Ranks). is placed at the disposal of O.C.Left Subsector. This party will stand to arms at their billets in M.14.c., sending an officer to report to Battalion Hdqrs.

6. **S.O.S.SIGNALS:-.**
   (a) The S.O.S. at present in use is a grenade bursting into two green and red stars. The signal to be repeated until the Artillery opens fire.
   The S.O.S. will be made only by order of an officer, and only if the enemy is seen actually advancing to the attack.
   The S.O.S. signal will be confirmed by telephone or any other available means.
   (b) The S.O.S. signal for the coastal area is a rocket bursting into a green and a white star, or a green and white flare.
   (c) Contact and patrol aeroplane will, in case of a hostile attack developing while they are flying, send the following S.O.S. signal.
   "White Parachute Flare follwed by a smoke bomb bursting into three streamers of smoke."
   The Signal to be repeated by the aeroplane until acted on by the Artillery.

7. **APPENDICES:-.** Sketch Map showing distribution of Battalion by day and by night. All posts, L.G's, French Guns, Observation and Sniping Posts and location of all dug-outs in which any portion of Coys. are located.

✱ *By night the front line system is occupied by the Coys. detailed less working parties and patrols.*

Capt.
Adjutant.

APPENDIX IV

SECRET.   O P E R A T I O N   O R D E R   No.40.   Copy.No......
6/10/17.

1. The 127th.Brigade on being relieved by the 123rd.Infantry Brigade will move into Divisional Reserve.

2. The Battalion will be relieved to-night 6/7th.by the 20th.DURHAM L.I.

3. On relief the Battalion moves back to Camp at ST.IDESBALDE,W.5.c.1.1.
   At 11-45 am.on 7th.the Battalion moves to billets at LA PANNE,W.22.a.

4. Advance parties have proceeded ahead to-day under Lt.F.G.BURN.

5. GUIDES:- for the relieving Battalion will assemble at Battalion Hdqrs. at 5-15 pm. 2 guides per Bn.Hdqrs. - 1 per each Coy.Hdqrs. - 1 per Platoon - and 1 per Post are required.
   All guides must be provided by Coys.with a note giving the dispositions of the unit they represent.
   The Asst.Adjutant will proceed in charge of these guides.

6. Defence Schemes, Trench & Secret Maps, Aeroplane photographs, Schemes for proposed work in progress,also Trench and Area Stores Ammunition,Flares etc., taken over from 5th.Manchesters will be handed over on relief.
   A copy of all receipts will be sent to Bn.Hdqrs.by 10 am.on 7th.inst.

7. 1 Officer from Bn.Hdqrs. and 1 Officer,1 N.C.O. and 2 Runners per Coy. will remain on after completion of relief till such time as their opposite numbers are satisfied. Coy.s.will notify Orderly Room the name of the Officer remaining behind. *Roebury. Hodge Richardson*
   These parties will then rejoin the Battalion independently.
   2/Lt.S.J.WILSON will be the Officer to remain from Bn.Hdqrs.

8. Platoons will move back independently on completion of their relief. Each Platoon must be complete. A distance of not less than 200 yds.must be maintained between them en route.
   A guide from Bn.Hdqrs.,each Coy.Hdqrs.and each Platoon will be picked up at the Cross Roads,COXYDE BAINS, W.6.a.9.6.

9. "B"Coy.will proceed to the New Camp ST IDESBALDE after their mid-day meal. O.C."B"Coy.will make all necessary preparations for the arrival of the Battalion.
   Blankets will be drawn if available and more guides provide if required. Hot tea will also be got ready for the Battalion on its arrival in Camp.

10. On the 7th.inst. 6 am. Reveille. 7-30am.Breakfast.
    10-30 am. all baggage must be ready dumped for loading,the R.S.M.providing necessary loading parties.
    The camp must be left perfectly clean and O.C.Coys.will report to this effect to the Commanding Officer by 11-15 am.
    O.C."C"Coy.will detail an Officer and 10 men to remain behind as a rear party to clear up the Camp and obtain a "clean"certificate.
    1 Motor Lorry will probably be available to move baggage.
    Marching Out States will be rendered to Orderly Room by 11 am.

11. Completion of reliefs in the Line will be wired to Bn.Hdqrs.by the cypher "PARTRIDGE". Completion of move to new Camp will be notified by Coys.to Orderly Room.

12. The refilling point for the 7th.inst.will be at W.18.d.9.4.

13. The Reserve Brigade Dump is situated on Cemetery Road at about X.13.a.4.9.
    This dump is for the use of the Reserve Brigade in case a sudden call forward is made.

14. The Battalion Transport and Q.M. Stores will complete move to new Camp as early as practicable during daylight to-day.

15. "C"Coy. (working strength 100) with necessary complement of Officers will report to 257th.Tunnelling.Coy. LA PANNE, W.21.a.3.7. at 9 am. on the 9th.inst.
    They will take their Cooker and rations for the 10th.

                                         (signed)
                              Adjutant.   ROOT.   Capt.

```
Copy No. 1   O.C. A Coy.
         2    "   B  "
         3    "   C  "
         4    "   D  "
         5   Transport Officer & Q.M.
         6.  File.
         7 & 8. War Diary.
```

19/10/17.   MOVE ORDER No.41.   Copy.No........

1. The Battalion less "C"Coy. moves into the Line tomorrow evening 20th and relieves the 1/5th.Lancs.Fus.s. in Brigade Support in the NIEUPORT SECTOR. "C"Coy. will remain attached to the Tunnelling Coy.

2. The Battalion will move to COXYDE after breakfast, have dinner there and continue the march in the afternoon at a time to be notified later.

3. 6-30 am. Reveille.   7-0 am. Breakfast.   7-30 am. Sick Parade. 10-0 am. Battalion will move in order:- Hdqrs. "D" "B" Coys. maintaining 200 yds between Coys Dress:- Marching Order without entrenching tools & haversacks.

4. "B" & "D"Coys. Field Cookers with their complement of Cooks will proceed ahead at 8-0 am. to COXYDE to prepare dinners for 1-0 pm.

5. O.C. "A"Coy. will arrange for guides to meet the Cookers outside CANADA CAMP to lead them to their standings.
   O.C. "A"Coy. will also make all arrangements for the accommodation of the Battalion at CANADA & AUSTRALIA CAMPS., and provide guides for Hdqrs. and each Company on arrival.
   Battalion Hdqrs. will be established at the old Brigade Hdqrs.

6. Blankets will be rolled tightly and neatly in bundles of ten and properly labelled and brought for loading to Q.M. Stores.
   "B"Coy. by 9-0 am.   "D"Coy. 9-10 am.   Hdqrs. 9-20 am.
   Companies will provide their own loading parties.
   "A"Coy. will hand their blankets in to Q.M. at COXYDE. at 11.30 am. tomorrow.
   Officers Kits, Orderly Room Boxes, Coy. & Mess Stores will be dumped at Q.M. Stores at 8-30 am. and loaded immediately under arrangements to be made by R.S.M. Baggage going forward to the Line should be properly labelled & loaded separately in limbers ready for the line. All packages for the Line should be small and easily handled.
                                                                    La Panne
7. All haversacks and entrenching tools will be handed in to Q.M. at COXYDE. except "A" Coy who will hand them in to Q.M. Dump Coxyde at noon tomorrow.

8. The Q.M. Stores and the Transport will take over from 1/5th.Lancs.Fus's. near COXYDE, 21st inst and remain there while the Battalion is in the Line.

9. A. B. & D. Coys. will take their 4 Lewis Guns and 24 drums per gun. Mobile reserve S.A.A. for Lewis Guns will not be taken. Limbers will be loaded to-day.

10. Rations for the 21st. will be carried up by the Transport. 50 Petroltins will be taken up and allotted 13 to each Coy. and 11 to Hdqrs. A further 50 tins should be taken over in the Line as Trench Stores.

11. All billets and thier surroundings must be left perfectly clean. Major G.B. HURST will inspect the Battalion billets after they are evacuated tomorrow and obtain a "clean certificate" from the Area Commandant.

12. Parade States will be rendered to B.O.R. by 9-p am.

13. An Advance Party under Lieut. C.S. WOOD of 2 representatives from Battalion Hdqrs. and one from each Platoon will proceed ahead to the Line at 9-0 am, carrying the day's rations. Party will assemble outside B.O.R. A N.C.O. from each Coy. should be included and he can look over Company Dumps etc.

14. Guides will be picked up at PELICAN BRIDGE: 3 for Battalion Hdqrs, 1 for each Coy. Hdqrs. and 1 for each Platoon.

15. Relief complete will be notified by the cypher "BLACK" or by Runner.

16. Acknowledge.

Adjutant. C.127.   Capt.

APPENDIX V

ADDENDA TO MOVE ORDER No. 41   19)10/17.

1. The Battalion will move from COXYDE in order D. B. A. Hdqrs., head of "D"Coy. to pass starting point, entrance to CANADA CAMP at 3-50 pm. and march via OOST DUNKERKE and WULPEN. Coy.Hdqrs will march in front of their Coys. 200 yds will be maintained between Platoons. Beyond WULPEN Platoons will march on Right edge of road in 2 deep formation.

   Halts will be made for 10 minutes at 10 minutes to the hour.

   Watches will be synchronised before starting.

2. Immediately after Companies have completed relief(except Lewis Guns) they will send parties to the unloading point to bring up their Lewis Gun equipment, rations etc.

   Arrangements have been made for one of the advance party to act as a guide to and from the unloading point.

Great care with Coke and Charcoal must be taken if used in cellars or dug-outs, particular attention be paid that all gasses from the fires are carried away.
No open fire in an enclosed space will be used.

[signature]
Adjutant. C.127.   Capt.

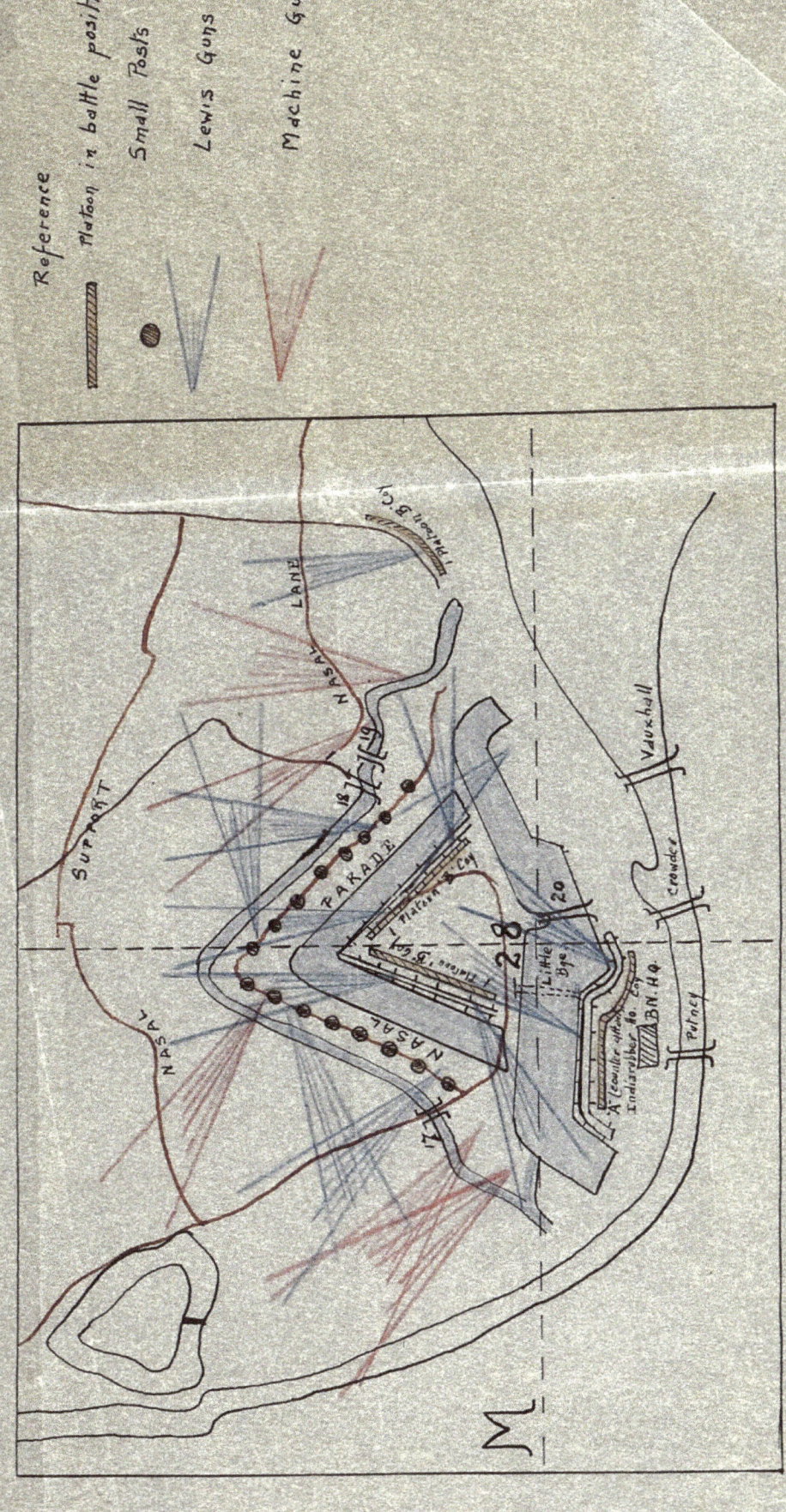

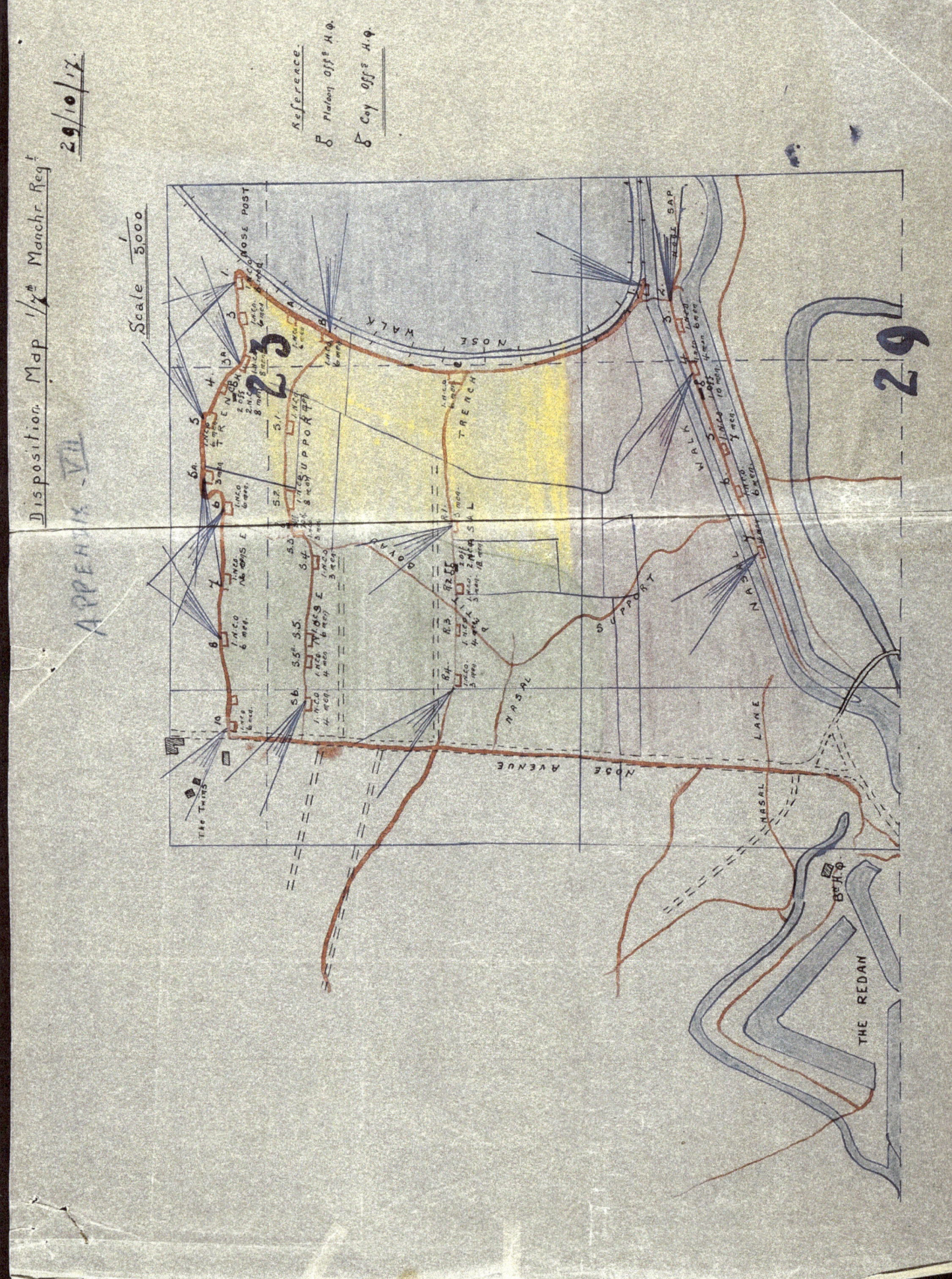

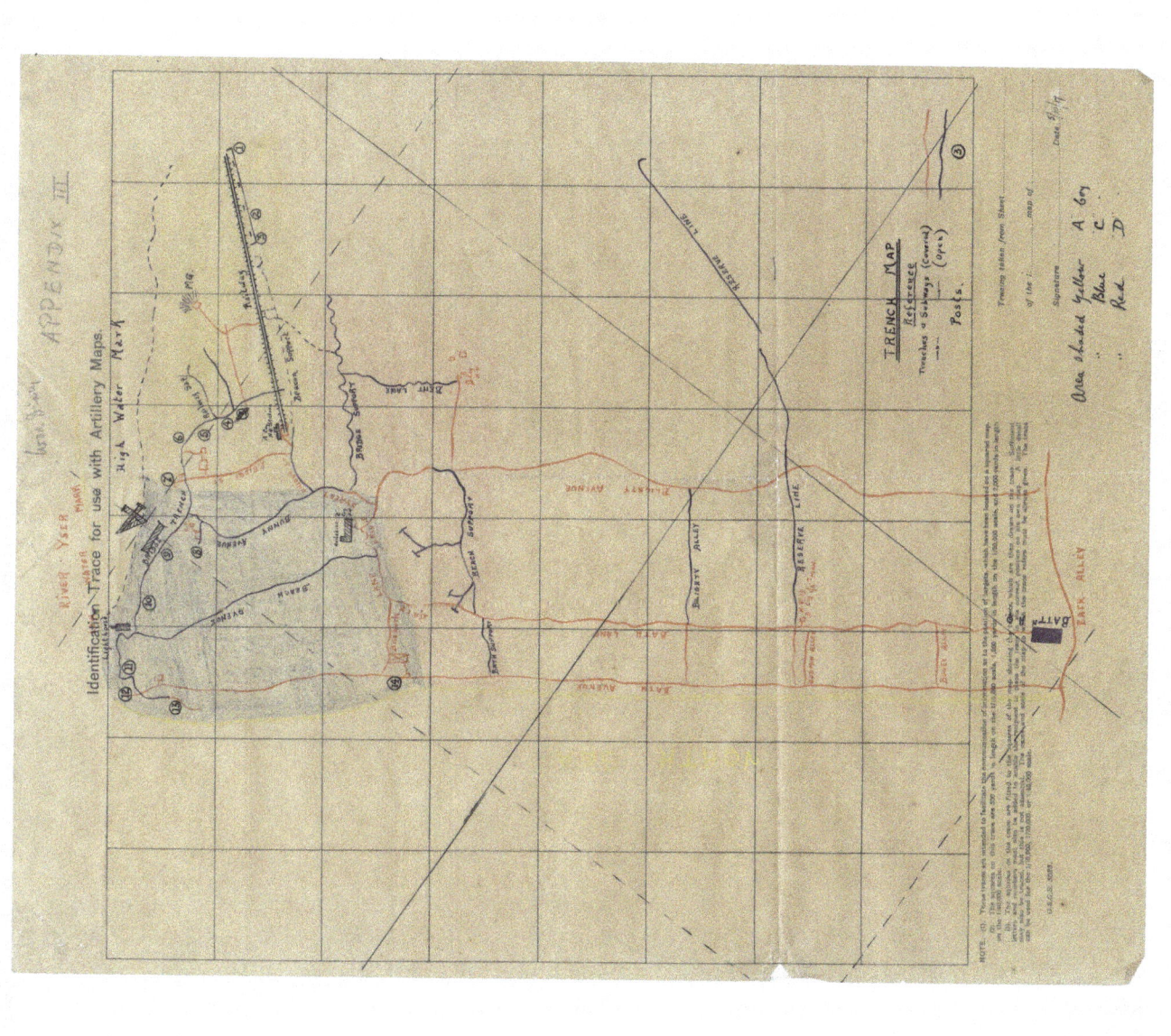

WAR DIARY
(CONFIDENTIAL)
OF
1/7th MANCHESTER REGIMENT.

PERIOD.

NOV 1st. to NOV. 30th.
1917.
VOL. II.

BELGIUM
Sheet 12 S.W. 20,000

Army Form C. 2118.
1/5 Bn: Manchester Regt.

WAR DIARY
INTELLIGENCE SUMMARY.
(Erase heading not required.)

Place	Date	Hour	Summary of Events and Information	Remarks and references to Appendices
REDAN NIEUPORT	1		Casualties during Oct. 1917.	
			Officers: Capt. H.H. NIDD and Lt. C.B. DOUGLAS, both slightly wounded & remain at duty.	
			Other Ranks: 4 killed, 13 wounded.	
			Bn 31/10/17. Total strength of Bn.	
			Officers 46 O.R. 898.	
			Actually with Bn:	
			Officers 31 O.R. 630.	
			Casualties today :- 1 officer missing (Lt. W.J. SIVEWRIGHT) 1 man killed	
			6 wounded	
			Lt. SIVEWRIGHT went out with an advance party of B Coy to reconnoitre line for tomorrows relief.	
			About 12.30 am, he went out into "No Man's Land" with 2 officers of the 5th from H.Q.'s	
			Whereon into the object of laying charges where the Dyke was to be crossed. Aircraft	
			Dyke, they came across a strong enemy party who bombed them. Lt. MATHER 4/5		302
			was killed and Lt. SIVEWRIGHT and JOHNSON (5th) are missing.	
N.28.6.5.2	2		The Bn: relieves A 127 in Right sub-sector of Bde front. Coys move forward 5.15pm 1 Coy	
			& not asking that. Relief complete 10.10pm without incident. Report ends of Strip:-	

Army Form C. 2118.

WAR DIARY
or
INTELLIGENCE-SUMMARY.
(Erase heading not required.)

1/7th Bn. Manchester Regt.

Instructions regarding War Diaries and Intelligence Summaries are contained in F. S. Regs., Part II. and the Staff Manual respectively. Title pages will be prepared in manuscript.

BELGIUM
Sheet 12 S.W. 20,000

Place	Date	Hour	Summary of Events and Information	Remarks and references to Appendices
M.28.b.5.2	2- (continued)		A Coy on Right Front (same as before) B Coy in Left Front. D Coy 1 Stokes and 4 L. Guns in Support in NASAL WALK D Coy & 1 L. Gun in REDAN Tunnel of D Coy & to occupy NASAL SUPPORT W. of Rembertyghe Rd. in case of alarm. The remng of D Coy to act as carrying parties. See APPENDIX VII of last month for sketch. 1 wounded prisoner brought in by A Coy; he died on way down.	
	3		No change. Roll A + B Coys sent out ????? patrols for offensive action if required, if not, they were to reconnoitre enemy wire & locate their posts. On enemy were encountered & no patrols obtained very useful information. 2/Lt. WARD took A Coys patrol and 2 Lt THORPE took B Coys.	
	#4		Turban passed on August 2/3 to those of Lt. SIVEWRIGHT were unsuccessful. Lt. Col. H.A. CARR to England on leave. Major T.H. ALLEN assumed command.	
	#4		Situation normal. 2/Lt. RICHARDSON took out a good patrol from A Coy. It worked through enemy wire opposite NOSE POST and bombed an of their posts.	
	5		No change.	
	6		Bn. HQ. struck by "Mininies" and practically wrecked; only 2 casualties, No officer hit. Place was same used for New Aid Post in REDAN. Bn. relieved in front line by 1/5 Lanc. Fusiliers without incident. Relief complete 10.25 P.M.	

A 5834. Wt. W4973/M687. 750,000. 8/16. D. D. & L., Ltd. Forms/C/2118/13

BELGIUM.
Sheet 12 S.E. 20,000

Army Form C. 2118.

WAR DIARY of 1/7 E. Bn. Manchester Regt.

INTELLIGENCE SUMMARY.

(Erase heading not required.)

Place	Date	Hour	Summary of Events and Information	Remarks and references to Appendices
CANADA CAMP COXYDE	1917 6 continued		Bn. moved back to Canada Camp COXYDE after 17 days in the line. Transport first to get out of this sector. Move complete 3.15 a.m.	
	7		Day spent in cleaning out bathing the men. Large working parties required. Leave to be opened up again. Not many men for training.	
	8		Practically the whole Battalion employed on working parties. None available for training. Weather much colder.	
	9			
	10		Working parties claim all available men during the day. The Major Genl. Comdg. Division & visit to the Camp and inspected the area generally. Showery & cold.	
	11		Working parties as usual.	
	12		Working parties as usual. Capt. T.R.CREAGH and Lt-C.S.WOOD to England on leave. Reduced working parties. Company available for training. Musketry. Rapid firing in morning. Recreational training in afternoon. Lt. F.G.BURN and T.P.WILKINSON returned from XI Corps S. of School. Much milder weather.	
	13		Working parties as usual. Also training. Another Coy just on for training - same programme as for 12 inst. Lewis Gun. Tactical Exercises + demonstration. 6 officers and 4 men attended.	
	14		Capt. A.H.TINKER and 2/Lt H.M.EVANS retd from Courses. Warm sunny day. Divisional Training & Trophies Parties. Brigade attended Tactical exercise by 1 Platoon - raid on a Strong Point - Officers & N.C.Os watched & Observed the operations afterwards. Much colder again.	

A 5834 Wt. W 4973/M 687 750,000 8/16 D. D. & L. Ltd Forms/C.2118/13

Army Form C. 2118.

Reference 1:100000 DUNKIRK Sheet A
1:40000 HAZEBROUCK "5A.
Sheets 11
12
19
20

WAR DIARY of 4/7th Bn
INTELLIGENCE SUMMARY. MANCHESTER REGT.
(Erase heading not required.)

Instructions regarding War Diaries and Intelligence Summaries are contained in F.S. Regs., Part II. and the Staff Manual respectively. Title pages will be prepared in manuscript.

Place	Date	Hour	Summary of Events and Information	Remarks and references to Appendices
CANADA CAMP. COXYDE	15/11/17. 16.		Working parties as usual. Day spent in preparations for the move on the 16th inst. 2/Lt W.H. BRADSHAW to hospital. Fine and cold. Bn. moved by train from COXYDE to LEFRINCKOUCKE and thence by road to TETEGHEM about 12 miles. No men fell out. The Bn was relieved in CANADA CAMP by a unit of the 133rd French Division. Capt. C.H. PHILP R.A.M.C. and Lt. T.P. WILKINSON went on leave to England. Fine and cold.	O.O. 46.
TETEGHEM	17.		Move continued by road to billets in ESQUEBECQ, about 11 miles. 3 men fell out and rejoined bn tr. Fine and cold.	O.O. 47.
ESQUEBECQ	18.		Move continued by road to billets in WEMAERS CAPPEL - about 6 miles. No men fell out. Than Emraked to the Feca Ambulance with frost trouble before the march commenced. Fine and milder.	O.O. 48
WEMAERS CAPPEL	19		Move continued by road to billets in the area between EBBLINGHEM and MALLON CAPPEL - about 8 miles. No men fell out. Fine and milder.	O.O. 49
MALLON CAPPEL	20		Move continued by road to billets in MAZINGHEM - about 13 miles. No men fell out. Transport generally very good. Slightly showery and fine late.	O.O. 50.
MAZINGHEM	21.		Day spent in cleaning up and attention to feet and anterior scrummy. 8 foot cross crane to 16 Field Ambulance. Showery and warmer.	
	22.		Light training during morning. Recreational training in the afternoon. General lectures to all ranks on Lewis Gun and its use by a staff sgt of the G.H.Q. Lewis Gun school. Capt. E. TOWNSON went on leave to England. Showery & mild.	
	23		Special demonstration of tactical scheme worked out by 2 Lt Tennin midly Staff Lyn of GHQ School Training during morning. Portion of "C" Coy rejoined from 257 Township Co. Lt Col W.T. BROMFIELD joined the Bn (taken on the strength accordingly). Marks and Kenny...	
	24		2 Corp. on XI Corps Range Musketry practice. Lewis gun and Rebels firm. A.L. practise in the middle area. Recreational training in the afternoon. Very windy and growing colder.	Ref.

Reference 1:100000. HAZEBROUCK 5A
1:10000. LA BASSÉE
RICHEBOURG.

WAR DIARY 1/7K Bn MANCHESTER REGT.
INTELLIGENCE SUMMARY.

Army Form C. 2118.

Instructions regarding War Diaries and Intelligence Summaries are contained in F. S. Regs., Part II. and the Staff Manual respectively. Title pages will be prepared in manuscript.

(Erase heading not required.)

Place	Date	Hour	Summary of Events and Information	Remarks and references to Appendices
MAZINGHEM	25/11/17		2 Corps or XI Corps Range carrying out practices as for the 24th inst. Church parade. Windy & cold.	
	26/11/17		Battalion moved by road to Gilletts in OBLINGHEM — about 12½ miles. 2 Men fell out. See O.O. 51. Fine and very cold wind. Lt H. ROSE left on short leave to England. Lt C.J.BRYAN to XI Corps School.	
OBLINGHEM	27/11/17		Battalion moved by road into GIVENCHY area and relieved the 1st R. Wiltshire Regt in the Support line. Lt. Col. H.T.BROMFIELD proceeded to furlough or leave. Maj. J. HOLLAN assumed command of the Bn. Lt. G.W.F. FRANKLIN proceeded to H.Q. LTC to report for duty. He took over the straight. Lt. C. WARD evacuated to Hospital. Lt. F.G. BURN appointed Acting Q.M. 2nd Lt. C.R. THORPE appointed Transport Officer. Lt. R.N.G. HEATHCOTE-HACKER reports from leave. Wet and milder.	O.O. 52.
A.14.a.9.9.	28/11/17		Bn in support line. Shell working parties found for 257th Tunnelling Co. Defence Scheme prepared. Fine and mild.	
	29/11/17		Working parties as usual. Copies of Defence Scheme issued. Capt. T.R. CREAGH and 2/Lt C.S. MOODIE sent from leave. 2/Lt C.R. TAAFFE returned from Divl Armrs Sch at NEWPORT.	
	30/11/17		Situation quiet. At 7 pm on the night (L.F.) Rose front to on the far side of the LA BASSÉE CANAL enemy bombard with this Gas Projectors as gas reached one trench. Enemy repeated operation at Mid-night.	

J.H. Allison Major
LIEUT.COLONEL
COMMANDING 1/7th BN. MANCHESTER REGT.

Reference
1:100 000 Dunkirk 1a
1:40 000 Sheet 19

OPERATION ORDER No.46. Nov.15th.1917.

1. Reveille.. 6-15am. Breakfast 6-45am.
    The Battalion will be relieved by a Battalion of the 133rd. French Division and will move from the XV Corps Area to the First Army Area, tomorrow.

2. The A.A.Lewis Gun Positions at present manned by the Battalion will probably not be relieved until the afternoon of the 16th.instt.
    Further details will be issued later.

3. Distance of 100 yds. will be maintained between Platoons in COXYDE VILLE and East of Coxyde. On the line of march 25yds. between every six vehicles West of COXYDE VILLE.

4. Transport of the Battalion will march in order in Brigade Column.
    1/6th.Manchesters, 1/7th Manchesters. etc. under Lieut.Crossley 1/6th. Man.Regt. to Cross Rds.in LA PANNE where it will come under the command of Capt.Fenner A.S.C.for the remainder of the march.
    This head of column will pass Starting Point W.18.c.5.7. at 12 Noon.

5. Baggage as follows will be stacked at the entrance to Camp near the Water Troughs: Blankets in bundles of 10, tightly rolled and labelled at 7-30am.
    The two Supply Wagons will be used for this purpose and sent to rendezvous at W.21.c.Central at 9-30am.to join 431st.Coy.A.S.C.
    2/Lt.C.R.THORPE, the RQMS, and 2 other ranks will accompany these wagons. On arrival at the destination TEREGHEM they will be unloaded and rations for the 17th.drawn on the wagons at the Refilling Point Q.15.b.26.
    The R.S.M.will find the necessary loading parties for the blankets. Officers Kits, Mess Stores, Orderly Room Boxes and Coy.Boxes etc.will be dumped at the same place at 9-30am.ready for loading on the remaining G.S.Wagons.
    The R.S.M.will supply the necessary loading parties.

6. Water will be drawn from Water Barges at either of the following points.
    Q.16.c.22. or C.27.b.9.8.

7. Railhead for Leave parties are as follows:-
    17th.inst. LEFFERINCOUCKE.
    18th.inst. ARNEKE.

8. Lieut.F.G.BURN and 4 N.C.O,s will proceed on bicycles as an advanced party for billeting to meet the Staff Capt at the Church LEFFERINCOUCKE Q(I.5.a.Central) at 10-0am. Billeting Area for the Battalion will be TETEGHEM.(North and Central Area.)

9. 1 Motor Lorry for the Battalion will be at AUSTRALIA CAMP at 9-0am.
    The Q.M.will send down a guide to take this to his Stores for loading.

10. Watches will be synchronised at the Orderly Room at 9-30am.

11. The Battalion will fall in on the open ground West of the R.E.Dump in Mass ready to move at 11-30am. Company Markers to report on Parade Ground to R.S.M.at 11-15am.
    Order of March. Hdqrs. A. B. C. D. Coys.
    Lieut.S.J.WILSON in charge of Hdqrs.will take the time to move from the rear Platoon of the 1/6th.Manchester Rgt. The Platoons will move in file Dress:-. Full Marching Order, Helmets, the Box Respirator will be worn slung over the right shoulder. No Packages or Sandbags will be carried.
    Rations will be issued to the men and carried in the haversack.
    Greatcoats in packs and waterproof sheets under the flaps of the pack.
    Marching Out States to be handed in to Orderly Room at 8-0am.
    Lieut.J.C.MORTEN and 1 Other Rank from each Coy.and Hdqrs.will report to

Orderly Room at 10-30am. to proceed ahead of the Battalion re entraining at COXYDE.
Instructions will be given when they report.

W H Barratt
Lieut.
Acting Adjutant. C.127.

OPERATION ORDER   No.47.   Nov.16th.1917.
Ref. 1:100,000 Sheet. DUNKERKE 1a.   1:40,000 Sheet 19.

1. The march of the 127th.Brigade to WORMHOUDT Area "A" will be continued tomorrow.

2. Advanced parties as for to-day, plus Sergt.T.BEAUMONT to represent Hdqrs. will proceed under Lieut.F.G.BURN at 7-30a .prompt to meet a Staff Officer of the 127th.Brigade at the Road Junction nearest the first "G"in GALGHOEK. (Map 19. I.22.a.7.2.) at 8-30am.

3. The two supply wagons will be loaded with the blankets as for to-day. Blankets will be tightly rolled in bundles of ten, labelled and dumped outside the Q.M.Stores ready for loading at 6-45am.prompt.
    The R.S.M.will detail the necessary loading parties.
2/Lt.C.R.THORPE, the RQMS, and 2 other ransk detailed by the Q.M.will go with these wagons under the same arrangemnts as for to-day. From the Starting Point they will march under the orders of an Officer of the 431st.A.S.C.
    Order of march. 1/7th.Manchesters leading after Brigade H dqrs.
    Starting Point same as for advanced party which will be past at 8am.

4. Officers Kits, Mess Stores and Orderly Room Boxes will be packed on the wagons by 7am. These wagons are outside the Q.M.Stores.
    Officers Batmen will attend to their Officers Kits.

5. The Battalion will move in order as follows:-.
        Hdqrs.   C.   B.   A.   D. Coys.
    The Mess Cart will follow Hdqrs.and the Field Kitchens will follow each Coy. Remainder of Transport will follow the Battalion. The head of the Column will pass the Starting Point at 8am.(the Road Junction below the "L" in INFLEEG on sheet 1a. or I.15.b.3.6.Sheet 19)
    Companies will have Marching Out States ready to hand in at the Starting Point. "D"Coy.will join the Column as it passes the Bye Road to thi their billets.
    Distances between Coys. 100 ysd. Between Battalions 500 yds.
    Dress:- Full Marching Order as for to -day.
Halts will be made from 10 minutes to the hour, to the hour, and from 5 minute to the ½ hour, to the ½ hour.
    Packs must be very promptly removed immediately the troops fall out on a ten minutes halt.
    Correct time will be sent to Coy. ommanders as soon as the Battalion has passed the Brigade Starting Point.

    Ther will be a halt for dinner from 11-50am. to 1-0pm.

6. Horses for Hdqrs Officers will be at "A"Mess at 7-45am.prompt and for Coy. Commanders at Starting Point at 7-55am.prompt. Feeds will be carried.

7. Sick Parade will be held outside Orderly Room at 7-0am.(I.15.b.1.3.)

8. Waterbottles can be refilled from Water Carts at mid-day halt. Water Carts will be filled before leaving. Companies will supply a hot drink at this halt and it will be prepared on the march. Hdqrs.will draw from their own Companies for this hot drink. The dry ration will be refunded later.

W.H.Barratt
                                                    Lieut,
                                        Acting Adjutant. C.127.

OPERATION ORDER No.48.   Nov.17th.1917.
eference 1:100,000   HAZEBROUCK   Sheet 5a.

1. The march of the 127th.Brigade to WORMHOUDT Area"B" will be continued tomorrow.

2. The Battalion will be billeted in WEMAERS CAPPEL. The Advanced party as for to-day will proceed under Lieut.F.G.BURN at 7-15am. The point of assembly will be at the Q.M.Stores, from where they will proceed to the Bridge over PEENE BECQUE South of WORMHOUDT and meet a Staff Officer of the Brigade at 8am.

The Refilling Point will be at ZERMEZEELE.

4. The Blankets drawn by Coys.will be tightly rolled in bundles of 10 and placed outside their billets on the road at 7am.and will be picked up by the supply wagons in the following order: B. A. D. C. Hdqrs.
   Officers Kits and Mess Stores will also be stacked at the same places and picked up at 8am.in the same order. The Orderly Room Boxes will be picked up at Hdqrs."A"Mess.
   The wagons will then pick up the remaining blankets at the Q.M.Stores. Coys.will find their own loading parties for blankets,Officers Kits.etc.
   These supply wagons will move with the transport section.
   Officers who are billeted in the village will send their kits to the Q.M. Stores for loading by 8am.
   The Mess Cart will call at "A"Mess at 8-30am.and then pick up the "B"Mess Stores. It will then proceed to the Transport Lines to join the column.
   The R.S.M.will find the Loading Party for blankets at the Q.M.Stores.

5. The Battalion will move in order as follows:-.
        Hdqrs. B. A. D. C. Coys.
   The Mess cart will follow Hdqrs.and the Field Kitchens will follow each Coy.
   The Head of the Column will pass the Starting Point at 9-30am.(the Rd junction nearest the first E.in ESQUELBECQ) Companies will have their Marching Out States ready to hand in at the Starting Point.
   Distance between Coys. 100 yds. 25yds.between each section of 6 vehicles.
   Dress. Full Marching Order as for to-day. Halts as for to-day. Watches will be synchronised at the Starting Point. The transport will move in rear of the column.

6. Horses will be picked up at the Starting Point as for to-day.

7. On arrival in billets O.C.Coys.will immediately send a Marching In State to Battalion Hdqrs. and if any men fall out,their rejoining the Coy.will be reported to Hdqrs.

8. As long as the Battalion is on the march Companies will send a Runner down to Hdqrs.for Orders for the following day as per previous arrangements.

9. The times as laid down in these orders will be strictly adhered to in every detail.

W.H.Barratt
                                                      Lieut.
                          Acting Adjutant.   C.127.

OPERATION ORDER No.49. Nov.18th.1917.
Reference 1:100,000 HAZEBROUCK. No.5a.

1. The march of the 127th. Brigade will be continued tomorrow to the STAPLE Area.

2. The Refilling Point will be at STAPLE.

3. Blankets drawn to-day will be rolled and placed outside Billets on the road at 6-30am. ready for loading on the Supply Wagons as for to-day.
   The order of collection will be C.D.B.Coys., and Coys. will find their own loading parties. A.Coy.& Hdqrs. will man handle their blankets and Officers Kits and Mess Stores to the Q.M.Stores for loading by 7am.
   The R.S.M. will detail the necessary loading parties.
   Officers Kits and Mess Stores of C.D.B.Coys will be collected on a wagon at 7-30am. under the same arrangements as for to-day.
   Orderly Room boxes will be loaded at the Q.M.Stores by 8am.
   The Supply Wagons will march with the Transport Section. The Mess Cart will call at "B"Mess at 8am. and A.Mess at 8-15am.

4. The Battalion will move in order as follows:-.
   Hdqrs. A. C. D. B. Coy.s Transport.
   The Mess Cart and Field Kitchens will take up their positions in the Columna as for to-day.
   The head of the column will pass the Starting Point at 9am.(the Cross Roads outside the Church in WEMAERS CAPPEL)
   Marching Out States will be handed in at the Starting Point and watches will be synchronised there.
   Distances and Halts on the March as for to-day.
   Dress:- Full Marching Order.
   The Transport will move in rear of the Battalion.

5. Officers Chargers will be waiting at the Starting Point for Coy.Commanders as for to-day.

6. Marching In States will be rendered on arrival and also the Runner reporting for orders in the evening will bring a billeting list showing the exact number of Officers and men in each billet.

W H Barratt
Acting Adjutant. Lieut.
C.127.

OPERATION ORDER No.50.   Nov.19th.1917.

Reference 1:100,000.   HAZEBROUCK.   5a.

1. The march of the 127th.Brigade will be continued on the 20thinst.to the
   AIRE AREA.

2. The Battalion will be billeted in MAZINGHEM. The Billeting Party will meet
   Lieut.F.G.Burn at the Hdqrs.of "D"Coy at 8-30am.with bicycles. They will
   proceed to the Hotel de la Ville,AIRE where they will meet a representative
   of the 127th.Brigade at 11-0am.

3. Officers Kits and Mess Stores of B. D.Coys.will be ready on the road
   outside their billets for collection at 6-30am.prompt. The Mess Cart
   will call at Hdqrs."A"Mess for Officers Kits,Mess Stores and Orderly
   Room Boxes at 7am. Cooking gear of Hdqrs.will be packed ready for putting
   on Mess Cart at "A"Mess at 7am.

4. The Battalion will move past the Brigade Starting Point in order as
   follows.   Hdqrs. B. C. D. A. Coys.Transport.
       The Battalion rendezvous will be at the Road Junction South West of
   the "W" in WALLON CAPPEL and the Head of the Battalion Column will pass
   this point at 9-15am.in the order shown.
       Companies will arrange their own route and time of parade to this
   rendezvous. Hdqrs will move at 8am.prompt. The Mess Cart will follow
   Hdqrs.and the Field Kitchens will follow each Company.
       Marching Out States will be handed in at the rendezvous.
       Distances and Halts as usual. There will be a halt for the mid-day
   meal from 11-30am. to 1pm.
       DRESS:_ Full Marching Order,and the Small Box Respirator will be
                carried on the top of the pack,instead of handing down on
                the left side.
       Watches will be synchronised at the Brigade Starting Point.
       Trabsport will march in rear of column including the A.S.C.Supply
   Wagons.

5. Hdqrs.Officers Chargers will be at "A"Mess at 7-30am,and Coy.Officers
   Chargers at each Coy.Hdqrs.at 8am. Yeams for the Field Kitchens will
   be at Coy.Hdqrs.at 8am.prompt.

6. Marching In States will be sent to Battalion Hdqrs as usual.

7. Acknowledge on attached slip.

                                              W H Barratt
                                                    Lieut.
                                     Acting Adjutant. 1/7th.Manch.Regt.

OPERATION ORDER No.51.   Nov.25th.1917.
Ref. 1:100,000 HAZEBROUCK Sheet 5a.

1. The Battalion will move to the BETHUNE Area tomorrow in the Brigade Group.

2. The route will be GUARBECQUE - BUSNES - ORBECQ - OBLINGHEM.
   The Battalion will be billeted in OBLINGHEM.

3. The Billeting Party will parade at 8-0am. at Orderly Room and proceed on bicycles to the Church at OBLINGHEM in charge of Lieut.F.G.BURN to meet the Billet Warden at 10-0am.

4. An Advanced Party of 1 Officer and 1 N.C.O. per Coy. and Battalion Hdqrs. will proceed by motor wagon to the Hdqrs. of the 7th.Brigade to reconnoitre the Line to be taken over.
   They will be at the Cross Rds.MAZINGHEM at 7-15am. to be picked up by a motor lorry. Advanced party will remain in the Line until the Battalion arrives to take over.

5. The Battalion will move in order as follows:-
   Drums. Hdqrs. C. B. A. D Coys.
   The head of the column will pass the Battalion Starting Point(on the MAZINGHEM - MOLINGHEM Rd. where the grid cuts it due South of the first "L" in L'OBLOIS) at 8-20am.
   Dress. "Over the top kit". Small Box Resporator slung down the left side
   The Mess Cart will follow Hdqrs. and the Field Kitchens each Coy.
   Halts will be as usual. Mid-day halt from 11-50am. to 1-0pm.
   Distances as usual.

6. The Refilling Point is at B.5.c.8.7. for the 26th.inst.

7. 5 Motor wagons will be at the Church MAZINGHEM at 7-15am. for surplus baggage. The Q.M.will detail a guide to meet them and take three of them to the Stores for loading. The other two will remain opposite the Orderly Room for the packs.
   The R.S.M.Will detail a loading party of 1 Sergt.and 20 men to report to the Q.M.Stores at 7-15am.   All surplus baggage will be loaded at once.

8. All blankets in possession will be tightly rolled in bundles of 10 and A. C. D. Coys. and Hdrq.s stacked on the standings opposite Orderly Room ready for loading by 6-50am.
   Two G.S.Wagons will call at "B"Coy.Billet No.35.at 6-30am. to collect blankets and Officers Kits and the mens' packs(see para 9.)
   Packs will be transferred to the motor wagons at the Orderly Room
   The surplus wagons will be used for these blankets.
   Orderly Room Boxes,Officers Kits of A.C.D.Coys.and Mess Stores will be dumped at the standings mentioned above by 7-15am.
   The R.S.M.will find necessary loading parties for this baggage.

9. All packs will be stacked separately by Coys.on the standings above mentioned ready for loading on two motor lorries at 6-50am.
   Greatcoats will be in the packs. O.C."D"Coy.will detail two other ranks. with two days rations to report to the Q.M.Stores to travel with the motor wagons as part of a working party on the surplus baggage.

10. The dump for surplus baggage will be at ECOLE de GARCON, BETHUNE.

11. Marching Out States will be handed in to Orderly Room at 7-50am.

12 Acknowledge on attached slip.

                                                      Lieut.
                                        A/Adjutant C.127.

OPERATION ORDER No.52.

Ref. 1:40,000 BETHUNE.   Sheet 36a. S.E.
   Sheet 36b. N.E.

1. The 127th.Infy.Brigade will relieve the 5th.Infy.Brigade in the GIVENCHY Sector on the 27th.& 28th.inst.

2. On the Right of the Brigade iis the 75th.Infy.Brigade which will be relieved by the 125th.Brigade on the 28th.inst.and on the left the front is held by the 1st.Portuguese Division/.

3. Battalions now going into the front line will probably be relieved after 6 days in the line.

4. The following distances will be maintained on the march.
   To BETHUNE:-. 100 yds between Coys.
   East of the line BUVRY-LOCON 200 yds between Platoons and groups of 4 vehicles.
   The Battalion will relieve the 1st.Wilts Regt.in the Support Line.

5. Defence Schemes,Aeroplane Photos,Trench Maps,Trench Stores,A.A.Lewis Gun Positions and Schemes for work in progress will be taken over on relief.
   A copy of receipts of all stores taken over will be snt to B.O.R.by 9 am.on the 28th.inst.

6. The Battalion will take greatcoats into the line,but will not take packs. Packs will be dumped at Transport Lines on the way up to the line.

7. The following working parties will be found daily by the Battalion for work with the 251 Tunnelling Coy.
   W. 13 men at 6-0am.   X. 13 mwn at 12-0 Noon.
   Y 26 "   " 6-0pm.   Z 26 "   " 12-0 midnight.
   No.Y party will be found on the 27th.inst by A Coy.at 6-0pm.
   Parties rendezvous at BRASSERIE PONT FIXE, A.14 b.20.00.

8. O.C."D"Coy.will detail 1 N.C.O and 9 Men to report to 7th.Infy.Brigade Hdqrs.at LOISNE(X.28.a.4.6.) at 10-30am.tomorrow to take over the Keeps etc
   This party will pick up packs at the Brigade Dump en route,proceeding there with the party leaving Hdqrs.at 7-30am.

8. Sgt.Livesley,Q Signaller and 3 Runners will report to the Signalling Officer of the 127th.Brigade at the 7th.Brigade Hdqrs.as above at 10-30am. tomorrow. The same orders for packs will be complied with

10. Dispositions in the Support Line will be "A" at WINDY CORNER, "B"at WINDY CORNER, "C"in Old British Line in Left Support "D"in the Keeps.
    The Coy.in the Keeps is not available either for work or for Counter attack.

11. The Transport Lines and Q.M.Stores will be taken over from the 1/8th.Bn. Loyal North Lancs Rgt. at F.3.d.1.5.
    Lewis Guns will be unloaded at the Transport Lines and carried forward by the Lewis Gun Teams. Tools will not be taken forward. Cookers will not proceed beyond Transport Lines. There is a central cook-house at Bn.Hdqrs.

12. Battalion Hdqrs.will be at A.14.a.9.9.

13. Guides on the scale of 4 per Coy.(including one for Coy.hdqrs.)and 1 for Battalion Hdqrs.will be picked up at Cross Rds.F.3.b.6.2. near GORRE Chateau at 1-30pm.

14. The mid-day meal(the meat ration will be made up)will be eaten at the Transport Lines immediately on arrival about 12-45pm.

15. The Refilling Point is the same as for to-day.

16. All baggage and Stores for loading on Transport will be ready loaded at the Q.M.Stores at 8-45am.. The Mess Cart will call at Hdqrs."A"Mess at 8-30am.

17. Completion of relief will be reported to Hdqrs.by the Code word"JINGO" followed by the code initials of the Coy.
    Position Calls will be used in future in the "Addressed to" and "addressed from" in all signal messages.

18. CORRIGENDUM. Valises will not be taken up. Para 7 of Wraning Order is cancelled.

19. Acknowledge on attached slip.

W H Barratt
Lieut.
26:11:17.   A/Adjutant. C.127.

WAR DIARY

(CONFIDENTIAL)

of

1/7th MANCHESTER REGT.

PERIOD

DEC. 1st to DEC. 31st.

1917.

VOLUME.

Army Form C. 2118.

MAPS
HAZEBROUCK 5A 1/100,000
LA BASSEE 1/10,000

WAR DIARY of 1/7th Bn. Manchester Regt.
or
INTELLIGENCE SUMMARY.
(Erase heading not required.)

Instructions regarding War Diaries and Intelligence Summaries are contained in F. S. Regs., Part II. and the Staff Manual respectively. Title pages will be prepared in manuscript.

Place	Date	Hour	Summary of Events and Information	Remarks and references to Appendices
GIVENCHY A.14.a.9.9	19.17 Dec		Officers Other Ranks Tot. strength of Bn. 44 806 Actually with Bn. 26 610 Battle casualties during December Officers O.R. Killed — 1 Missing 1 [Lt Sivewright] — Wounded — 15	10/13
	2		Situation quiet. Lt. G. NORBURY rejoin Bn. from divisional duty. No change.	
	3		11th Bn. Cheshires (1/7 Manchesters in support) carried out night raid on Sch[e]. front. Left company went over at 9.45 am & was completely without incident at 11.50 am. B[omb]d[ing] & Lewis gun parties D centre and C to the left sector. A in support. Raid B & D Coys. See attached sketch. APPENDIX I.	10/13 APPENDIX I
1/5 Devons	4		Situation very quiet & normal. In scheme of defence taken over in crater sector i.e. the lights of Craters' posts to Sch. Neuds are the main line of resistance.	10/13

WAR DIARY of 1/7th Bn. Manchester Regt.
INTELLIGENCE SUMMARY

Army Form C. 2118

BM +PS FRANCE
BETHUNE MAP M36a
36 SW, 36 NE, 36C NW, Map of LA BASSÉE 1/10,000

Place	Date 1917	Hour	Summary of Events and Information	Remarks and references to Appendices
A.8.d.55.45	4 continued		This is being modified & it is hoped to put a 2nd line into the main line of resistance when sufficient wire has been constructed and the left flank is well secured.	10/B APPENDIX I
	5		Whilst they will be in reserve line, our defence scheme APPENDIX II. Rather more enemy artillery activity. Bn. HQ bombarded for 15 minutes. White light from at mid-night. Opposite our reconnoitring patrols each night. Enemy patrols have got so far from encounters.	10/B
	6		Relatively very quiet. Plans are being formed to counter-attack front occupied by Man: to the Tunnelers & the Bn HQ. Generally, enemy examined at about 30 little more than ordinary. Except to extend front as Bullart Bns.	10/B
	7		No change. Weather has disappeared.	4/B
	8		Enemy artillery more active. Bombarded Bn: HQ area at 7 h.m. + 12 h.m. with 4.2.5 and 77 mm. Also entire of Left Coys standard zone 2 killed & 1 wounded at Bn HQ.	11/B
GORRE	9		Bn: was relieved in the line by 1/5 Manchester and moved into billets in GORRE. Relief on being adjusted at follows: Relieved by 1/5 Manchester: after relief Bn moved back & remained. Reserve at GORRE. Move complete 7 h.m. A, B, C Coys billeted in GORRE CHATEAU. Bn is in Reserve to 6 Coys.	10/B

GORRE

MAPS FRANCE (Belgium)
BETHUNE HOLLAND
LA BASSEE

WAR DIARY
or
INTELLIGENCE SUMMARY.

Army Form C.

of 1/5th Manchester Regt.

(Erase heading not required.)

Instructions regarding War Diaries and Intelligence Summaries are contained in F.S. Regs., Part II. and the Staff Manual respectively. Title pages will be prepared in manuscript.

Place	Date	Hour	Summary of Events and Information	Remarks and references to Appendices
GORRE	10		Bn. strength 14 and Anthony	6/13
	11		A & B Coys had all the Coys Lewis Gunners for the Rngt	6/13
			2 am D Coy doctor heavy and Lewis gun drill	
	12		Evening in the morning, Sunday Evening by Pioneers	6/13
	13		Train Major J.H. ALLAN seconded to Holding Battn	10/13
			G.B. HURST assumes Command of the Bn.	
	14		Issued orders & Permission for tactical attack on GIVENCHY	10/13
			RIDGE as adjt & 2 officers and 3 O.R. from each	
			of the Coys to reconnoitre and give in detailed criticism showing	
			how this would encounter.	
ABUSSUS	15		Battalion relieved 5th Manchesters in right subsection of 126 front L.S.	6/13
			by L.L. relief. First Coy moved from GORRE 12.45 pm, relief finished	
			without incident 3.50 pm.	
			Dispositions – Front line B Coy right, A Coy centre, C Coy Left.	
			Support D Coy	
	16		Lt.Col. H.C. DARLINGTON C.M.G. (7th Bn.) takes command of Bn. Brit. Major HURST	1/13
			2nd in Command. Leicestershire Regt.	
	17		Lt.Col: W.T. BROMFIELD returns from leave and assumes command of the	1/13
			Battalion. Situation very quiet. Weather cold, ruined at Aug 16	
			Unchanged. Mr. WILKINSON took out a patrol from R Coy centre Coy.	

MAP
FRANCE
LA BASSÉE. 1/20,000

WAR DIARY
of 1/7th Bn. Manchester Regt.
INTELLIGENCE SUMMARY.
(Erase heading not required.)

Army Form C. 2118.

Place	Date 1917	Hour	Summary of Events and Information	Remarks and references to Appendices
A.8 ѕᵈ 85.45	18		Another cold, quiet day. Patrols got from B and A Coys. Enemy much quieter than usual & specially their artillery. Near four any enemy patrols out.	/OB
	19		Hard frost. Situation normal. 1 man sniped & killed at E.Sy. Learn that 2/Lt. H.A. CARR has been ordered a medical Board in England & therefore goes off on change.	/OB
			Lt. GRESTY reposts from Hohibe	
	20		2/Lt. WARD reposting from Hohibe. Hard frost continues. Coys. Commanders (Major Van HOLLAND) and 2.O.B. Bns. (Major General SOLLY FLOOD) go round Bn. line. Situation very quiet	/OB
	21		No change.	/OB
E.17.d.9.9 BETHUNE	22		7th Lancs. Fusiliers relieved the Bn. in the line about mid-day but the Bn. moved back to billets in the Tobacco Factory BETHUNE. Move completed without incident at 6 pm. The factory holds all the men of the Bn. Frost continues. E.A. bombed town 3 pm.	/OB
	23		Church Parade only. E.A. bombed town at 5 p.m.	/OB
	24 25		Section and platoon training. Holiday. M.G.R. X mas dinner 1 pm.	/OB

MAP
FRANCE. LA BASSÉE 20000/1
BETHUNE (embraced) 40,000

WAR DIARY
or
INTELLIGENCE SUMMARY

of 1/7th Bn. Manchester Regt. Army Form C. 2118.

(Erase heading not required.)

Instructions regarding War Diaries and Intelligence Summaries are contained in F. S. Regs., Part II. and the Staff Manual respectively. Title pages will be prepared in manuscript.

Place	Date 1917 Dec	Hour	Summary of Events and Information	Remarks and references to Appendices
BETHUNE E.17 c.9.9	25	continues	Lt. Col. A.E. CRONSHAW T.D. (late of 1/7th Manchesters) and Capt. J.R. CREAGH were mentioned in C. in C.'s despatches dated 21/12/17 for gallantry in the field.	NB NB
	26		Front of snow continues.	NB
	27		Training to Brigade. Capt. C.E. HIGHAM rejoins Bn. fr. 1/10th Manchesters.	NB
	28		No change.	NB
FERME DU ROI E.6.c.7.4.	29		Bn. moved quarters to FERME DU ROI; gents comfortable quarters.	NB
	30		2 coys training. 2 coys working of the line.	NB
	31		2 coys training. 2 coys working of the line from + to 11 hrs. Lt. H. HODGE goes to 1/5th East Lancs to take command Ja coy. F.A. bombed BETHUNE between 5 and 5.45 pm. Several dropped near the town.	NB

W.J. Bromfield
LIEUT-COLONEL,
COMMANDING 1/7th BN. MANCHESTER REGT.

APPENDIX I

Reference
Company areas Shaded
Posts manned by B Coy ● D ● C ● A ■ Sept.
" " " ● ▲ ■ alternative
"2" T.M. position in use
Coy H.Q.
Batt. H.Q.
M.G. direction of fire
L.G.

Scale 1/10,000

12-18-1917

APPENDIX II

GIVENCHY FRONT --- RIGHT BATTALION SUBSECTOR.

DEFENCE SCHEME.   8/12/17.

1. **BATTALION FRONT:-.** WOLFE ROAD to WARWICK SOUTH both inclusive.

2. **COMPANY FRONTAGES:-.**
   (a) Right Company from WOLFE ROAD (inclusive) to HALF MOON ST. (exclusive)
   (b) Centre Company from HALF MOON ST. (inclusive) to WARE ROAD (inclusive)
   (c) Left Company from WARE ROAD exclusive) to WARWICK SOUTH (inclusive)
   (d) Support Company (a) This Coy. holds various posts in Support as garrison as shown on Disposition Map.
   (b) After finding these posts the remainder of the Coy. is at the disposal of O.C. Centre Coy. and is quartered at his Hdqrs. in CALEDONIAN ROAD.

3. **DEFENCE SCHEME.** (a) The front line of resistance is the Sap heads.
   (b) Each Company has a small reserve.
   (c) There is no Battalion Reserve.
   (d) In case of attack two Companies support Battalion are at the disposal of O.C. Right Subsector.
   (e) It is proposed to turn the front line trench into the line of resistance and the sapheads (except on extreme R. & L. of Subsector) into an outpost line and work is now proceeding.
   (f) All posts are to hold out at all costs.

4. **TRENCH MORTARS:-.**   6 inch.   1   ) Hdqrs.
                            2 "   4.) CAVAN
                            Stokes.   3.) ROAD.

5. **VICKERS GUNS:-.**   8.

6. **MINES:-.**   We have defensive mine galleries under the front line trench of the Right and Centre Companies.
   Hdqrs. Tunnelling Section - In mine under Centre Coy. H Q

7. Trench Mortar Officers call at Battalion Hdqrs. at 10 a.m. every morning.

                                                    Capt.
                            Adjutant.   C.127.

Received DEFENCE SCHEME for RIGHT BATTALION SUBSECTOR.

Time. .... Date...............

                                            Signed.

APPENDIX II

REPORT ON FIRETRENCH WEST OF THE CRATERS.

The problems along this trench are different in different points and it is better to divide it into four sections from R. to L. and deal with each part separately.

1. From SAP "A" to SAP "D".

    The fire trench is close up to the Sapheads and the field of fire from the trench is nil except in one place between SAP "A" and SAP "B" where it is proposed to firestep.

    SAPS "B" & "C" are close together and it is proposed to connect them up and so make a short length of fire trench on the hill crest

    Immediately SOUTH of SAP "D" there are two bays in the fire trench which would cover the N. flank of the proposed trench between SAPS "B" & "C".

    To protect our Right flank it is proposed to make a fire bay in WOLFE ROAD just SOUTH of SAP "A".

    This flank would be safer if the Battalion on our Right could make a post in the heap of sandbags about 100-150 yds. SOUTH of SAP "A".

2. From SAP "D" to SAP "F".

    There will be sufficient firesteps in this part of the trench when a few under construction and repair are finished.

3. From SAP "F" to SAP "J".

    There are only 7 Fire steps in this length and more will have to be made.
    My " " Cy. is going on with this work.

4. SAPS "J" and "K".

    I consider these sapheads could be held as part of the line of resistance.
    There are some firebays in SCOTTISH TRENCH which give the sapheads very good support.

NOTES:- 1. There is very little dug-out accommodation in the front trench and a great deal of work will be required to provide this.
    I will report further on this point.

2. PICCADILLY would make a good support trench.

3. Revetting, firestepping, thickening of parapets, rebuilding of parados. Drainage and Dug-outs are all being considered in conference with R.E. and some of the work is now being done.

WAR DIARY (CONFIDENTIAL)

OF

1/7th Bn. MANCHESTER RGT.

PERIOD

JANUARY 1st to JANUARY 31st

1918

VOLUMN 1

MAPS
FRANCE 1
LA BASSÉE 1/40,000

WAR DIARY of 1/7th Bn Manchester Regt.
INTELLIGENCE SUMMARY

Army Form C. 2118.

Instructions regarding War Diaries and Intelligence Summaries are contained in F. S. Regs., Part II. and the Staff Manual respectively. Title pages will be prepared in manuscript.

(Erase heading not required.)

Place	Date 1918 Jan	Hour	Summary of Events and Information	Remarks and references to Appendices
BETHUNE	1		Total strength of Bn. with Unit — Officers 42, O.R. 799	O.B.
			— 28, 876	
			Casualties during Dec:— killed — 5	
			missing — 1	
			wounded — 6	
	2		Routine. Training and Baths. E.A. bombed BETHUNE	O.B.
			Foot treatment and inspection of Kits	
KING S. CLEAR A.15.c.15.23	3	7	The Bn. relieved 1/5th East Lancs in the left sub-sector of the right Bde: front i.e. astride the LA BASSÉE Canal. Relief was delayed for the morning tret owing to poor visibility, was postponed till afternoon 3:30 pm. Relief completed without incident by 8:30 pm. All 4 Coys are in the line in order from the right B, D, C, A. Coys are attached APPENDIX I. sketch APPENDIX I.	D.B. APPENDIX I
	4		Situation very quiet. Had feet continued.	O.B.
	5		Situation quiet. 2 Patrols of 1 night Boy encountered enemy parties tight. Took places + 1 of our men was wounded. Col. BROMFIELD went to inspect 42nd Div: lying at ALOUAGNE.	O.B.

MAP FRANCE
LA BASSÉE 1/10,000

WAR DIARY
of 1/7th Bn. Manchester Regt.
INTELLIGENCE SUMMARY
(Erase heading not required.)

Army Form C. 2118.

Place	Date 1918 Jan	Hour	Summary of Events and Information	Remarks and references to Appendices
RINGSCLERE A.15.C.6.8.23	6		Situation normal till afternoon when enemy heavily bombarded our area S. of CANAL and L. Bn. on our right with T.M.s of all calibres & a few light shells mixed with some gas shells, from 3 pm till 5:30 pm. A good deal of damage was done to trenches & about 10 casualties caused. Pte. Saunderson of B Coy tackled & bayonetted in our trench a man in BRICKSTACKS clothes & bayonetted in but hastily only wounded. Two Bavarian caps and 1 very pistol were found.	103 103
	7		Quiet until about 5 p.m. when a number of lighter shells were dropped around Bn: H.Q. 2/Lt. G. WARD to hostile.	103
	8		1/5 Manchester relieved Bn. in the Line during morning without incident. Bn. Bn: moved back to Béthune Dugouts. Disposition of Coys.:	103
WOBURN ABBEY A.20.f.8.3	9		A Coy — ½ Coy ORCHARD KEEP A.15.a.3.4 ½ Coy SPOIL BANK KEEP A.15.c.8.9 B " — ½ Coy BRADDEL CASTLE A.20.d.8.6 ½ Coy MOUNTAIN KEEP A.21.a.3.1 C " — MARYLEBONE Rd 80.A.Q. A.21.c.0.3 This Coy is in support to centre garrison of Rt Bn. D " ½ Coy GUNNERS SIDING A.15.a. ½ Coy ESPERANTO TERRACE A.15.a This Coy is in support to these garrison of Left Front Bn.	103
	10		Situation quiet. Lieut. J.Hurst to autonomie. All Coy parties R.E. working parties 103 D. Murphy & 2nd Bathurst to England. Capt. C.E. HIGHAM assumes duties of 2nd in Command	103

MAP
FRANCE
LA BASSÉE 1/7 Bn Manchester Regt   Army Form C. 2118.

WAR DIARY
or
INTELLIGENCE SUMMARY.
(Erase heading not required.)

Instructions regarding War Diaries and Intelligence Summaries are contained in F. S. Regs., Part II. and the Staff Manual respectively. Title pages will be prepared in manuscript.

Place	Date 1918 Jan	Hour	Summary of Events and Information	Remarks and references to Appendices
WOBURN ABBEY A.20.6.83	11		No change. Three witnesses. Lt. E. JESSOP taken off strength (in England)	} DR
	12		No change. 2/Lt. J.O. RICHARDSON invalided & taken off strength.	
	13		No change	
	14		No change	
KINGSCLERE A.15.c.65.23	15		Bn. relieved 1/5 Manchesters in Left Bde sector during the Morning. Relief was completed without incident at 11 am. Dispositions of Coys from right to left C, A, B, and D Coys: all Coys have their line + one platoon in depth, see sketch APPENDIX I.	
	16		Very stormy. Trenches falling in & becoming very bad (blown). All work stopped except clearing of trenches which have fallen in. Very badly est dug-outs of trenches flooded. 2/Lt MILNE rejoins from hosps. Lt. GRESTY to England on leave. Situation quiet. All available labour including Support + Reserve Bns. turned on to trenches	} DR
	17		Situation quiet. No change.	
	18		No change. Weather mild.	
	19		No change. No. 275276 Sergt. J. HOLBROOK (ASC) awarded D.E.M. (also No. Manch Div) in rear	
	20		Situation quiet. Every man active at work clearing trenches.	
	21			

MAP FRANCE
Sheet 36 B.NE. 1/20,000

WAR DIARY
INTELLIGENCE SUMMARY.
(Erase heading not required.)

Army Form C. 2118.

Place	Date	Hour	Summary of Events and Information	Remarks and references to Appendices
LE PREOL F.15.d.05.90	22		Bn. relieved in the line by 5th Manchesters in the afternoon without incident. Relief complete 6.40 p.m. Bn. moved back to Bde Reserve into Billets at LE PREOL. Move complete 8.55 p.m.	A.O.2
	23		All Bn. bathing & cleaning up.	
	24		Training to a limited extent i.e. L. Gun class for 2 hours per day. B.F. and P.T. class for N.C.O's. Large R.E. working parties in & to work in line every evening from 4.30 p.m. till nearly midnight. These parties do 1 hour close order drill & 2 hour practice in firing Rifle Grenades each morning.	LOST
	25		Lance Cpl ??? G	
	26- 27		Training & working parties. Training parties this morning.	
			Brig. Gen. Hon. A. M. HENLEY to gallant work on 4.5 gun in silencing telephone wires during heavy bombardment.	LOST
	28		No change.	
HINGETTE	29		Bn. relieved by 1/6 Lanc. Fusiliers in E. morning. Bn. moved back to HINGETTE and went into Bde: in Divisional Reserve. Move complete about 12.30 p.m. Bn. billets dry & natural.	LOST

MAP
FRANCE

BETHUNE

WAR DIARY
INTELLIGENCE SUMMARY
(Erase heading not required.)

Army Form C. 2118.

1/7th Bn. Manchester Regt.

Place	Date	Hour	Summary of Events and Information	Remarks and references to Appendices
MINGETTE	1916 Jan 30		Training & cleaning up. 2/Lt F.T.R. WOODWORTH reports for duty with Bn.	
	31		Training.	

W.F. Bomfield
LIEUT.-COLONEL,
COMMANDING 1/7th BN. MANCHESTER REGT.

17TH
MANCHESTER REGT.

APPENDIX I

CANAL (A). SECRET. N° 60.

WAR DIARY

(Confidential)

OF

1/17th. Battalion Manchester Regt.

Period

1st. Feb. 1918 to 28th. Feb. 1918.

Volumn. 2

MAP FRANCE
BETHUNE (included) 57D.N.W.

WAR DIARY
or
INTELLIGENCE SUMMARY
(Erase heading not required.)

of 1/7th Bn. Manchester Regt.

Army Form C. 2118.

Place	Date	Hour	Summary of Events and Information	Remarks and references to Appendices
HINGETTE	1918 Feb 1		Total strength of Bn. Officers 36, O.R. 821	/OB
			Strength 1st Bn. 24, 617	
			Battle Casualties during January 1918	
			Killed — Wounded — Missing	
			3 O.R. 7 O.R. —	
	2		Training. "C" Coy is detached from the Bn. at CAMBRIN where it forms working parties for 2 Tunnelling Coys. Capt. C.E. TOWNSON evacuated to Corps Rest Station on 29.9 Jan.	10B
	3		Training. Church Services. Gas demonstrations by D.G.O. Lt. DOUGLAS & 2/Lt SMITH rejoin from Lewis. Capt. J. BAKER proceeds on Army Musketry Course.	10B
	4		Training.	10B
	5		Working parties. 2 officers, 82 O.R. "C" Coy returned from CAMBRIN, leaving only 26 O.R. attd to Tunnelling Co.	10B

Ref: FRANCE
BETHUNE (confined) 1:40,000
sheet

Army Form C. 2118.

WAR DIARY
or
INTELLIGENCE SUMMARY.
(Erase heading not required.)

of 1/7th Manchester Regt.

Instructions regarding War Diaries and Intelligence Summaries are contained in F. S. Regs., Part II. and the Staff Manual respectively. Title pages will be prepared in manuscript.

Place	Date	Hour	Summary of Events and Information	Remarks and references to Appendices
HINGETTE	6.		Training. Capt. J.R. CREAGH and H.A. NIDD left for 6 days leave.	WB
	7.		Training. Lt.Col. W.T.B. BROMFIELD attended acting Byde. Commander. 9/Lf. Bgte. Theatre bathe - equally and suit. Lt. P. PELL-ILDERTON to England for 6 mths.	WB
	8.		Wining parties at LOCON under Hd Qr. Field Co. R.E. Capt. D. MORBURY-RELF to Bd a assumed Command of "B" Coy	WB
	9.		Wining parties at LOCON - Lt. W.S.T. THORP proceeded to England on 1 months leave.	WB
	10.		Wining parties at LESTREM. Lt. J.C. MORTEN to First Army School. Lt. E.M. LUDLAM to G.H.Q. Lewis Gun School. Lt. C.B. DOUGLAS in Command of "D" Coy.	WB
	11.		Training	WB
	12.		Move to BURBURE by Route march. Lt.Col W.T. BROMFIELD proceeded to Bgde H.Q.	WB
BURBURE	13.		Training.	WB
	14.		Training. Lt. F.G. BURN rejd from leave. Capt. CREAGH and NIDD from leave. "A" Coy moved to HURIONVILLE to Regt Billets	WB
	15		Reinforcements of 7 Officers and 187 "other ranks" join Bn. They are a complete Coy (B Coy) from 9th Manchesters. The officers are posted to Coy's as follows:- A Coy { Lt. J. McALMONT, Lt. H.L. POVEY B Coy { Lt. H. ABBOTT, Lt. W.C. WILSON C Coy { 2/Lt. T. COCKSHOOT 2/Lt. J.A. HARLAND D Coy { Lt. I. LEWIN All men officers a good lot. Under this Re-organisation Reserve Brigades are reduced to 3 Battalions. The 5th Manchesters leave our Bde and join the 126th Bde as a complete unit.	WB

Of: FRANCE
36A. 1/40,000

3

1/7th Bn: Manchester Regt.

Army Form C. 2118.

WAR DIARY
or
INTELLIGENCE SUMMARY.
(Erase heading not required.)

Instructions regarding War Diaries and Intelligence Summaries are contained in F. S. Regs., Part II. and the Staff Manual respectively. Title pages will be prepared in manuscript.

Place	Date 1918	Hour	Summary of Events and Information	Remarks and references to Appendices
BURBURE	16		Training.	WB
	17		Whitsunday Church Parade and inspection.	WB
	18		Training.	WB
	19		Training.	WB
	20		Training. 2/Lt: J.A. HARLAND goes to Div: Grenade Course.	WB
	21		Training.	WB
	22		Lt Col: W.T BROMFIELD who has been commanding the Bde: during the absence on leave of the Brigadier rejoins the Bn: and resumes command.	WB
	23		Training. Col: SLAUGHTER instructs Bn: Transport & Rds: Competition.	WB
	24		All Coy: Offrs: on ALLOUAGNE Ranges. Church Parade. Officers & N.C.Os go to ALLOUAGNE to see demonstration by H.A.C. Platoon.	WB
	25		Training. Major HIGHAM and Lt.BARRATT to PARIS on leave.	WB
	26		Training. 2/Lt. J.V. SPREADBURY (2/10th Manchesters) joins the Bn:	WB

MAP FRANCE 36 A. 4.0.10.0.

WAR DIARY
INTELLIGENCE SUMMARY of 1/7th Bn. Manchester Regt.

Army Form C. 2118.

Place	Date	Hour	Summary of Events and Information	Remarks and references to Appendices
BURBURE	1918 July 27		Training.	WMB.
	28		Training. Capt. D. NORBURY to England on 6 months tour of duty. Lt. A.S. WOOD (at 1/9th and 2/6 Manchesters) joins Bn.	

W.T. Rumpfuff
LIEUT.-COLONEL,
COMMANDING 1/7th BN. MANCHESTER REGT.

42nd Division
127th Infantry Brigade.

1/7th BATTALION

MANCHESTER REGIMENT

MARCH 1 9 1 8

WAR DIARY

CONFIDENTIAL

of

1/7th MANCHESTER Rgt.

FROM 1st March 1918
To. 31st March 1918

VOL. III

MAP: FRANCE
36 A 40,000

WAR DIARY
or
INTELLIGENCE SUMMARY of 1/7th Manchester Regt.

Army Form C. 2118.

Place	Date 1918 March	Hour	Summary of Events and Information	Remarks and references to Appendices
BURBURE	1		No Battle Casualties in Bn. during Feb.	
			Strength Total strength Officers 43 O.R. 956	6.J.B.
			Number with Bn. 29 818	
	2		Training.	6JB.
	3		Training in Morning. Half Holiday known.	6JB.
			Bn. shoots (by Coys) on ALLOUAGNE Range: 5 rounds application at 300 yds.	
	4		15 rounds Rapid (fixed targets) in 1 minute at 300 yds. Bn. ctd.	6JB.
			Bn. moves at 1 p.m. to billets at BUSNES than complete 3 p.m. Bny. ctd.	
			1/5th Manchesters (of 6th Bde) take over our billets at BURBURE.	
BUSNES	5		Billets at BUSNES good but as training grounds.	6JB
			Reconnaissance of Robecque 2nd Lows. Coy Route March.	6JB
			Lt. Col. W.T. BROMFIELD to England on leave.	6JB
	6		Training.	6JB
	7		Training.	6JB
	8		1 Athletes Platoon from each Coy shoot off A.R.A. Competition on OBLINGHEM Range.	6JB
			C Coy won.	

MAP: FRANCE
36 A 1/40,000 36A S.W. 1/20,000

Army Form C. 2118.

WAR DIARY
or
INTELLIGENCE SUMMARY.
(Erase heading not required.)

Place	Date 1918	Hour	Summary of Events and Information	Remarks and references to Appendices
BUSNES	9		Everything in immediate readiness to reinforce Portuguese Front. Bn. would occupy localities in R.28.d, R.29.c.Centre, R.29.c.8.5, R.23.d. From the night the line will be garrisoned by A C & B Coys with D Coy in reserve at Bn. H.Q. about R.21.c.9.5. Lt. E.B DOUGLAS sailed for England on leave. Received warning that enemy may attack Portuguese tomorrow 10th.	693
	10		Church parades.	693
	11		Training. Lt. MILLAR (U.S.A.) our M.O. return from Paris leave & Lt. TABUTEAU appoins Field Ambulance.	693
	12		Training.	693
	13		Lt. W.T.THORP appoins from leave in England. Training.	693
	14		Training. 1 Station of A Coy Officers & N.C.O's of A Coy do a Tactical outdoor topo. Divisional & Brigade Commanders.	693
	15		Training.	693
	16		Training. No 9 Platoon representing the Bn. in the Platoon Competition won the A.R.A Cup Lt. J.A. HARLAND. 2/Lt J.A. HARLAND commands No.9 Platoon.	693
	17		Church parades. 2/Lt W.B SMITH returned from leave.	693
	18		At the Bn. on a O.16 been part of CHOQUES. Scheme of attack & defence.	693

Army Form C. 2118.

FRANCE
36A S.E. 20,000
1/40,000

WAR DIARY
~~INTELLIGENCE SUMMARY~~
of 1/7 Bn Manchester Regt.

(Erase heading not required.)

Instructions regarding War Diaries and Intelligence Summaries are contained in F.S. Regs., Part II. and the Staff Manual respectively. Title pages will be prepared in manuscript.

Place	Date 1918 March	Hour	Summary of Events and Information	Remarks and references to Appendices
BUSNES	19		D and C Coys shot on Range at LABEUVRIERE. Remainder Training. S.O.S. Lt: MORTEN rejoins from Army School. Lt: S.J.WILSON fm ~~hospital~~ Army and Lt: C.S. WOOD fm Siv: Signal School.	LNB
	20		Lt: WOOD becomes Bn: Signalling Officer. 2nd Capt: M. BATEMAN is posted to A Coy. Training. Capt: E. TOWNSON rejoins from Hospital	LNB
	21		Bn: box returns on No 16 Arm. No 9 Platoon Coy Tactical schemes in order. Bn: Competition under Brig: Gen: A.M. HENLEY. No 9 does well but is not upto Standard to be 6 Manchester. Lt: Col: W.T BROMFIELD rejoins Bn: from leave.	LNB
L'ECLEME	22		Bn: moves to billets at L'ECLEME. Bodies proceed Independently at 7.75 pm. to dump surplus baggage (at BUSNES) in train of Another trestle. All baggage entrained by 11.30 pm.	LNB
AYETTE	23	7.30 am 10.20 am	Transport ~~orders~~ to ~~HORRY~~ TINQUES by rail Bde. Ambuses Bde: de-buses near AYETTE in squares I + Sec 1/100,000 Bn: immediately to revised defences of its defences. on Ayer fm ABLAINVILLE to X roads on AYETTE — COURCELLES Rd: in order A B D with C in close Support. Bn: H.Q. Ainotroise. Receive orders to relieve tonight 6 40 Div: in the	LNB
	~~mid-night~~ 24			LNB

(A7092). Wt. W.12839/M4293. 750,000. 1/17. D. D. & L., Ltd. Forms/C.2118/14

MAP
LENS roll 100,000 Sheet
57c N.W.

Army Form C. 2118.

WAR DIARY of 1/7th Bn: Manchester Regt.
or
INTELLIGENCE SUMMARY.
(Erase heading not required.)

Instructions regarding War Diaries and Intelligence
Summaries are contained in F.S. Regs., Part II.
and the Staff Manual respectively. Title pages
will be prepared in manuscript.

Place	Date 1918 March	Hour	Summary of Events and Information	Remarks and references to Appendices
500 yds S. of GOMMECOURT	24 continued		MDRY sector of the line ~ the 127th Bde to move up at 8 P.m. At GOMMECOURT en route to line. Relief cancelled & Bde takes up Defensive Position S. of GOMMECOURT, to Br. Relief left of line in G.5.b. Front positions give way and 42nd Bde heavily engaged all day holding on. A & B Coy remain all day in position in G.5.b. C & D Coys 9th Bde Reserve about noon to relieve 6th Manchesters sent to relieve BIHUCOURT.	10B
	25		D Coy been attacked 5.5th Manchesters & successfully counter attack with them & B (Capt. J. BAKER, RndE.C. HOSKYNS and 2/Lt G.B. TAYLOR wounded. O.R. casualties light. C Coy held defensive flank along trench in G.5.c Receive orders to withdraw at 2 am. Garrison, whole line goes back. At 2am. Bn is withdrawn in conformity with general retirement & takes up a defensive line in front of LOGEAST WOOD through A.27.B.&c. to A.2.d. this line renewed 11.2.am. This line evacuated at 7.15 am. & line taken up from N.E. BUCQUOY to S. ABLAINZEVELLE. Enemy attack guards get in touch with coy Support with coy following this withdrawal on our southern flank. Give line from F.28.a.72 to E.29.a.27 established 9.45 am. 6.2nd Bn. on our right Bn. on our left 5th Man. to Bde Reserve 1/6 & 8th Bde Res. left sector.	
57D N.E. Bn. H.Q. F.29.c.9.2	26		From dawn enemy bombards our position first with light guns from 3 tan orchards to 7 a.m. with 5.9's. Enemy infantry then assemble to attack 600/800 yds in front but it is Mown down. F.2 am + 1pm got good targets.	10B

Army Form C. 2118.

WAR DIARY
of 1/7th Bn. Manchester Regt.
or
INTELLIGENCE SUMMARY.
(Erase heading not required.)

Instructions regarding War Diaries and Intelligence Summaries are contained in F. S. Regs., Part II. and the Staff Manual respectively. Title pages will be prepared in manuscript.

Place	Date 1918 March	Hour	Summary of Events and Information	Remarks and references to Appendices
F.22.c.9.2.	26		Casualties at 27th Capt. C.H. PHILP M.O. Rifle Casualty at 26th Capt. C.H.PHILP M.O. Rifle Casualty at 26 night quiet.	
	27		Casualties Lt. A.S. WOOD wounded (since died) Lt. J.E. MORTEN wounded.	
			Night 26/27th Quiet except for enemy bombardment between 3 and 4 a.m.	
		10.15 a.m.	Enemy commences shelling with the Bn. front between 5.9's	
		11.30 a.m.	Shelling increases to a bombardment and continues until dusk.	
			Constant enemy movement in front during day. Lines of them advance apparently to attack behaviour not pushed home on our front. Enemy assembling in NISSEN HUTS N. of ABLAINZEVELLE and	
			when they were bombarded by our artillery & to inflicted persons states they suffered heavy casualties. Enemy is apparently endeavouring to recover his recently position in shell-torn shell ground.	673
			About 2.00 p.m. from our front 6 in rifles & 2 Lewis Guns did a lot of execution. Our casualties considerable. 1 Platoon sent with 6 aeroplane box forward.	
			Patrols of 6 p.m. from the types C.D.B.A. did fresh troops a broken Rd. BUCQUOY - ABLAINZEVELLE on the least shelled all day. Night again quiet.	
	28		After sometime Heavy 5.9 barrage commenced soon after daylight on all Bn. position & continued all day. Enemy M.G. enfiladed Sunken Rd. from ABLAINZEVELLE village.	
			All along front formidable enemy movement. Enemy still endeavouring to establish a forward position. Periodically long lines of enemy infantry advance in extended order but no general attack developed. Counter attack through villages in between front lines from Krupports	673

MAP
57D NE 20000
5½ D NE of 1/7th Manchester Regt.

Army Form C. 2118.

WAR DIARY
of 1/7th Manchester Regt.

INTELLIGENCE SUMMARY.

Place	Date	Hour	Summary of Events and Information	Remarks and references to Appendices
E.22.c.9.2	28 Continued		Met 2nd Reserve Jaeger Bn. 16th Regt. in front of us. This Bn has not been in action since Oct 1917. 6 Other casualties :- Killed Capt. A.H. TINKER. Lt. M.T. THORP. 2/Lt. B.W. LUDLAM. Wounded Capt. H.H. NIDD (at duty) Lt. D. McLAINE.	WD
F.10.d. 1500 yds N.W. of BUCQUOY	29		Night 28/29th Bn. relieved by 7th Lanc. Fusiliers Bn. with to Bde. Reserve. Moved on to Bde. Reserve. Quiet day.	WD
	30		Night 29/30th Bn. relieved 1/5th HANTS in support S. of GOMMECOURT with four R.H.a. and R.F.C. dispositions of Coys from Rt. Aghin :- D Coy R.4.c.8.4 to K.4.a.3.4 A " R.4.a.3.4 to R.5.c.0.2. C " R.5.c.14 to R.5.a.9.1 B " in front support R.4.d.4.8 to R.4.b.8.2. Bn. H.Q. R.3.b.9.1. Day quiet. 5th L.F. on Bn. left. 5th Manr. on right behind HEBERTERNE. 6 Others in Bde. Reserve. E.28.a. 5th L.F. is in support to 4th Australian Bde + Bn. is immediately behind 4th Australian Regt.	
	31		1275 Bde is in support to 4 Australian Bde + Bn. is immediately behind 4th Australian Regt. Day quiet. Some excitement in B Coy from artillery.	WD

A.T. Bromfield. Lt Col.
Cmdg. 1/7 Manchester Regt.

127th Inf.Bde.
42nd Div.

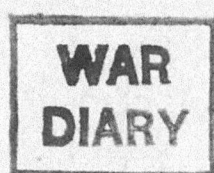

1/7th BATTN. THE MANCHESTER REGIMENT.

A P R I L

1 9 1 8

Confidential.

"War Diary".

No 4.

Apr 1st 1918 to Apr 30th 1918.

17th Bn. Manchester Regt.

Army Form C. 2118.

MAR. 57TH M.i. 1/10.000

WAR DIARY of 2/6th Bn Manchester Regt

INTELLIGENCE SUMMARY.

(Erase heading not required.)

Instructions regarding War Diaries and Intelligence Summaries are contained in F. S. Regs., Part II. and the Staff Manual respectively. Title pages will be prepared in manuscript.

Place	Date 1918 April	Hour	Summary of Events and Information	Remarks and references to Appendices
F.20 b and d	4		Situation calm. Heavy rain made trenches bad in absence of drainage system. Bn. takes over left sector of front line, being ABLAINZEVELLE, and Bn's in Bde. reserve. At night relieved 1/8th Manch.R. in F.21, 22 & 27, dispositions as follows:- A Coy from F.27 b 2.8 to F.27 b 5.7 D " F.21 d 1.5 to F.21 d 5.9 C " F.22 a 0.5 to F.22 b 2.2 Relief complete 10.30 p.m. Capt BATEMAN wounded by same shell.	EYM
F.21, 22 & 27	5		Capt BATEMAN wounded keeping up men from near H.Q. 2.A.M. bombarded & gas shelling by same shell. At 5 a.m. enemy commenced a heavy gas bombardment of battery positions & HY MG ESPORTS. Some few reached Batt's positions. Rear of the Batt's with the Composite Batt's formed from South supplied capture casualties in this area from the trenches behind which lasts 3 hours. BUCQUOY has also heavily shelled. Then enemy attacked 125th Bde of our right, capturing half BUCQUOY village. Counter attacks caused heavy fighting in the village, but our line finally readjusted through the middle of the village. Heavy rain all day made trenches very bad - no shelter for the men. 2/Lt WOODWORTH wounded. Shell arrived in transport lines at SOUASTRE causing casualties. Total casualties. 10 O.R. killed, 15 O.R. wounded, 4 Officers 2 O.R. gassed.	EYM
"	6		Day quiet. At night Batt's relieved 1/5 th Manch. in front (Capt Inst creator) disposition - Bn. H.Q. F.22 Central. 'B' coy in reserve in trench near 18th M.Q. Coy's in rela C.A.D. from F.22 d 8.7 to F.16 d 9.0, a right post being held at F.23 c 1.6	EYM

Army Form C. 2118.

AP 57D N.E. 1/20,000

WAR DIARY
or
INTELLIGENCE SUMMARY.

1/7th Manchester Regt.

(Erase heading not required.)

Instructions regarding War Diaries and Intelligence Summaries are contained in F.S. Regs., Part II. and the Staff Manual respectively. Title pages will be prepared in manuscript.

Place	Date	Hour	Summary of Events and Information	Remarks and references to Appendices
GOMMECOURT	1918 6/3/18	1	Batt. Casualties during March in the Batt⁸. Officers Killed — 4 Severely Wounded — 1 Wounded — 9 Missing — — Strength Total strength — Officers 33 O.R. 806 Serving with Batt⁸. — 20 510 The Batt⁸. continues to occupy trenches in K.4.c.y.d. and K5c, the Bde. being supported by the 4th Auz. Bde. There is no change in the situation. "B" Coy had some casualties from shell fire = 3 O.R. killed & 3 wounded.	E.M.M.
"		2	Quiet day. In the night, the division taking over the line from BUCQUOY to N. of ABLAINZEVELLE from the 41st division, the Batt⁸ is relieved by 13th Regt Rifle Bde. (37th Div.). Batt⁸ is in reserve and Batt⁸ occupies position in F.20 b and d, taking over from a detachment of R.A.'s of the 41st Div. There was much congestion on the road between GOMMECOURT and ESSARTS.	E.M.M.
F 20 b and d		3	Situation unchanged. Heavy shelling in neighbourhood of BUCQUOY at night.	

Army Form C. 2118.

MAP. 57D N.E. 1/20000 and LENS II 1/40000

WAR DIARY of 3 Y & L R: Manchester R.

INTELLIGENCE SUMMARY.

Instructions regarding War Diaries and Intelligence Summaries are contained in F. S. Regs., Part II. and the Staff Manual respectively. Title pages will be prepared in manuscript.

(Erase heading not required.)

Place	Date 1918 April	Hour	Summary of Events and Information	Remarks and references to Appendices
F 22 & 23	7		Day - Quiet. At night divisional relief by 62nd Div?. Bn relieved by 2/7th W. Ridings - relief complete by 1 a.m. Bn moved by route march back to SOUASTRE via MONCHY. Three enhances via taken to Corps School Camp at VAUCHELLES.	E.J.M.
VAUCHELLES	8		Bn moved in the afternoon into billets in LOUVENCOURT. Draft of 37 O.R. and the following officers from the Bath - 2/Lt E.E. HARRIS M.C., 2/Lt F.J. HOWELL, 2/Lt H.S. STANIER, 2/Lt J.W. DAVIES, 2/Lt J.M. JONES, 2/Lt S. MAWSON.	E.J.M.
LOUVENCOURT	9		Bn resting & cleaning up. Lt Col. H.T. BROMFIELD evacuated to hospital sick. Major C.E. HIGHAM assumes command of Battn.	E.J.M.
"	10		Capt J. BAKER rejoins. Draft of 99 O.R. joins Battn. Training &c.	E.J.M.
"	11		CAPT. G. W. HANDFORTH and 2/Lt S.G.E. KIMBER joined the Battn. Battn took part in inspection of Brigade by Divisional Commander in VAUCHELLES.	E.J.M.
"	12		Training &c. LT J.L. SPENCER joins Battn. LT H.N. KAY returns from Div. Wing and to O.R. again. Draft 100 O.R. join Battn.	E.J.M.
"	13		Church parades in the morning.	E.J.M.
"	14		Training &c. Advance party proc. to reconnoitre line at HEBUTERNE. 2/Lt S. MAWSON attached to 137. L.T.M.B.	E.J.M.
"	15		Bn entrained and from LOUVENCOURT at 2.28 p.m. to valley west of SAILLY AU BOIS remained there until dusk & then proceeded to HEBUTERNE. Relieved the 13th R.B. in the line. Relief complete 12.10 a.m. 2/Lt H.L. POVEY evacuated to hospital sick.	E.J.M.
"	16			E.J.M.

Army Form C. 2118.

MAP. 57D NE. 1/20,000

WAR DIARY
INTELLIGENCE SUMMARY of 1/7th 18th Hackesh Ry

Place	Date April	Hour	Summary of Events and Information	Remarks and references to Appendices
	16 (Contd)		Dispositions - Bn N.Q. K9 a 4.8 A Coy - K16c 2.8 to K16c 5.6 B Coy - K16c 2.8 to K16a 5.3 with forward post at K16a 2.6 D Coy - K16a 7.3 to K16a 9.6 " to K16 b 4.0 C Coy in CATACOMBS around K9a 3.7.	EJM
HEBUTERNE	17		Bn trained to further attack next day, & change hits in dispositions. 'B' Coy withdrawn from line to 'C' Coys from Catacombs to form offensive flank on N. of HEBUTERNE. Switch line formed from K9a 2.2 K15d 9.9 with platoon localities around K15d 7.8 and K15.6.3.5. Patrons were upily day and three to K15d 9.9 with platoon localities around K15d 7.8 and K15.6.3.5. Patrons were upily day and three point. 'A' & 'D' closed in with boundary at K16a 3.2. 'D' taking over forward post of K16d 2.6 'A' coy attempts to obtain an identification by sending raiding party (3 platoons) to locate of enemy.	EJM
"	18		Captive enemy post in K16c o.d. They went out three times but no sign of enemy. Expected attack did not develop - quiet day. A daylight patrol of 'A' Coy found these German (26 I.R.) in K16c. A daylight patrol of 'D' Coy located enemy post at K16 b central. Raiding party at night did not succeed in capturing this post.	EJM
"	19		Quiet day. Relieved in front line by 17th Hunck.R. Relief complete 12:10 a.m. 18th moved into HEBUTERNE LOCALITY. A Coy - Catacombs B " K9a 9.8 C " K8d 9.6 & K15 b0.9 D " K15d.9 & K9 a 7.7 N.R. in Catacombs	EJM
"	20		Abid batt on R.E. fatigues.	O.M.M.
"	21		R.E. fatigue. Nl J.M. JONES evacuated to hospital sick. LT. W.H. BARRATT returned to unit from hospital.	CMM
"	22		R.E. fatigue. Capt H.H. MIDD evacuated to hospital sick from battle symptoms.	O.M.M.
"	23		Quiet day.	B.M.M.

MAP. 57 D N.E. 1/20000

Army Form C. 2118.

WAR DIARY
or
INTELLIGENCE SUMMARY. of 1/7th Manchester Regt
(Erase heading not required.)

Instructions regarding War Diaries and Intelligence Summaries are contained in F. S. Regs., Part II. and the Staff Manual respectively. Title pages will be prepared in manuscript.

Place	Date April	Hour	Summary of Events and Information	Remarks and references to Appendices
HÉBUTERNE	24		Bn. moved into divisional reserve. Bn. relieved by 2nd Auckland N.Z. during the afternoon, moved back to J6d near CHATEAU de la HAIE. Was despatch had to be made to accompany the Battn. They	8PM
J6d	25		consisted of elephant shelters dug into the front. Day employed in clearing up & completing elephant shelters. Two companies on R.E. fatigues.	6AM
"	26		" " Drill & rest. 2/Lt. C.L.THORPE reverted to hospital sick.	6AM
"	27		" " 2/Lt. E.E. HARRIS M.C. reverted to hospital sick, slightly wounded	6AM
"	28		Work as before, weather still bad. 2/Lt. R.V. SPREADBURY posted to Battn. Surplus. Bn. relieved 1.2.5th Bde. in the line. Bn. moved up to Bde. support in GOMMECOURT LOCALITY, relieving 1/5th L.F.	6AM

Disposition -
H.Q. K4a 2.5
A Coy K4c 5 8
B. " K4c 9 6
C. " K4b 6 1
D. " K4b 2 6

| GOMMECOURT | 29 | | 10 O.R. reinforcement joined Bn. Work on improvement of trenches. Lt. W. CRESSY arrived from Bath. Surplus. | 6AM |
| " | 30 | | R.E. fatigue day & night. Dull & wet. Lt.Col. E.V. MANGER of the D.L.I. arrived to take command of the Battn. | 6AM |

E.V. Manger Lt Col
Commdg 1/7 Manchester Regt

WAR DIARY
(CONFIDENTIAL)
OF
1/7th BATTALION
MANCHESTER REGT.

PERIOD.

MAY 1st TO MAY 31st.
1918.

VOLUMN: 5.

Army Form C. 2118.

WAR DIARY
INTELLIGENCE SUMMARY of 1/7th Bn. Manchester Regt.

MAP: 57D NE. 1/40000

Place	Date May	Hour	Summary of Events and Information	Remarks and references to Appendices
GOMMECOURT	1		Battle Casualties during April in the Battn.	6th
			Officers O.R. Honours & Awards	
			Killed — 20 Capt. H.H. NIDD M.C.	
			Died of Wounds — 6 Lieut E.C. HOSKYNS Cr. "	
			Wounded 2 44 Lt. K. BAGSHAW "	
			Missing — — Lt. J.L. SPENCER "	
			2/Lt. J.A. HARLAND "	
			Officers O.R.	
			Strength Total Strength 41 877 24 O.R.'s M.M.	
			Number in Battn. 24 636 2 O.R.'s Bar to M.M.	
			The Battn continued to hold forts in K4b & c, with H.Q. at K4a 2.5	
			All available men on trenching parties clearing fire trenches. 4 O.T.'s training.	6th
	2		Lt. Col. E.V. MARGER D.L.I. assumes Command of Battn. Major C.E. WIGHAM assumed 2/Cmd.	6th
	3		Day quiet. Working parties as for the 1st.	6th
	4		Working parties clearing trenches & firing at night.	6th
	5		All available men digging new trench from K4C.05.10 through K4C 65.25 to K4d 2.4 at night.	6th
			Divisional relief by 57th Division commenced.	
HENU	6		Battn relieved in daylight by 9th King's Liverpools. Relief complete 6.45 p.m.	6th
			Moved back to Camp near HENU in D.13.f. Battn. supplies required from MARIEUX	
			Col. H.R. NIDD M.C. returned from hospital.	
	7		Battn cleaning up & Kit inspecting &c. R&S Line near SOUASTRE reconnoitred.	6th
			Heavy rain during night & early morning, so that Camp kept to & specially drained	
			during afternoon.	

WAR DIARY or INTELLIGENCE SUMMARY

Army Form C. 2118.

57D N.E. of 1/7th Bn Manchester R/t

Place	Date May	Hour	Summary of Events and Information	Remarks and references to Appendices
HENU	8		Training commenced.	EtM
"	9		Battn took part in Divisional practice alarm & marched out of camp at 9 a.m. to new Red Line i.e. E.13 & 19 and D.24. Major G.B.L. RAE, 10th K.L.R. (Scottish) posted to Battn as 2nd in Command vice Major C.E. NUGHAM. 2/Lt. W.H. CRICK	EtM
"	10		Battn training & on working parties taking dugouts near camp vic J.6.	OtM
"	11		E. for 10th. 2/Lt. K. BAGSHAW M.C. evacuated to hospital sick.	OtM
"	12		Church Parade in the morning.	OtM
"	13		Training & working parties. 2/Lt. F.J. HOWELL left Battn to England for R.A.F.	OtM
"	14		Training & working parties. Very hot in the day. II Battn 307 Regt U.S. Army joined Brigade and encamped near Battn.	OtM
"	15		Officers & a few NCOs took part in skeleton Counter attack on BEER TRENCH in E.22 & 28. 2/Lt. H.V. SPREAD AUX. evacuated to hospital sick.	OtM
"	16		Training & working parties. Hot weather continued. 2/Lt. G. WARD evacuated to hospital sick.	OtM
"	17		" " 2/Lt. J.W. DAVIES left Battn to England for R.A.F.	OtM
"	18		" " Lt. J.L. SPENCER M.C. left Battn to regain.	OtM
"	19		15th Hants. Major C.E. NUGHAM left Battn on leave to England.	StM
"	20		Church parade in the morning. Capt G.W. HANDFORTH left Battn to Depot on Mngmt of AMBRICK. Lieut C.B. DOUGLAS evacuated to hospital sick.	OtM
"	21		Training & working parties. "B" Coy on ROSSIGNOL RANGE (500 yds) in the morning. TRSM L. ANEZARR resumed duties of RSM in Battn vice A/RSM S. CROUGHMORE relinquished his rank. Training of the afternoon Battn did tactical exercise in presence of D.C. & General Sir JULIAN BYNG	BtM

MAR. 57TH N.E.

Army Form C. 2118.

WAR DIARY
or
INTELLIGENCE SUMMARY
1/7th Bn. Manchester Regt.

(Erase heading not required.)

Instructions regarding War Diaries and Intelligence Summaries are contained in F.S. Regs., Part II. and the Staff Manual respectively. Title pages will be prepared in manuscript.

Place	Date	Hour	Summary of Events and Information	Remarks and references to Appendices
HÉNU	22		Training & working parties. All two Officers convened inspection of Manchesters. Capt J.R. CREAGH (Adjutant) evacuated to hospital sick.	6MM
"	23		W2 Lt. J.M. JONES returned from hospital. Lt/QM. ROSE evacuated to the Base injured. Hot weather still continues.	6MM
"	24		Training & working parties. 2/Major C.E. NISHAM relinquishes acting rank.	6MM
"	25		Continuous rain interfered with training. S.O.R.'s joined as reinforcement.	6MM
"	26		Training & working parties. Capt C.R. ALLEN M.C. joined Batt: and assumed command of 'A'Coy vice Capt F.G. BURN.	6MM
"	27		The D.C. presented medal ribbons to recipients in the Brigade on the Batt's parade ground. The Brigade being formed to the ceremony. The following Officers & W.O.'s of the Batt's were mentioned in the C.in.C's despatch of April 7th: Major (A/Lt.Col.) A.E.F. FAUCUS M.C., Lieut. W.T. THORP, Capt C. NORBURY, 275/03 C.S.M. S. CLOUGH and 275493 C.S.M. J. SHIELDS.	6MM
"	28		Working parties & training, including tactical exercises.	6MM
"	29		" Lt L. WEYDER D.C.M. and Lt C.T. LOFTHOUSE joined the Batt: and 1 O.R. as reinforcement. Lieut P. PELL-ILDERTON rejoined from England. Capt G.W. HANDFORTH was struck off the strength being employed as P.S. Officer.	6MM
"	30		Training & working parties. & the Divisional history commenced. The Batt: took second place in aggregate number of points gained. Cpl (L/Cpt.) A. GOODER of the Batt: "granted a divisional commission to the Y/7 Bn. Manchester Regt for the distinguished leadership & fine fighting qualities displayed by him during the fighting around BUCQUOY and NISLANZIVELLES in March & April 1918." He is taken on the strength as an Officer.	6MM
"	31		Training & working parties. Lieut P. PELL-ILDERTON evacuated to hospital sick.	6MM

[signature] Lt. Col.
Comg. 1/7th Bn. Manchester Regt.

BRIGADE

WAR DIARY
(confidential)
OF
1/7th. Bn. Manchester Regiment.

PERIOD

June 1st. to June 30th. 1918.

Volume: 6.

MAR. 57 N.E.

Army Form C. 2118.

WAR DIARY
INTELLIGENCE SUMMARY. of 7th Bn. Yorkshire Rgt

(Erase heading not required.)

Instructions regarding War Diaries and Intelligence
Summaries are contained in F. S. Regs., Part II.
and the Staff Manual respectively. Title pages
will be prepared in manuscript.

Place	Date June	Hour	Summary of Events and Information	Remarks and references to Appendices
HENU	1		Battl Casualties during May in the battn: O/R. 3 Killed, - Wounded, 2 Missing. - O.R. Total strength O/R 43, 916 26 819	E.P.M.
"	2		Battn continues training out of the line. Working parties also supplied. Church parade with the S.F.A. also attended by the D.C. It was rejoined as Reverend Service for June & July 25.	E.P.M.
"	3		Training & Working parties. Hot dry weather still continues.	E.P.M.
"	4		"	E.P.M.
"	5		Officers recommenced to line at HÉBUTERNE. Capt C.E. HIGHAM returned from leave in England. 2/Lt N.N. KAY rejoined battn from Divisional Wing. 2/Lt J. MCCALMONT and 2/Lt N.V. SPRADBURY rejoined battn from hospital. Capt J.R. CREASH rejoined battn from hospital. Capt C.E. HIGHAM proceeded to England & was taken off strength.	E.P.M.
"	6		Battn relieved the 2nd Battn WELLINGTON N.Z. Rgt in the front line at HÉBUTERNE in the right, being the left Battn of the left Brigade. Trench strength 20 Offs. 566 O.R. Quiet relief.	See map marked 'A'
HÉBUTERNE			dispositions — A.1 H.Q. K9£ 15.30 "A" coy. K10c 7.2 "B" " K16 b 4.8 "C" " K16 b 2.7 "D" " K16 b 6.2 Rear H.Q. and Transport lines — LOUVENCOURT. I 29c	

Army Form C. 2118.

MAP: 57D N.E.

2. WAR DIARY
or
INTELLIGENCE SUMMARY of 1/7 & 1/8 Hawick Kys

(Erase heading not required.)

Instructions regarding War Diaries and Intelligence Summaries are contained in F. S. Regs., Part II. and the Staff Manual respectively. Title pages will be prepared in manuscript.

Place	Date JUNE	Hour	Summary of Events and Information	Remarks and references to Appendices
HEBUTERNE	7		Quiet day.	6thh
"	8		" " One man wounded. Lt C.B. DOUGLAS rejoined at North Lupus from hospital.	O/H/h
"	9		Enemy shelling concentration at 3.30 a.m. for 20 mins. One man killed, one wounded.	6thh
"	10		Quiet day. Major RAE relieved Col. MANSFIELD in the line, the latter coming to near H.Q.	O/H/h
"	11		Inter-company relief took place during the day. 'A' + 'B' Coys relieved each other, and 'C' + 'D' Coys.	O/H/h
"	12		Quiet day. An Austrian Recomp. from our lines on our positions behind HEBUTERNE.	6thh
"	13		Quiet during the day. A good deal of enemy howitzer seemed to indicate a relief in the early evening. Special reconnaissance of FUSILIER TRENCH was carried out in the night in preparation for raid on the 15th. Routine Bos. with special bombed carried out at night - one wound per shelling falling in the signal.	O/H/h
"	14		At the early morning 300 under 6" T.M. shells fired into CEDRIC trench on the right of St Cony - good casualties being inflicted on the enemy. The Bath was relieved in the line by the 7th LF's. Moved to SAILLY. All Boys in the night. Dispositions as follows	6thh
			St. MA: J, 18 a 4.9	
			R. Coy J, 12 a 4.4 SAILLY.	
			B " J, 18 c 6.8	
			C " K, 8 c 5.6	
			D " K, 13 c 2.1	
			Lt Batts is in reserve to the 125th Inf. Bde.	
SAILLY AU BOIS	15		'B' Coy rehearsed raid before D.C. at SAILLY. They moved into line at HEBUTERNE in the night.	6thh
"	16	10 a.m.	Raid carried out according to programme the following taking part in it - 2/LIEUT D.O.M., 2/Lt MILNE, 2/Lt GOODIER and 60 O.R. of 'B' Coy. Enemy position in FUSILIER TRENCH + K7a being the objective. Sixty nine trench were inflicted in spite of artillery barrage + counter bombing from M.G. and bombing.	6thh E/A See File marked 'B'

MAP. 57D N.E.

Army Form C. 2118.

3. WAR DIARY

INTELLIGENCE SUMMARY. 1/7th Bn Manchester Regt

(Erase heading not required.)

Place	Date JUNE	Hour	Summary of Events and Information	Remarks and references to Appendices
SAILLY au BOIS	16 (cont)		One prisoner was brought in, and 6 or 8 German dead were seen in the trench. Our casualties in the raid were 2/Lt MENDER missing, 2/Lt MILNE wounded, 2/Lt GOODIER slightly wounded (at duty) our O.R. missing, 7 14 O.R. wounded.	EyMm
"	17		Other casualties were Lt C.L. WOOD wounded and Lt S.L. WILSON wounded (at duty). 2/Lt B.G. KINDER went to U.K. for transfer to R.A.F.	EyMm
"	18		Batt's employed working parties. Capt J.C. PALMER joined batt's from the Base.	EyMm
"	19		" " " Capt W.K. CRICK proceeded to England for transfer to M.G. Corps.	EyMm
"	20		" " Working parties.	EyMm
"	21		" " "	EyMm
"	22		" " " Major R.A.E. evacuated to hospital sick. Capt J.R. CREAGH assumed Command of Batt's	EyMm
"	23		Batt's relieved 7th Bn Manchesters in Brigade reserve on the right sector, and occupied localities near COLINCAMPS as follows— Bn H.Q. K25a 5.9 A Coy K 32a and K 26c 9.2 B " K25a and K25b C " K26a 7.6, K20c and K19d 8.2 D " K19c	EyMm
COLINCAMPS	24		Lieut J.G. EVANS and 2/Lt H. GORST and 14 O.R. joined batt's from the Base. Work continued on localities. Capt H.T. TINTO, Lt W. EDGE and 2/Lt F.D. THRUTCHLEY joined batt's from the Base.	EyMm
"	25		R.E. fatigues.	EyMm

MAP. 57 D N.E.

WAR DIARY
INTELLIGENCE SUMMARY of 1/7th & 1/8th Manchester Rgt

Army Form C. 2118.

Place	Date June	Hour	Summary of Events and Information	Remarks and references to Appendices
COLINCAMPS	26		R.E. working parties. C'oy area slightly shelled & 2 men killed.	6/7th
"	27		" " "	8/7th
"	28		" " " Coys rehearsed in skeleton forming defensive flank in vicinity of NORTHERN AVENUE (K20c and K19d, c) facing north.	8/7th
"	29		R.E. fatigues.	8/7th
"	30		" " Col. MANGER resumed command of Batt'n on return of Brig. Gen. HENLEY to Brigade from leave. Lieut. H. Jos joined Batt'n from the base.	8/7th

Col. Mangord-al
1/7 Manchester Regt

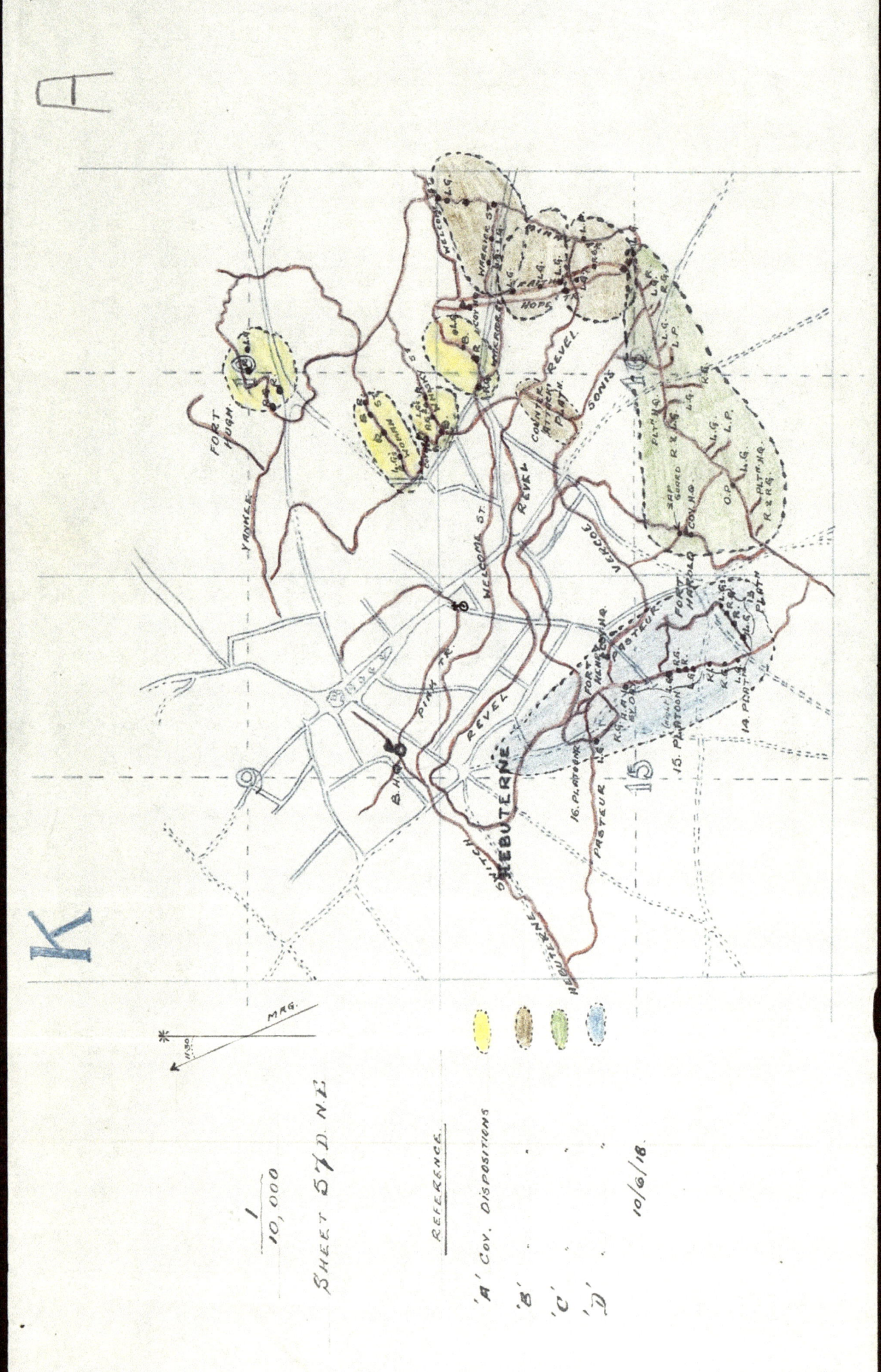

SECRET.

Headquarters.
127th Infantry Brigade.

42 DIV 2661

Report on raid carried out by the 1/7th Bn.
The Manchester Regiment on night 15/16th June 1918.

The raid was carried out at 1 hour 3' a.m. by 'B' Company. Strength 3 Officers and 70 Other Ranks, and 10 regimental stretcher bearers.

Identification was secured, and one prisoner captured. Machine Guns were located but could not be captured.

The raiders were divided into four platoon parties, approximately 16 O.Rs. Right, Centre, Left & Support.

The preliminary arrangements worked without a hitch. *what about shelling on HEBUTERNE?*

Right party leader Lieut. L. WENDER, D.C.M.

Party proceeded as per orders, but inclined too much to the right after leaving its guide tape and came within 50 yards of an enemy post. After carefully approaching this post, Lieut. WENDER gave the order to charge. The charge was held up by wire and heavily bombed. Party moved left and were entering enemy trench by gaps in wire when a bomb dropped in centre of party wounding six. Only four entered trench, killing one German.

Lieut. WENDER though wounded entered enemy trench leading, and was seen to fall.

Sergt. FLEETWOOD, 2nd in Command, took charge and on whistles sounding got his men out of enemy trench. He himself searched for Lieut. WENDER without success. He found L/Cpl. HAYDOCK of the same platoon lying on parapet of Bosche trench incapable of movement with a fractured leg. He without help and long after his men had regained our lines, carried this man across No Mans Land under M.G. fire to the control post. Having reported the arrival of his party and the loss of his Commander, he saw L/Cpl. HAYDOCK down to the advanced dressing station.

The last seen of Lieut. WENDER was on the German parapet under heavy bomb fire.

Sergt. FLEETWOOD looked very carefully for his Commander before he left for our lines with L/Cpl. HAYDOCK, and he considers Lieut. WENDER fought his way in and was again wounded or killed.

Centre party leader. 375395 Sergt. J.W. GREEN, M.M.

This party left MINNY Trench at Zero 3. On reaching the junction of WATSON STREET and FUSILIER Trench they were met with a shower of bombs and a very light was sent up. The party now came under M.G. fire from a position about twenty yards to the East. Sergt. GREEN silenced the M.G. with a bomb and ordered one Section to capture the gun. This section was held up by wire and driven back by bombs and rifle fire. Remainder of party jumped into FUSILIER Trench at its junction with WATSON STREET.

Just left of this point a German Machine Gunner jumped on to our side of the trench and was bayoneted by Pte. PICKERING, placed under escort and sent back to our lines. Sergt. GREEN killed a second with his revolver, it being found impossible to get him out. A party detailed to capture a second M.G. located some distance up the C.T. was unable to reach the gun in time owing to enemy bombing and the withdrawal being ordered. Party returned bringing in all its wounded. The wounded prisoner, two German rifles and one German Helmet were all safely retrieved.

Left party leader. 2/Lt. A. GOODIER.

This party got quickly across No Mans Land, but on entering FUSILIER Trench found it blocked on the South (towards Centre Party) with loose barbed wire. Party proceeded along parados and parapet bombing to the right, meeting with opposition, which as they pushed forward became stronger. The trench was found to be held by strong posts at intervals of about 25 yards.

One post was driven off but the second held up our attack. Six German dead were seen in trench. Party were unable to dislodge enemy who were behind old wire. Party withdrew at 1-15 a.m. when whistles were sounded. No dugouts were seen, but small shelters were found in trench. The garrison of trench was strong. Fire heavy. More could have been done had time allowed been longer.

-- 2 --

Covering party leader. 2/Lt. J.H. MILNE.
Fulfilled to the letter the task set them. They covered the withdrawal of the force.
Sergt. GLEESON and L/Cpl. TITTERINGTON assisted by stretcher bearers searched a wide area for wounded before returning, and report that no one was left in front of German Trench.
There was continuous fighting throughout the operation and I am satisfied the enemy casualties greatly exceed our own.
The artillery barrage was extremely accurate and efficient, although the raiders were close up to the 18 pdrs barrage not a single casualty occurred. It gave the men the greatest confidence.
The enemy sent up green and red rockets mostly in pairs, and orange lights without visable results.
His barrage if any was negligible.
German wire in front no obstacle but loose wire in his trench on the flanks of posts greatly impeded our work.
The time allowed i.e. 13 minutes was too short for the overcoming of the unexpected resistance and the unusual determination of the garrisons.
To obtain a better bag or to capture M.Gs., it seems imperative to penetrate to the second line, at least, and this I consider would lessen casualties.
The raiders returned in good order at Zero 15 to Zero 25.
The equipment of raiders was satisfactory.
A list of casualties is attached. Most of them are slight.
I regret very much that any attempt to search for Lieut. WENDER and Pte JOHNSON after the raid was considered by me impracticable, and would have led to further casualties.
The reconnaissance work of 2/Lt. STANIER and Lieut. WILSON was invaluable.
The work of Capt. GREY BURN in training the N.C.Os. and men before the raid, in practising the operation on tapes at SAILLY, and his conduct of the operation from our front line, very largely contributed to its success.
The Medical arrangements worked without hitch and were in every way satisfactory.
In preparing for the raid my Chaplain, The Revd. HOSKYNS was of great assistance in actually raising the Morale of the men.
Recommendations for immediate awards follow.

16th June 1918.

Lieut. Colonel.
Cmdg. 1/7th Bn. Manchester Regt.

Wounded at Duty.   Officers - 2.

Missing.   Officers - 1.   O.Rs. - 1.

Wounded.   Officers - 2.   O.Rs. - 14.

SECRET. War Diary 1/7th. BN. MANCHESTER REGIMENT. **B** COPY.....13.....

OPERATION ORDER NO. 77.
by
LIEUT. COL. E.V.MANGER   Commanding "C" Battalion.

REF. MAP 57D.N.E.
1:20,000.

(1) RAID   (a) The Battalion will raid the Enemy Posts in FUSILIER
                     TRENCH on Z day.
    OBJECT   (b) To take prisoners, secure identifications (Caps, Shoulder
                     Straps, Documents, Very Lights) destroy his dugouts ,
                     capture and bring back Machine Guns.
    OBJECTIVE   (c) Enemy Front Line, FUSILIER TRENCH, between K.16.b.98.70.
                     and K.16.b. 95.30.
    APPROXIMATE
    STRENGTH: (d) 3 Officers and 70 other ranks of "B" Company.
    O.C.RAID: (e) Capt. F.GREY BURN, O.C. "B" Company.

(2) ASSEMBLY   The assembly of the raiders will be complete in proper
    AND FORMING   order of parties in CROSS STREET TRENCH, North of WHISKY
    UP: TRENCH by Zero - 3 hours.
                     They will proceed to Front Line (MINNY TRENCH) by parties
                     observing absolute silence.
                     Parties will be in position opposite their objectives
                     and the gaps prepared in our wire ready to go over the
                     top by Zero - 30 minutes.

(3) PLAN OF OPERATION:
                 (c) At Zero plus 3 the raiders will advance and assault
                     when our barrage lifts from Enemy Front Line and wire
                     The Scouts under Lt. H.A.STANIER will on Zero -
                     1 night prepare gaps in our wire, clearing all loose
                     wire for at least 30ˣ towards the German Lines and lay
                     telephone line through gaps towards German Line.
                     Steps will also be cut in parapet of MINNY TRENCH at
                     points of exit, opposite the prepared gaps in our wire.
                     At Zero - 60 on Z day white tapes will be placed along
                     these guides wires and men of the Battalion Scout Section
                     will be out in front to cover the assembly.
                     At Zero - 15 covering party will eeeeeeeeeup withdraw
                     and form Battle Police.
                     The raiders will be formed up as follows in MINNY TRENCH:-
                                                         Point of entry into
                                                           Enemy Trench.
                     Right Party: Lt. L.WENDER D.C.M. No......Platoon, K.16.b.97.30.
                     Centre Party:Sergt. J.GREEN M.M. No......Platoon, K.16.b.97.47.
                     Left Party :2/Lt. A.GOODIER ....No......Platoon, K.16.b.99.70.

                     Lewis Gun and covering party under 2/Lt. W.H.MILNE in
                     rear of Centre party.
    FORMATION   (d) In column of files well closed up , Commanders on
                     Left Flank, Senior N.C.Os in rear.
3)ACTION: On barrage lifting at Zero plus 3 the raiders will advance
                     and rush Enemy's line, and carry out their several tasks
                     as quickly as possible, returning to our lines as detailed
                     in Party Orders.
                     The covering party will be responsible for laying out
                     a tape line from over our parapet, across No Mans Land
                     up to and into Enemy Trench to assist the returning
                     raiders back to our lines. Tape to be pegged in Enemy
                     Trench.
                     The Command "(Over the top)" will be given by Commanders
                     of parties at Z plus 3 by the watch.

(4) GENERAL PLAN OF ATTACK:

Right Party (16 other ranks) will on entering Enemy's Trench capture Machine Gun North of BOUILLON C.T., and mop up to the left, Bombers on top, covered by Rifle Grenadiers until the centre party is met at the junction of Enemy's C.T. an FUSILIER TRENCH.

They will assist in holding this junction until the moppers up, of the centre party have returned after clearing the C.T.

The left and centre parties will then return to our lines by the tape, at Zero plus 13, not before.

Centre Party (16 other ranks), 8 other ranks under Cpl. .... to mop up the C.T. for 50 yards from point of entry, the remainder of party to hold point of entry and exit, covering the return of mopping up party.

On Right party joining the centre party, the combined forces will return along guide tape back to MINNY TRENCH with their prisoners and booty at Zero plus 13, not before.

Left Party, (16 other ranks) enter German Line at the JUNCTION OF FUSILIER TRENCH with the Sunken Road.

They will proceed to the right along and on top of Enemy's Trench to deal with the Strong Point shown on Map and the Machine Gun, bombing any dugout there.

K.J. Grenades will be carried for this purpose and sent down just before leaving at Zero plus 13, not before.

Stops will not be formed but Rifle Grenadiers will form Protective barrages as detailed in Party Orders.

Covering Party. (16 other ranks), will follow centre party and take up a position on parapet of FUSILIER TRENCH covering centre party and prepared to assist in capture of trench: they will remain in position and withdraw after centre party covering their withdrawal with Rifle Grenade and Rifle Fire.

Lewis Gun Team take up a position in No. Mans Land and cover Right Flank of raiders.

Withdrawal of Gun at Zero plus 15 covered by Rifle Fire of Team.

(6) WITHDRAWAL AND SIGNAL:

At Zero plus 13 the withdrawal will commence, each party will have a rear guard composed of Rifle Grenadiers and Rifle men with Egg Bombs.

These covering party will not commence to withdraw until the remainder of the raiders have passed them.

The Signal for withdrawal will be short and long blasts on the Whistle by Commanders of parties who will all carry reliable watches.

A Searchlight will be used as an additional guiding mark to assist returning raiders back to our wire.

It will play from Zero plus 13 to Zero plus 25 at intervals.

Suggested position for light :- On Road below ROSIGNOL FARM.

Seconds in Command of all parties will also be in possession of Whistles and Synchronised Watches.

Right and Centre Parties will withdraw along the tape, covering party follow, covering withdrawal.

Left party withdraw parrallel with Sunken Road.

(7) REPORTING ON RETURN:

On return of raiders Officers and N.C.Os in charge of Platoon Parties will report to O.C. Operations at K.10.c.70.3 left Support Coy. H.Qrs. HEBUTERNE SWITCH.

All others will proceed at once to Battalion H.Qrs. and hand in their Special Identity Discs and be provided with hot tea, rum and food.

(8) LEWIS GUNS: O.C.Right &&&.Front Coy. will kindly bring Lewis Gun Fire to bear on K.16.d.60.20. with as many Guns as possible at Zero.

(9) MEDICAL/ R.A.P.in Tank Trap on the Road K.16.b.10.32.
10 Stretcher Bearers and Personnel will report to R.A.P. one hour before Zero to assist in bringing down wounded.
Wounded brought back by Regimental Bearers will be provided with relays at junction of FAITH TRENCH and Sunken Road, K.16.b.40.80.

(10) PRISONERS ESCORTS & DOCUMENTS: Prisoners and identifications will be sent at once to Raid H.Qrs., for disposal under escorts previously detailed for this duty.
Prisoners will be sent on to Brigade under Special Escort, documents will be placed in sandbags, sealed and forwarded to Brigade.
Lt. S.J.WILSON will collect information from the returned raiders at Battalion H.Qrs.

(11) COMMUNICATIONS:
Telephone and Buzzer Communication will be installed at junction of MINNY and WARRIOR TRENCHES, K.16.b.80.75. and an Amplifier at H.Qrs Raid at K.10.c.70.20.
Direct telephone Communication will be arranged between K.10.c.70.20. and Brigade H.Qrs.

(12) HEAD QUARTERS:
Raid H.Qrs. K.10.c.70.20.
O.C.Raid, Post at junction of MINNY and WARRIOR TRENCHES, K.16.b.80.75.

(13) SYNCHRONISATION OF WATCHES:
Watches will be compared at 5-0 p.m. on Z day and corrected by Battalion Signalling Officer at Battalion H.Qrs. SAILLY.

(14) CODE: Attached for those concerned.

(15) RETURNING RAIDERS: At .... a.m. returning raiders will be marched from Battalion H.Qrs. HEBUTERNE SWITCH, to SAILLY by their own Officers.

(16) DRESS AND EQUIPMENT:
Hands, faces and Bayonets will be darkened, Steel Helmets Rifles and Bayonets - 8 rounds in Magazine, 1 in Chamber, 20 rounds in the pocket, will be carried by N.C.Os and men.
Each N.C.O. and man will carry two Egg Grenades.
Selected Bombers will carry 4 Mills Grenades No.23,
Rifle Grenadiers, 6 No. 36 in Haversack, Cup on Rifle.
Box Respirators in Alert Position.
Wire Cutters distributed to parties.
Breech Covers will not be taken.
Equipment will not be worn. All ranks will remove every mark, paper or other means whereby the enemy could identify them.
Rifles will be loaded and inspected by an Officer.
Faces and hands blacked before leaving CROSS STREET.

(17) Barrage Tables will be explained to all concerned.
(18) 18 Pounder Barrages will fall on Enemy Front Line at Zero and lift to his Support Line at Zero plus 3 remaining stationery for 25 minutes.
(19) R.E. will sandbag and render splinter-proof the Tank Trap to be used advanced R.A.P. and the post at junction of WARRIOR TRENCH, H.Qrs. O.C.RAID.

In the Field.
12:6:18.

Lieut. Col.
Commanding 1/7th. Bn.Manchester Regt.

Very SECRET.

CORRIGENDA TO OPERATION ORDER
NO. 77 of 12:6:18.

(a)   During the whole of the Operation, No Rifle Grenades will be used.

(b)   The covering party will use only No. 5 Mills Hand Grenades, and not No. 34 Egg and No. 36 Rifle Grenades.

(c)   It is not necessary to remove Regimental Flashes.

(d)   The Small Box Respirator will not be worn.

(e)   In addition to or in place of the Searchlight Rockets will be sent up from the direction of FAITH TRENCH to show the returning raiders the way back to our lines.

(f)   A small issue of Rum will be made to each member of the raiding party at the Assembly point in CROSS STREET at 10-0 p.m. on Zero night.

In the Field.
14:6:18.

E.H. Manger   Lieut. Col.
Commanding 1/7th. Bn. Manchester Regt.

Code referred to in Operation Order No. 77 issued to

    O.C. OPERATIONS.

    O.C. RAID.

@@@

Operations postponed 60 minutes...................... CABBAGE.
(This must be sent 30 minutes before Zero hour)

Operation cancelled....................... POTATO.
Have formed up............................ CRESS.
Raid successful........................... MUSTARD.
All doing well............................ CELERY.
Much resistance........................... BEANS.
Weak   "   .... PEAS.
Prisoners returning....................... SEEDS
Many casualties........................... ONIONS.
Few casualties............................ TOMATO.
Held up................................... LETTUCE.
Party all in.............................. CARROT
Artillery to continue an extra 10
minutes, viz., Zero $+$ 50 to
Zero $+$ 60 .... CUCUMBER.

@@@@@ @@@@@@@@@@@@@@@@ @@@@@@@@@@

                    (Sgd) E.V. MANGER   Lieut. Col.
    Commanding 1/7th. Bn. Manchester Regt.

In the Field
11:6:18.

RAID ORDERS ~~BY~~ by FOR CENTRE PARTY
Lieut. Col. E. V. MANGER   z   Commanding "C" Battalion.

----

1. N.C.O. COMMANDING   Sergt. J. GREEN M.M.

2. FORMING UP.   This party will form up on the left of Lt. WENDER'S party and be the second party to leave CROSS STREET at Zero - 2 hours 50 minutes.
   It will form up opposite its point of exit 120 yards South of the Sunken Road in FUSILIER TRENCH, left of party opposite exit steps ~~cuttin~~ cut in parapet.

3. ASSAULT AND ACTION ON ENTERING ENEMY TRENCH.   The advance will commence at Zero plus 3 minutes by the watch when the party will cross No. Man's Land in file keeping well closed up, Commander on the left, 2nd. in Command bring up the rear.
   On entering enemy trench one section (8 other ranks under Command of ....) will mop up the C.T. from K.16.b.97.47. to a point 50 yds. beyond its junction with FUSILIER TRENCH.
   Remainder of party hold point of entry covering the return of the moppers up.
   On the right raiding party joining up, the combined force will return along guide tape back to MINNY TRENCH with their booty at Zero plus 13 not before.

4. PRISONERS.   Any prisoners taken will be at once evacuated under previously detailed escort to the left Support Coy. H.Qrs.

5. WITHDRAWAL AND SIGNAL.   By time at Zero plus 13 not before.
   Short and long blasts on whistle by O.C. Party and 2nd. in Command.
   Party will return to our Front Line covered by Rifle Grenadiers of covering party, and be guided accross No Mans Land by the white tape to the gap in our wire and a searchlight in our back areas.
   The tape will be run out by covering party to FUSILIER TRENCH at point of entry of centre party K. 16.b.97.47.
   Order of withdrawal, Centre party followed by Right party covered and followed by covering party

6. STRETCHER BEARERS.   Two Regimental Stretcher Bearers for this party will accompany the covering party.

7. REPORTING ON RETURN.   Sergt. J. GREEN will report at H.Qrs. Left Support Company on return, to O.C. Operations.
   All other ranks to Battalion H.Qrs. HEBUTERNE SWITCH. under the 2nd. in Command, where they will hand in identity discs and be provided with tea.

In the Field   (Sgd) E. V. MANGER   Lieut. Col.
12:6:18.   Commanding 1/7th. Bn. Manchester Regt.

RAID ORDERS FOR RIGHT PARTY
by
Lieut. Col. E.V. MANGER   Commanding "C" Battalion.
                                             12:6:18.

Map Reference Sheet 57D.N.E.
   1:20,000 and Special Sketch.

---

1. O.C. PARTY.	Lt. L. WENDER D.C.M.
2. FORMING UP.	This party will leave Cross Street at Zero - 3 hours and form up in MINNY TRENCH opposite its point of exit about 200x South of Sunken Road right of post opposite exit steps.
3. ASSAULT AND ACTION. ON ENTERING ENEMY TRENCH.	The advance will commence at Zero + 3 minutes by the watch. The party will cross No Mans Land in file keeping well closed up Commander on the left, 2nd. in Command bringing up rear. On entering enemy trench at K.16.b.97.30 the party will deal with M.G. Post at junction of BOUILLON C.T. and FUSILIER TRENCH and mop up FUSILIER TRENCH to the left.
4. PARAPET PARTY.	Bombers along parados, covered by Rifle Grenadiers until the centre party is met at the junction of enemy C.T. and FUSILIER TRENCH. They will assist the centre party in holding this junction until the moppers up have cleared the C.T. and rejoined. Right and centre parties will then return to our lines by the tape at Zero + 13 not before. Withdrawal to ~~commence by Rifle~~ be covered by Rifle Grenadiers of covering party.
5. PRISONERS.	Any prisoners taken en route will be immediately evacuated under previously detailed escort to Left Support Coy. H.Qrs.
6. WITHDRAWAL AND SIGNAL.	By. time at Zero + 13 not before. Short and long blasts on whistles by O.C. Party and 2nd. in Command. Party will return to our Front Line MINNY TRENCH, and be guided accross No. Mans Land by the white tape to gap in our wire and a searchlight in our back areas. The tape will be put out by covering party to FUSILIER TRENCH at point of entry of centre party, K.16.b.97.47. Order of withdrawal, Centre party followed by Right party covered and followed by covering party. Lt. L. WENDER D.C.M. on return will report at H.Qrs Left Support Company to O.C. Operations. All other ranks under 2nd. in Command of party to Battalion H.Qrs. HEBUTERNE SWITCH, where they will hand in identity discs and be provided with tea.
8. STRETCHER BEARERS.	Two Stretcher Bearers will accompany this party.

In the Field.
12:6:18
                                      (Sgd) E.V. MANGER   Lieut. Col.
                                      Commanding 1/7th. Bn. Manchester Rgt.

RAID ORDERS FOR COVERING PARTY
by
Lieut. Col. E. V. MANGER   Commanding "C" Battalion.

---

1. **O. C. PARTY**   2/Lt. W. H. MILNE.

2. **COMPOSITION AND FORMING UP.**   10 Riflemen and Lewis Gun Team (No. 8 Platoon).
   This party will form up in MINNY TRENCH on left of the centre party, Lewis Gun and team on left.
   Party leave CROSS STREET after centre party at Zero - 2 hours 40 minutes.

3. **ADVANCE AND ACTION DURING OPERATION.**   The party will be led out immediately after the centre party are clear of MINNY TRENCH.
   The Riflemen under Sergt............ supporting the advance of the centre party, if necessary, assisting in the capture of enemy post.
   They will lie down on parapet of enemy trench covering with their fire the work of centre party.
   They will remain in position and withdraw after centre party, covering their own withdrawal with Rifle Grenade Fire.

4. **LEWIS GUN.**   The Lewis Gun of the covering party will take up a position in No Mans Land covering Right of the operation.
   Their duties are to watch the right flank of the area raided and to cover the withdrawal of our raiders.
   An "all round" look out must be kept.
   The party will return in rear of the last man of covering party, covering its own withdrawal with Rifle Fire.
   12 Drums will be carried.

5. **WITHDRAWAL AND SIGNAL.**   The left, centre and right party will return at Zero plus 13.
   Signal for withdrawal whistle blasts.
   Order of withdrawal, Centre party followed by the Right party followed and covered by covering party.

6. **REPORTING ON RETURN.**   2/Lt. W. H. MILNE and Sergt. .... will report the return of their covering party at H.Qrs. Left Support Coy. to O. C. Operations.
   All other ranks to Battalion H.qrs HEBUTERNE SWITCH, under 2nd. in Command when they will hand in identity discs and be provided with tea.

7. **STRETCHER BEARERS.**   6 STRETCHER Bearers will accomany the covering party and two the covering Lewis Gun Team.

8. **GUIDE TAPE.**   One N. C. O. and two other ranks will be detailed to reel out the line of tracing tape from point of exit in MINNY TRENCH to and into German Trench where it is to be securely pegged.

In the Field.
12:6:18.

(Sgd) E. V. MANGER   Lieut. Col.
Commanding 1/7th. Bn. Manchester Regt.

RAID ORDERS FOR LEFT PARTY
by
Lieut. Col. E.V. MANGER　　　　　　　　Commanding "C" Battalion.

1.	O.C. PARTY.	2/Lt. A. GOODIER.
2.	FORMING UP.	This party will form up in MINNY TRENCH between the Sunken Road and the covering party opposite the prepared steps cut in the parapet of MINNY TRENCH about 50 yds. South of junction of Sunken Road with MINNY TRENCH.

It will leave CROSS STREET at Zero - 2 hours 30 mins. 10 minutes after covering party.

3. ASSAULT AND ACTION ON ENTERING ENEMY TRENCH.

The advance will commence at Zero plus 3 by the watch.

The party will cross No Mans Land in file keeping well closed up, Commander on left 2nd. in Command bringing up the rear.

Enemy trench will be entered near Sunken Road.

The party will proceed quickly along and above trench to the right and deal with the M.G. and Strong point shown on Map, bombing any dugout there immediately on arrival.

K.J. Smoke Bombs will be carried for this purpose and three sent down each dugout.

The party will leave enemy line at Zero plus 13 not before.

Stops will not be formed, but Rifle Grenadiers will form local protective barrage if necessary on the Sunken Road.

This party will return alongside the Sunken Road.

4. PRISONERS. Any prisoners taken will be sent back without delay under a previously detailed escort and be taken to Left Support Coy. H. Qrs.

5. WITHDRAWAL AND SIGNAL. By time at Zero plus 13 not before.

Short and long blasts on whistles by O.C. Party and 2nd. in Command.

Party will return to our lines covered by Rifle Grenadiers and be guided accross No Mans Land by Sunken Road and Searchlight in our back areas.

6. REPORTING ON COMPLETION. On return 2/Lt. A. GOODIER will report at H.Qrs. Left Support Company to O.C. Operation.

All other ranks to Battalion H.Qrs. HEBUTERNE SWITCH under 2nd. in Command, where they will hand in identity discs and be provided with tea.

7. STRETCHER PARTY Two Regimental Stretcher Bearers will accompany this party.

　　　　　　　　　　　　　　　　　　(Sgd) E.V. MANGER　Lieut. Col.
　　　　　　　　　　　　　　　Commanding 1/7th. Bn. Manchester Regt.

In the Field.
12/6/18.

ARTILLERY, T.M. and MACHINE GUN BARRAGE.

On night preceding Zero 4.5 HOWITZERS and 60 Pounders to send over Gas Shells mixed with Smoke on to the old German Front and Support Line, between K.17.d.30.30. - K.17.b.10.90.

At Zero Smoke Shell on old German Front and Support Line between above limits.
(A) Intense 18 Pounder Shrapnel on FUSILIER TRENCH from K.16.b.65.62 K.17.a.65.80. Three Batteries.
(B) Intense 18 Pounder H.E. and Shrapnel Barrage on old German Front Line K.17.d.30.20 - K.17.b.00.70. Three Batteries.
(A) will lift to line K.17.a.60.60. - K.17.a.60.05. at Zero plus 3
(B) will be stationary until Zero plus 25.

All known and suspected T.M. and M.G. positions to be dealt with by the 4.5.Howitzers including the Strong Point, 16 Poplars and K.18.c.25.15.
Battalion and Coy. H.Qrs. in old German Front and Support Line in K.17.b.
Counter Battery arrangements are to be made.
M.G.Cross Barrage to be arranged for in depth on both flanks.
6" H.T.M. on K.16.d.50.80. and K.22.b.3. 5" Zero to Zero plus 15.
Light T.Ms on same point as 6" H.T.Ms. Zero to Zero plus 15.
From Zero to Zero plus 5 Battalions on both flanks will kindly arrange for continuous Lewis Gun Fire on their Fronts.
At dusk odd Gas and Smoke Shells on old German Front and Support Line.
At Zero - Chinese Barrage on ROSIGNOL WOOD (Smoke and H.E.).

In the Field.
12.6.18.

[signature] Lieut. Col.
Commanding 1/7th. Bn. Manchester Regt.

APPENDIX "A".

TABLE OF TASKS FOR 18 POUNDERS.

Phase I. Battery.	Zero to Zero + 3. No. of Guns.	Target.	Rate of Fire.	Ammunition
C/286.	6.	Trench K. 17. a. 01. 67. to K. 17. a. 00. 20.	4. r.p.g.p.m.	A.
3rd. Bde. N.Z.F.A.	4.	Trench K. 17. a. 00. 20. to K. 17. c. 05. 80.	do.	A.
do.	2.	C.T. K. 17. a. 00. 40. to K. 17. a. 43. 64.	do.	A.
do.	4.	Road. K. 17. a. 04. 70. to K. 17. a. 55. 65.	do.	A.
Rt. Group, 57th.) Div. Artillery)	6.	Trench K. 17. b. 02. 70. to K. 17. b. 02. 00. to	do.	AX.
)	6.	Trench K. 17. b. 02. 00 to K. 17. d. 20. 30.	do.	AX.

Phase II. Battery. C/285.	Zero + 3 to Zero + 15. No. of Guns.	Target.	Rate of Fire.	Ammunition
C/268.	6.	Trench K. 17. a. 43. 64. to K. 17. a. 31. 32.	3. r.p.g.p.m.	A.
3rd. Bde. N.Z.F.A.	6.	Trench K. 17. a. 31. 32. to K. 17. a. 60. 00.	do.	A.
do.	4.	Trench K. 17. b. 00. 55. to K. 17. b. 00. 25.	do.	A.
Rt. Group 57th.) Div. Artillery.)	6. 6.	)) Same as Phase I.	do.	AX.

Phase III. Zero + 15 to Zero + 25.

Same as Phase II with rate of Fire of 1 r.p.g.p.m.

APPENDIX "B".

TABLE OF TASKS FOR HOWITZERS.

Phase I   Zero + to Zero + 3.   Target.   Rate of Fire.   Ammunition

Battery.	No. of Hows.	Target	Rate of Fire	Ammunition
D/286.	1.	K.17.b.03.71.	2.r.p.h.p.m.	BX.
do.	1.	K.17.b.00.55.	do.	BX.
do.	1.	K.17.b.00.28.	do.	BX.
do.	1.	K.17.b.00.15.	do	BX.
do.	1.	K.17.d.10.86.	do.	BX.
do.	1.	K.17.d.18.58.	do	BX.
3rd Bde.N.Z.F.A.	2.	K.16.d.50.13.	do.	BX.
do.	2.	K.17.a.57.68.	do.	BX.
do.	1.	K.16.d.99.81. M.G.	do.	BX.
do.	1.	K.17.c.12.76. M.G.	do.	BX.
6" Howitzers.	1.	K.17.b.02.85. Coy.H.Q)	1.r.p.h.p.m.	---
do.	1.	K.17.b.11.61. Coy.H.Q)	do.	---
do.	1.	K.17.b.33.01. Coy. H.Q.)	do.	---
do.	1.	K.17.d.40.42. Dugout	do.	---

Phase II.   Zero + 3 to Zero + 15.

Same as in Phase I.

Phase III   Same as in Phase I with rate of Fire of 1 r.p.h.p.m.

Copy of Telegram received from 127th. Brigade dated 16:6:18

Following message received from G.O.C. THIRD ARMY aaa
Please congratulade all ranks of 1/7th. Bn. Manchester Regt. on successful Raid.

                                42nd. Division.

SECRET.
      LEFT GROUP 42ND. DIVISIONAL ARTILLERY.
        OPERATION ORDER NO. S.I.
                             June 13th. 1918.
Ref. Map, 57D.N.E. 1/20,000.

1. At a date and hour to be notified later a party of the 1/7th. Manchester Regt. consisting of 3 Officers and 80 other ranks will raid the enemys trenches in K.16.b. and K.17.a.

2. The Artillery supporting this raid will be commanded by Lieut. Col. E.B.COTTER, D.S.O. R.A. and will be compased as under:-

   286 Bde. R.F.A.   6 - 18 pdrs.   6 - 4.5. hows,
   3rd. Bde. N.Z.F.A.   10 - 18 pdrs.   6 - 4.5. hows.
   Rt. Group 57th. Div. Art
             12 - 18 pdrs.
     Total.   28 - 18 pdrs.   12 - 4.5. hows.

   One Battery of 6" hows will also take part.

3. The tasks for individual Batteries are tabulated in the Appendix.

4. No registration of any nature must be carried out in the vicinity of K.16.

5. Time and place for synchronisation of watches will be notified to all concerned later.

6. C.B's will be asked to neutralise enemy Batteries as required.

7. Acknowledge.

                    (Sgd) E. COTTER. Lieut. Col.
                    Commanding Left Group, 42nd.
                       Divisional Artillery.

SECRET.

Head Quarters,
   127th. Inf. Brigade.

Report on raid carried out by the 1/7th. Battalion The Manchester Regiment on night 15/16th. JUNE 1918.

@@@@@@@@@@@@@@@@@@@@@@@@@@@@@@@@@

The raid was carried out at 1 hour 3' a.m. by "B" Company.
Strength, 3 Officers and 70 other ranks, and 10 Regimental S.Bearers.
Identification was sequired, and 1 prisoner captured.
Machines ~~were located~~ Guns were located but could not be captured.
The raiders were divided into 4 Platoon Parties, approximate 1 Officer 16 other ranks. Right, Centre, Left, and Support.
The preliminary arrangements worked without a hitch.
Right Party Leader Lieut. L.WENDER D.C.M.
Party proceeded as per orders, but inclined too much to the right after leaving its guide tape and came within 50 yards of an Enemy Post.
After carefully approching this post, Lt. WENDER gave the order to charge. The charge was held up by wire and heavily bombed.
Party moved left and were entering enemy trench by gaps in wire when a bomb dropped in centre of party wounding 6. Only 4 entered trench killing one German.
Lt. WENDER though wounded entered enemy trench leading and was seen to fall.
Sergt. FLEETWOOD, 2nd. in Command, took charge and on whistle sounding got his men out of enemy trench. He himself searched for Lt. WENDER without success. He found L/cpl. HAYDOCK of the same Platoon lying on parapet of BOSCHE trench incapable of movement with a fractured leg. He without help and long after his men had regained our lines, carried this man accross No.Mans Land under M.G.Fire to the control Post.
Having reported the arrival of his party and the loss of his Commander he saw L/cpl. HAYDOCK down to the advanced Dressing Station.
The last seen of Lt. WENDER was on the German parapet under heavy Bomb Fire.
Sergt. FLEETWOOD looked very carefully for his Commander before he left for our lines with L/cpl. HAYDOCK, and he considers Lt. WENDER fought his way in and was again wounded or killed.

Centre Party Leader. 375395 Sergt. J.W. GREEN M.M.

This Party left MINNY TRENCH at Zero 3. On reaching the junction of WATSON STREET and FUSILIER TRENCH they were met with a shower of Bombs and a Very Light was sent up. The party now came under M.G.Fire from a position about 20 yards to the East. Sergt. GREEN silenced the M.G. with a Bomb and ordered one section to capture the gun. This section was held up by wire and driven back by bombs and rifle fire.
Remainder of party jumped into FUSILIER TRENCH at its junction with WATSON STREET.
Just left of this point a German Machine Gunner jumped on to our side of the trench and was bayoneted by Pte. PICKERING, placed under escort and sent back to our lines. Sergt. GREEN killed the second with his revolver, it being found impossible to get him out.
A party detailed to capture the second M.G. located some distance up the C.T. was unable to reach the Gun in time owing to Enemy bombing and the withdrawal being ordered. Party returned bringing in all its wounded. The wounded prisoner, two German Rifles and one German Helmet were all safely retreaved.

Left party Leader 2/Lt. A. GOODIER.

This party got quickly accross N° Mans Land, but on entering FUSILIER TRENCH found it blocked on the South (towards centre party) with loose barbed wire. Party proceeded along parados and parapet bombing to the right, meeting with opposition, which as they pushed forward became stronger. The trench was found to be held by Strong Posts at intervals of about 25 yards.

One post was driven off but the second held up our attack.
6 German dead were seen in the trench. Party were unable to dislodge enemy who were behind old wire. Party withdrew at 1-15 a.m. when whistles were sounded. No dugouts were seen, but small shelters were found in the trench. The garrison of trench was strong, Fire heavy. More could have been done had time allowed being longer.

Covering Party Leader. 2/LT. J.H. MILNE.
Fulfilled to the letter the task set them. They covered the withdrawal of the force.

Sergt. GLEESON and L/cpl. TITTERINGTON assisted by Stretcher Bearers searched a wide area for wounded before returning, and report that no one was left in front of German trench.

There was continuous fighting throughout the operation and I am satisfied the enemy casualties greatly exeed our own.

The Artillery barrage was extremely accurate and efficient, although the raiders were close up to the 18 pdrs. barrage not a single casualty occurred. It gave the men the greatest confidence.

The enemy sent up green and red rockets mostly in pairs, and orange lights without visible results.

His barrage if any was negligible.

German wire in front no obstacle but loose wire in his trench on the flanks of posts greatly impeded our work.

The time allowed i.e.   13 minutes was too short for the overcoming of the unexpected resistance and the unusual determination of the garrisons.

To obtain a better bag or to capture M.Gs. , it seems imperative to penetrate to the second line, at least, and this I consider would lessen casualties.

The raiders returned in good order at Zero 15 to Zero 25.

The equipment of raiders was satisfactory.

A list of casualties is attached. Most of them are slight. I regret very much that any attempt to search for Lt. WENDER and Pte. JOHNSON after the raid was considered by me impracticable, and would have led to further casualties.

The reconnaisance work of 2/Lt. STANIER and Lt. WILSON was invaluable.

The work of Capt. GREY BURN in training the N.C.Os and men before the raid, in practicing the operation on tapes at SAILLY, and his conduct of the operation from our front line, very largely contributed to its success.

The Medical arrangements worked without hitch and were in every way satisfactory.

In preparing for the raid my Chaplain, the Rev. HOSKYNS was of great assistance in actually raising the morale of the men

Recommendations for immediate awards follow.

(Sgd.) E.V. MANGER Lieut. Col.
16:6:18.   Commanding 1/7th Bn. Manchester Regt.

WOUNDED AT DUTY.   Officers - 2.

MISSING.   Officers - 1   Other ranks - 1.

WOUNDED.   Officers - 2   Other ranks - 14.

Confidential

War Diary

1/9th Battalion Manchester Regiment.

July 1st to July 31st 1918

Volume 1.

Vol 18

Army Form C. 2118.

WAR DIARY
INTELLIGENCE SUMMARY. of 1/7th Bn Manchester Regt
(Erase heading not required.)

MAP 57 D.N.E.

Place	Date July	Hour	Summary of Events and Information	Remarks and references to Appendices
			Batt. Casualties during June in the Battⁿ	
			Off. O.R.	
			Killed - 3	
			Wounded 4 26	
			Missing 1 -	
			Died of Wounds - 1	
			Strength- Off. O.R.	
			Total strength 39 900	
			Members with Battⁿ 21 630	
			Awards during June - Military Medal - 275397 L/Cpl H. OGDEN and 275021 Sgt BAMBER	
			Military Medal - 2782 Pte W. PICKERING, 276635 Pte A. MISKIN and 276171 Pte L. HYDE	
			Sgt J. HORSFIELD	
COLINCAMPS	1		Battⁿ continue to occupy localities in brigade reserve	One
"	2		Battⁿ relieved 16th Manchesters in the front line. Disposition as follows -	See map marked "A"
			B.H.Q. PIONEER TRENCH K25a 7.4 K25. K26, K32 and K19 & 20.	
			'C' Coy Front line from BORDEN AVE. K34c18 to K33 6.6	
			with two platoons in support.	
			'B' Coy Front line from K33 6.6 to K27a 2.6 with two platoons in support.	
			'D' Coy Right support in K32b	
			'A' Coy Left support in K26a	
"	3		Quiet day - Lieut N. EDGE evacuated to hospital sick.	One
"	4		" " weather fine.	One
"	5		6" Westons finished enemy trench south of LA SIGNY FM. Major T.J. KELLY M.C. joined Battⁿ	One
			Awards 2/Lt A. GOODIER awarded the M.C. and 275161 Sgt A.S. FLEETWOOD & 275395 Sgt J.W. GREEN awarded the D.C.M. for gallant conduct in the raid on June 16th.	

2. WAR DIARY or INTELLIGENCE SUMMARY.

Army Form C. 2118.

MAP. 57D N.E.

of 1/7th Bn Manchester Regt

Place	Date JULY	Hour	Summary of Events and Information	Remarks and references to Appendices
COLINCAMPS	6		Inter-Company relief took place. 'D' relieving 'C' Coy & 'A' relieving 'B' Coy. HQrs was projected at the enemy in the vicinity of Lt SIGNY F24 2nd Lt A. GOODIER M.G. proceeded to U.K. on leave for 14 days.	gre
"	7		Enemy gas shelled COLINCAMPS and K25 & vd in the night. Lt H.N. BARRATT proceeded to U.K. on leave for 30 days. Major T.J. KELLY M.C. posted to 1/5 Manchester for temporary duty. Capt J.R. CREAGH assumed duties as 2nd in Command. Lt S.J. WILSON assumed duties as acting adjutant.	gre
"	8		In view of anxiety of Corps about enemy dispositions a daylight raid was carried out by N.C.O. GORST and 8 O.R. of 'D'Coy. It was a complete success. A dead German was bro't in & he had no shoulder straps. Identification - 30th R.I.R. - 16th Res. Div. at K34a 20.05	gre
"	9		An abortive effort was made by Sgt ALDRED & 9 O.R. of 'C' coy to quietly enter a post at K34a 25.25. They were held up by wire hoover, and attempt bombed, M.G. 2d. & obtaining two casualties they proceeded for more than three hours & finally had to give it up. Lt P. PELL-ILDERTON rejoined batt.n from hospital.	See No Man's Land Sketch marked "C"
"	10		The batt. moving back into divisional reserve, batt.n was relieved by the 1/8 L.F. & in the line in daylight & by 10.30 pm, all batt.n in camp vacated by 1/5 L.F. & at BUS in J20 a.	gre
BUS	11		Batt.n cleaning up etc.	gre
"	12		Various R.E. working parties in vicinity of COLINCAMPS formed. 2nd Lt MANGER 1/4 to command the temporary during absence of LUIS. KENSEY.	gre
"	13		Rev: E.C. HOSKYNS M.C. Lyft batt.n, being posted as S.C.F. to 6th Division. Capt CRENSHAW [?] handed to batt.n working parties & training. Qr.Mr. & Hon Capt. A. ABRAHAMS joined batt.n from the Base. CREDGE reported to hospital.	gre
"	14		" chiefly parades	gre
"	15		" training. One or two crashes about 11.45 pm. close to the camp.	gre
"	16		" training. Heavy thunderstorm in early morning caused discomfort.	gre
"	17		Capt N.R. M.D. M.C. left for the Base being declared unfit for service by medical board.	gre

MAP. 57D N.E.

WAR DIARY
or
INTELLIGENCE SUMMARY. of 1/8th Manchester Regt

Army Form C. 2118.

Place	Date July	Hour	Summary of Events and Information	Remarks and references to Appendices
BUS	19		Battn taking over the line from the 126th Bde, the Battn relieved the 10th Manchesters in the right sub section on a one company frontage. Three companies relieved in daylight, & the front coy. at night. Dispositions.	g.e.
			B⁴ H.Q. K19.c.6.1	
			'C' Coy front line (N° 1 Coy) - from K27a.2.6 to K27b.1.9	See appendix I
			2	platoons moved K27a.8.7
			'B' " support (N° 2 ") - Platoons at K27c.7.9, K26b.5.1 – 5.3 and 9.7	
			'D' " Second Support (N° 3 ") " K26a.8.5, K20.c.6.2 and 5.3 and K28.c.5-9.2	
			'A' " reserve (N° 4 ") - In FORTCHARLES and PIONEER TRENCH.	g.e.
COLINCAMPS	19		In conformity with the advance of the N.Z. division in front of HEBUTERNE the Brigade was ordered to advance to his	
			support. This Battn was to occupy the Road K26.a.0.7 along NORTHERN AVE. A party departed	
			about 5.00pm. 'C' Coy carried out the operation with Lieut N. EDGE in charge of its attacking	
			parties. The post was captured about 1 a.m. and one prisoner taken.	
			Party of 14 O.R. Lift to O.R. in close support. The post was captured about 1 a.m. and one prisoner taken.	
			Consolidation & wiring was immediately begun & NORTHERN AVENUE was found empty. A patrol of 'D' Coy.	See appendix II
			On a further reconnce of the front it was decided to attack & occupy the triangular system of trenches joining	
			the points K27b.9.2, K28c.1.9 and K27d.6.9. This was known to be fairly strongly held by the enemy with	
	20		a further post at K28.a.0.4.	
			'B' Coy, supplied the attacking force under Lieut GREGSTY assisted by 2/Lt BORST. The assault idea being to	
			front along from K28.a.0.7. Operations commenced about midnight, the assault was a complete success. The	
			TRIANGLE was cleared, 3 prisoners being secured, & a good many enemy killed. Four posts were established & a	
			very quantity of material. Nurse Mary W. th. Janison had been between 40 & 50. consolidation and	See appendix III
			commenced at once & wire put round the three posts K28.c.1.9, K27b.9.2 and K28.a.0.4. whilst CENTRAL	
			AVENUE was opened up forward through the TRIANGLE.	g.e.
			Our casualties were 2/Lt BORST wounded & one man killed.	

Ref. 57 D NE.

Army Form C. 2118.

WAR DIARY
or
INTELLIGENCE SUMMARY of 17th Bn Manchester Rgt.
(Erase heading not required.)

Instructions regarding War Diaries and Intelligence Summaries are contained in F. S. Regs., Part II. and the Staff Manual respectively. Title pages will be prepared in manuscript.

Place	Date July	Hour	Summary of Events and Information	Remarks and references to Appendices
COLINCAMPS	21		Quiet during the day. The night was spent in consolidating & wiring the new forward posts. Captured material "B" Coy relieved "C" Coy in the front line. Work on outpost line continued. One of the Company positions	J.P.C.
"	22		Coy W is an enemy light M.G. which had obviously been dropped in a shell hole during the enemy's flight on the night of the 20th.	J.P.C.
"	23		Enemy commenced to shell our outpost positions on the night with heavy shells during the day. Work continued in the night. A good daylight patrol indicated that enemy did not occupy CETORIX TRENCH.	J.P.C.
"	24		"A" Coy relieved "B" in front line & "D" relieved "C". Dispositions of Coys. slightly altered.	J.P.C. See byd Op (contd) "D"
"	25		Work continued on forward posts. 2/Lt McCALMONT carried out good patrol & located enemy post at K28a S.4.	J.P.C.
"	26		Major G.B.L. RYLIE returned from sick leave in England, & assumed command of Batt.	Wnd
"	27		"A" Coy attempted to occupy posts along CETORIX, but owing to heavy rain during the day they found the trench untenable. One of the parties returned too far & had with hostile bombing. 2/Lt RODIER M.C. was wounded and 7 O.R. of this party wounded with bombs.	
"	28		In the operations of July 14th & 21st Military Medals were awarded to Sgt HORSFIELD DCM, Sgt BURNHAM, L/Cpl CRAVEN, Pte ROTHAM, ROURKE A, & EDWARDS R.	2RLR
"	29		Trenches in very bad condition owing to rain. Wiring the front posts at night. Weather improved. Work concentrated on wiring front posts at night.	2RLR
"	30		"D" Coy relieved "A" Coy in front line.	2RLR
"	31		Quiet day.— Work continued on front line. Weather hot. Obtained another enemy division in front of us.	2RLR

In the display fireworks activity used is have apparent. No mans land. He very seldom sends up flares.

2/Lt Mc ?? 19.7 Italian light M.G. captured in the advance of the 20th has been earmarked as a trophy.

G.B.L. Rae Major

War Diary I

C 127.

18:7:18.

OPERATION ORDER   NO. 19.

1. A party of "C" Coy. will attack Enemy Post at K.27.b.95.60. and occupy it tonight.

2. Party will be composed of :-
    (a) Attacking Party. - Lieut. N. EDGE, 2 N.C.Os & 12 men
    (b) Supports   - 1 N.C.O. & 9 men with shovels.
    (c) Flank Party   - Each with 1 N.C.O. & 3 Men with L.G.

3. "D" Coy will supply No. 1. - One Wiring Party of 1 N.C.O & 5 men.
                    No. 2. - One digging Party of Lieut. W. GRESTY and 40 men.

4. ZERO Hour :- 10-30 p.m.

5. When Post has been established endeavours will be made to get into touch with B 127 along trench leading North from Post.

6. DISPOSITIONS :- Party A will leave Front Line Trench at PALESTINE AVENUE and moving along old sap enter the Post silently as possible.
   Blocks will be immediately constructed in the trenches on both flanks and as far forward along NORTHERN AVENUE as possible.
   Parties C will immediately follow party A and move to positions as shown in attached sketch. They will protect the flanks of the attacking party and remain in position till daylight.
   Party B will follow party A at ZERO plus 5 and keep in close support taking as much cover as possible. Immediately Post is established they will enter and consolidate as quickly as possible. This party will be responsible for escorting prisoners back to the Front Line only, returning again to their work.

   The Wiring party will remain in Front Line Trench at K.27.b.15.80 till objective is gained when word will immediately be sent to them. French concertina Barbed wire will then be carried forward and put out at least 40 yards principally North East and South of the captured post.
   Party A will supply covering party.

   The Digging party, immediately this objective has been gained will commence cleaning and deepening NORTHERN AVENUE backwards from the captured post. This party will also dig a Small Supporting Post about K.27.b.60.55 to hold 4 men which will be garrisoned in daylight by Right Flank Party.

7. A dump of Bombs, Rifle Grenades, "P" Bombs and S.A.A. will be made off the Front Line in PALESTINE AVENUE at K.27.b.1.8.
   O.C. "C" Coy will arrange carrying parties for these if required.

8. Before dawn the garrison of the new post will be relieved by 1 N.C.O & 10 men who will carry forward with them supplies of water and rations for 24 hours.

9. 2/Lieut. STANMIER and the Scouts will be responsible for keeping in close touch with the operation of B 127 on Enemy's Post at the junction of NAIRN ST. with CETORIX TRENCH and equally giving them up to date information of our situation.

10   An accurate Nominal Roll will be kept of all parties engaged.

11   In case they should be wanted one 3" Stokes Mortar is available for harrassing fire.

12   An Advance Stretcher Post will be established at "C" Coy's H.Qrs. where there will be 2 wheeled Stretchers.
      Casualties will be taken to R.A.P. in RAILWAY AVENUE.

13   Advance Coy H.Qrs. will be established at Platoon H.Qrs.K.27.b.1.7.

14.   Two daylight patrols will go out at 8-15 p.m. to find out if bombardment had made any gaps in the wire.

J.Wilson Lieut
/Adj.

Commanding 1/7th. Bn. Manchester Regt.

C 127. *Wardean* II

OPERATION ORDER No. 20.   July 20th. 1918.

1. A party of "D" Coy. will tonight attack enemy positions in the TRIANGLE north of LA SIGNY FARM around K.27.b.8.0., and occupy it.

2. The party will be composed as follows :
    - X   1 N.C.O. and 8 men.   bombers.
    - Y   "   "   "   "   "
    - Z   "   "   "   "   "

    Two reserve teams of bombers, each of 1 N.C.O. and 8 men.
    Two parties each of 1 N.C.O. and 6 men to be used as consolidating parties.
    OFFICERS :- Lieut. W. GRESTY & 2/Lt. H. GORST.

3. "B" Coy. will detail two parties of 1 N.C.O. & 6 to remain in reserve for emergency.

4. Zero hour -- 10-30 p.m.

5. Point of Exit -- the post captured last night at K.28.a.0.6.

6. DISPOSITIONS :   FIRST OPERATION
    Party X will move South from K.28.a.0.6. along the trench, and bomb out any post found in this trench as far as K.27.b.9.2. On reaching this point they will attack the post near there with bombs and enter it. After this they will make a block along the trench running S.W.

    Party Y will follow 10 yards behind party X and having reached K.27.b.9.2. proceed along the trench running S.E. and clear it. They will bomb the enemy out of post at K.28.c.05.90. and establish a block at K.28.c.06.85.

    Party Z will follow 10 yards behind party Y and on reaching K.28.c.05.90. turn into trench running East and establish a block there.
    The two reserve teams will move into the trench between K.27.b.9.2. and K.28.c.05.90., and await orders and will be available to watch trench running west from K.28.c.05.90.
    The two consolidating parties will move behind the two reserve teams to consolidate with wire and by digging the posts at K.27.b.9.2. and K.28.c.05.90.

7. SECOND OPERATION :
    2/Lt. GORST will keep close touch with Lt. GRESTY and when K.28.c.05.90. has been made good will receive orders from him to mop up the two sides of the TRIANGLE, leading out party X for this purpose from K.27.b.9.2. and any further men from the reserve teams he may require.

8. Touch will be obtained with the 5th. L.F's. along RAILWAY AVENUE after occupation of K.28.c.05.90.

9. O.C. "D" Coy. will make arrangements to man the posts as follows at 2 a.m. :
    - K.27.b.9.2.   --   1 N.C.O. and 8 men.
    - K.28.c.05.90. --   2 N.C.O's. & 16 men.

    These will relieve the troops taking part in the assault.

(2) contd.

10. O.C. "C" Coy. will man a post at K.28.a.0.5. approx with 1 N.C.O. and 6 men drawn from the garrison at K.28.a.0.6.

11. MEDICAL ARRANGEMENTS : An advanced stretcher post will be established at "C" Coy. H.Q's. where there will be two wheeled stretchers. Casualties will be taken to R.A.P. in Railway Avenue.

G. Wilson Lieut
    Adj.

20:7:18.

                                                            Capt.
                        Commanding : 1/7th. Manchester Regiment.

REPORT ON
OPERATIONS - JULY 19th. to 21st
1918.
1/7th. BN. MANCHESTER REGT.
=======================================

FIRST OPERATION : Night July 19th. 20th.

In the afternoon of the 19th. the Battalion was ordered to capture an enemy post at K.28.a.0.6. and to maintain touch with the 1/6th. Manchesters who were to carry out a similar operation on the left.

A daylight patrol was immediately sent out along NORTHERN AVENUE and they reported the post held but that the wire appeared to offer no obstacle.

ATTACKING PARTY : This was composed of Lieut. EDGE and 14 Ors. with 10 other ranks in close support and 4 o.Rs. with L.G's on each flank.

A consolidating party was held in reserve in the front line to dig out NORTHERN AVENUE as soon as post was taken and to wire the post

Artillery support not called for.

THE ATTACK. As surprise was to be the chief element in this operation, the attacking party moved out along the direction of NORTHERN AVENUE stealthily, using the hedge as cover. They left K.27.b.1.8. at 10-30 p.m.

Movement was difficult and progress therefore slow. By 12-30 am. they had reached the post. After a careful reconnaissance the party rushed into the post. One prisoner was captured, but the remainder of the garrison managed to escape owing to the extremely broken up condition of the ground.

CONSOLIDATION : Blocks were quickly constructed on three sides of the post an a belt of concertina wire placed around it. NORTHERN AVENUE was opened up from the old front line to the post.

There were no casualties in this operation.

SECOND OPERATION : It was decided in the after noon of the 20th. that the triangular system of trenches (TRIANGLE) north of LA SIGNY FARM around K.27.b.8.0. should be captured that night.

ATTACKING PARTY: Lieut. GRESTY was put in charge of this opertion, assisted by 2/Lt. GORST. The party was composed as folows:-

Three Bombing teams of 1 N.C.O. & 8 men each with two similar teams in reserve. These were followed by three consolidating parties of 7 other ranks each, and three special parties of 5 O.Rs. each for wiring. Two parties of 9 other ranks each were held in reserve at K.28.a.0.6.

The special idea was to emerge from the post established the previous night at K.28.a.0.6. and move South along the trench to the TRIANGLE.

It was expected that enemy posts would be met with at K.28.a.0.4. K.27.b.9.2., K.28.c.05.85. and K.27.d.6.9. Each of these was to be taken in turn by bombing.

No artillery support was called for.

THE ASSAULT : 2/Lt. GORST led out with the leading party from K.28.a.0.6. along the trench to the South, and had only proceeded about 100 yards when they encountered an enemy working party in the open. The latter fled very hurriedly and the garrison of the post in the trench also quickly evacuated. They were persued by Bombs and bullets and one wounded prisoner remained in our hands. Our men pushed on and then bombed the post at K.27.b.9.2. and entering it found the garrison had again departed. The first party then turned to the right making for K.27.d.6.9. whilst the second and third parties under Lieut. GRESTY proceeded straight on. The first party came upon a large party of the enemy issuing stew and tea. They immediately threw bombs amongst them and the enemy quickly replied with a shower of bombs. 2/Lt GORST was wounded by one of these but he chased the enemy down the trench killing some with his revolver until wounded again with a bullet. Sergt. J. HORSFIELD D.C.M. then took charge of this party emptying his revolver three times into the fleeing enemy. The latter however temporarily made a stand with bombs at K.27d.6.9., and one of our men was killed.

A bombing attack was then made upon them whereupon they fled once more.

Meanwhile Lieut. GRESTY saw a number of the enemy running over the top from our first attacking party towards LA SIGNY FARM and he and his men hurried along the trench to intercept them. Going was difficult however, owing to the exremely broken up state of the trench. They encountered a post as suspected at K.28.c.05.85. and proceeded to bomb it. The enemy did not wait for the final rush and we occupied it without difficulty.

Later two more prisoners were discovered hiding in shell holes and after dawn an Officer was seen. He was fired on and wounded but he managed to escape in the direction of the farm.

The enemy garrison in their surprise and hurry to get away had left almost everything behind them except the machine guns, and from the quantity of rifles and material collected it is estimated that these posts contained a total garrison of from 35 to 50 men.

A Granaten werfer was found and several ammunition boxes for M.G's at various points. On the night of the 22nd. a Light M.G. was found by a patrol in a shell hole in front of the captured position.

CONSOLIDATION :

Blocks were established in all trenches leading towards the enemy. The wiring parties hurried up and quickly ran out a belt of concertina in front of each post to make it habitable, and working parties commenced to open out CENTRAL AVENUE so as to join up the old front line with the TRIANGLE.

Meanwhile the work of deepening NORTHERN AVENUE was continued.

This operation was carried out exactly according to orders, and the speed with which our men pushed on prevented the enemy from making any effective resistance, nor had he opportunity to call upon artillery support or for reinforcements.

The casualties were 1 man killed and 1 Officer wounded.

The whole operation advanced our line about 400 yards on approx. 500 yards front, and touch was obtained with the 1/6th. Manchesters on our left.

Capt.
Commanding 1/7t. Bn. Manchester Regt.

War Diary

COPY OF CONGRATULATORY MESSAGE FROM BRIGADIER GENERAL A. HENLEY
Comdg. 127th. BRIGADE.(Acting G.O.C. 42nd. Div.)

"23rd. July.

My Dear Colonel MANGER,

I have been hoping for a detailed account of the operations which have led to the successful advance of our line, on the whole of 127th. Brigade Front.

I have been waiting for it before sending my congratulations to the Battalions concerned and to you.

However they are quicker at tackling the Hun than they are at writing the story afterwards, so you must be content with my judgement by results. Will you please, therefore, convey to all concerned my appreciation of the promptitude, determination, and skill with which each stage in the advance was made.

Everything was done in the accustomed manner of 127th. Brigade and in accordance with the invariable spirit of 1/6th. & 1/7th. Manchester Regts.

(Sgd) Yours sincerely,
ANTHONY HENLEY.

P.S. I wish to thank you personally for getting the show started so promptly. "

O. C.

    1:7th. Bn. Manchester Rgt.

Lieut. Col. E.V.MANGER desires his congratulations may be conveyed to all who took part in last night's most successful Minor Operation.

It was exceedingly well planned and carried out with great determination.

It is realised that the Operation was a most difficult one, the Right flank being exposed and the distance of the objective great.

The fact that an Enemy Advanced Post and a valuable Idenification was obtained shows how silently and well the plan of Operation was s supported by all concerned.

                                                   (Sgd) E.V.MANGER, Lt.Col

20:7:18.   O.C. 127th. Infantry Brigade.

Copy of Divisional Memo. dated 27:7:18.

"127th. Inf. Brigade.   G.S.120/1/41

     On his return, the Divisional Commander has read with satisfaction the account of the minor operation carried out by 127th. Inf. Brigade between 19th. and 21st. July, and heartily congratulates the Brigade and the 1/6th. and 1/7th. Battalions Manchester Regt. on their work.

                                                                        (sd) R.F.GUY,
                                                                        Lieut. Colonel,
                                                                        General Staff,
27th. July 1918.   42nd. Division.

Copy of wire from 42nd. DIVISION dated 20:7:18.

"Wire from Third Army begins :-

Best congratulations on successful operation from GENERAL BYNG aaa Divisional Commander adds his congratulations."

(sgd) RANDOM.

Copy of
Congratulatory Message

The following remarks on our recent operations have been received from the Army Commander:-

"A very satisfactory operation.
The 127th Inf. Bde. are to be congratulated on the result of the well planned advance"

(sd) J BYNG
General

31/7/18

WAR DIARY
(CONFIDENTIAL)
OF
1/7 (17th) BN. MANCHESTERS.

PERIOD

AUGUST. 1st. 1918. to
AUGUST. 31st. 1918.

VOLUMN: 8.

1/7th. MANCHESTER REGT.
- :-:-:-:-:-:-:-:-

Copy of wire received from 42nd. Divisional Commander :   3:8:18.

" The Divisional Commander sends ROOT his heartiest congratulations on their excellent performance "

MAP. 57D NE.

Army Form C. 2118.

WAR DIARY
INTELLIGENCE SUMMARY. of 17th Bn Manchester Rgt

(Erase heading not required.)

Place	Date August	Hour	Summary of Events and Information	Remarks and references to Appendices
COLINCAMPS	1		Battle Casualties during July in the batt'n	
			Off. O.R.	
			Killed — 2	
			Died of Wounds — 1	
			Wounded 2 52	
			Missing 1 —	
			Strength.	
			Off. O.R.	
			Total strength 39 942	
			Number with batt'n 18 636	
"	2		Batt'n continue to hold the right sub-sector of the left brigade front in K27b &c. Quiet day - very hot.	
"	3	4 a.m.	"B" Coy relieved "D" Coy in the front line. Day quiet. 86 W.O.'s N.C.O.'s & men of 1/27th Manchester joined the batt'n. Preceded by a deliberate barrage on line of resistance & bombardment of forward posts with T.M.'s the enemy made a determined attack with about 80 men on our own & the 8th Manchester forward posts in the vicinity of LA SIGNY F'm at 4.5 a.m. after A.P.O.I. The first parties of the enemy were seen at 4.5 a.m. & rifle fire & the enemy did not get beyond the wire. They however was immediately opened & with fire fire & were harassed with fire along the wire to the left evidently trying to find a gap & were harassed with fire by small groups of our men along the trench. L/Cpl THORPE M.M. (N°276540) displayed great coolness & power of Command on this occasion & hours afterwards proceeded to Expand for his good work. Eventually the enemy gave up the attempt & retired in confusion. Lieut PEEL-INGERTON took out a small bombing party to follow them up, but found that they had gone back to their	WWD WWD

MAP. 57D N.E. 1/20000 and 57D 1/40000

Army Form C. 2118.

WAR DIARY

INTELLIGENCE SUMMARY of 7th B: The Lancashire Fus.

(Erase heading not required.)

Place	Date August	Hour	Summary of Events and Information	Remarks and references to Appendices
COLINCAMPS	3 (cont)		Own lines. A dead German was brought in & all identification had then removed except a Prussian cockade in his cap which indicated that the 26th Inflantry Div. had been relieved. Another German who had been wounded lost his way & wandered into the 6th Bn. on our left. He revealed the Div. on our right is the 183rd Div. Search was made again at night and another dead German N.C.O. was brought in. The Batt⁵ was relieved during the day & early night by the 8th L.F. the brigade moving back into reserve. Relief complete by 10.15 p.m. Batt⁵ marched billets at LOUVENCOURT.	See attached slip tacked on I
LOUVENCOURT	4		Capt J. MARSHALL appointed Staff Capt 7th 125th Bde. & is taken off the strength. Rest & clean up. 2/Lt MANSER returned from Bde. & resumed command of Batt⁵.	MSB
"	5		2/Lt EDGE, 2/Lt GREASTY and 2/Lt GORST all received M.C. for the operations of July 19-21.	MSB
"	6		Inspection parades & kit inspection.	MSB
"	7		Training - special attention to double L.G. action. Following officers arrived from the Base, principally remainder of officers from 17th March Reft - Capt D. NELSON, Lt A. SMITHIES, Lt J.C. HAMMOND, Lt L. J.C. GOODALL, 2/Lt H. WILCOCK and 2/Lt A.A. LAMB. Batt⁵ paraded at J.31.c.2.9. - Tactical handling of L.G. practiced.	MSB MSB
"	8		" " " "	MSB
"			Batt⁵ gave his appreciation of the work done in the last tour in the line. Brig. Gen. HENLEY addressed the	MSB
"	9		'B' Coy gave a demonstration of the tactical handling of the double L.G. section.	MSB
"	10.		Short training and Coy. Exercises in Tactical Schemes.	MSB
"	11.		Training and Routine as normal. Reconnaissance of line at COLLINCAMPS preparatory to taking over.	MSB
COLLINCAMPS	12.		Relieved 1/5th Manchester Regt. in Support Line of Right Brigade Sector. Battalion Head Quarters J.30.d.4.0.	MSB

Reference Maps: 1:10000 57D. NE. SE
57D. NW. SW
57C. NW. SW

Army Form C. 2118.

Instructions regarding War Diaries and Intelligence Summaries are contained in F.S. Regs., Part II. and the Staff Manual respectively. Title pages will be prepared in manuscript.

WAR DIARY of 1/7th Battalion The Manchester Regiment

INTELLIGENCE SUMMARY.
(Erase heading not required.)

Place	Date August	Hour	Summary of Events and Information	Remarks and references to Appendices
COLINCAMPS.	13.		Harvelling Parties supplied. Work on maintenance of trenches, etc. Lieut. Col. E.V. MANGER to leave. 2/Lt. H.V. SPREADBURY and Lieut. GOODALL to leave in U.K. Lieut. C.J. BRYAN reported from Base.	WD
	14.		Enemy retreat commenced and our pursuit. One Company moved up to RAILWAY AVENUE N. Locality. Coy H.Q. K.26.d.5.3. 2/Lt. A. HARLAND, M.C. returned from leave. Lieut. T.P. WILKINSON do do do 2/Lt. J. McALMONT to U.K. on leave.	WD
	15.		Enemy retreat and our pursuit continued. 1 Coy moved up to APPLE TREES Rockery. A/Q at Q.2.a.7.6. One Coy moved to RAILWAY AVENUE S. Locality in K.26. Coy H.Q. at K.26.d.5.3. Battalion H.Q. moved up to K.31.b.4.7. Lieut. W. CRESTY, M.C. to U.K. on leave. Pursuit of Enemy held up.	WD
	16.		Battalion holding same position as on previous day.	WD
	17.		Situation unaltered. The Battalion relieved the 1/6th Battalion Manchester Regt. in the left sub sector of the Brigade front during the night 17/18th. 2 Coys. in advanced outpost positions. 2 Coys. in Old B.L. and LEGEND Trench. Battalion H.Q. at K.33.a.3.2.	WD
	18.		Lieut. N. EDGE, M.C. to 3rd army Infantry School. Situation unchanged. Patrols. In touch with Enemy, whose positions were held by M.G. posts on high ground. Movement by day very difficult owing to Enemy observation. Enemy put down barrage on our Main Line (MUNICH Trench) from 5 a.m. to 5.30 a.m. causing only 2 casualties.	WD
	19.		Position unchanged. Enemy snipers and M.G. fire persistent and accurate. 2/Lt. H.R. STANIER returned from leave. Patrols constantly in touch. Aircraft active above normal.	WD
	20.		Position unchanged. Preparations made for attack on Enemy positions in ridge overlooking MIRAUMONT.	WD
	21.		At 2 am. The Battalion moved in assembly formation in the vicinity of PENDENT COPSE. L.31.a.5.6. 1/7th Battalion Battle H.Qrs. on the SERRE ROAD, K.35. a. 9.9.	WD

WAR DIARY of 1/7th Bn. The Manchester Regt.
INTELLIGENCE SUMMARY.
(Erase heading not required.)

Army Form C. 2118.

Place	Date	Hour	Summary of Events and Information	Remarks and references to Appendices
	2(continued)		An attack had been ordered in conjunction with the NEW ZEALAND Division on the left of the 42nd Division and the 21st. Division on the right. The 127th Brigade was to attack with 1/7th Bn. Manchester Regt. on the left and the 1/6th Bn. Manchester on the right — the 125th Brigade was to attack on the left of the 127th Brigade. The Brigade objectives were 2 important pieces of high ground overlooking the River ANCRE & MIRAUMONT. The first objective was to be a crest in L.32.d. L.26.d. & L.33.a. and the second objective the high ground overlooking MIRAUMONT around L.33.central. "D" Company (Capt. J BAKER) and "A" Company (Lieut S DOUGLAS) were detailed to take the first objective and consolidate where "B" Coy.(Capt. F GREY BURN) would leapfrog and take the 2nd objective. "C" Coy. (LIEUT. H. ABBOTT) was detailed to be in Support and 1 Coy. of the 1/5th MANCH. REGT. was detailed to be in Reserve. Zero hour 4.55 a.m. at which time there was an exceedingly thick mist and it was impossible to see 50 yards ahead. At 8.30 a.m. "A" and "D" Coys were reported to be consolidating on the first objective with "B" Coy. in position for moving forward to the final objective. Prisoners were coming in and the casualties reported to be light. At 8.55 a.m. the Creeping Barrage commenced again and "B" Coy attacked the second objective and were reported in position and consolidating at 11.30 a.m.	
		At 11.30 a.m.	Battalion H.Q. moved up to MUNICH TRENCH.	
		CASUALTIES.	Lieut. H.N. KAY killed. LIEUT. C.T. LOFTHOUSE wounded. 2/Lt. J.A. HARLAND M.C. wounded. 4 other Ranks killed. 40 Other Ranks wounded.	

WAR DIARY of 1/7 Bn. Manchester Regt.   Army Form C. 2118.

of

INTELLIGENCE SUMMARY.

(Erase heading not required.)

Place	Date	Hour	Summary of Events and Information	Remarks and references to Appendices
	2 (cont) August		ESTIMATED PRISONERS: 2 Officers (1 Field Officer) 1 Warrant Officer. 95 Other Ranks. Of these Prisoners 53 were captured by "B" Coy. and all brought down in one party in the evening.	
	22.		COMMENTS. Owing to the long distance which was reached in taking the objective & to the exceedingly hot day the work required from Stretcher Bearers and Running Escorts was excessive and it would appear necessary that arrangements should be made to lessen the work of the attacking infantry in both these respects.	MPB
	23.		At dawn the enemy attacked our new position and the Left Brigade, after a heavy Barrage in which several casualties occurred — the attack which was made favourably by the 52nd Naval Division and fresh to the line was completely repulsed. During the afternoon there were indications of another attack but continuous gun fire from our artillery was asked for and this probably broke up the attack. Lieut. H.A. STANIER was severely wounded. Shortly after dawn following upon information received from his Patrols Capt. F. GREY-BURN pushed the line 300 yards further forward to a better line of observation facing MIRAUMONT and the Left Brigade & Right Battalion subsequently conformed. "C" Coy. here moved up to our new line.	MPB MPB MPB

WAR DIARY of 7th Bn. Manchester Regt.
or
INTELLIGENCE SUMMARY

Army Form C. 2118.

Place	Date	Hour	Summary of Events and Information	Remarks and references to Appendices
	August 24.		Following upon information received from our patrols and Brigade H Qrs. that the enemy were in retreat and the River ANCRE leading 67.a of the Brigade (7th & 1/6th) crossed the River without much opposition between 9.45am and 12 noon and took up a position on the high ground R.11. central to R.11. d. 8. 9. The left Brigade experienced considerable M.G. opposition and did not get through MIRAUMONT till the afternoon about 3 p.m. At 3.30 p.m. 8th Bn. 7th Manch. Regt. passed through MIRAUMONT and took up a position in support. At 8 p.m. the 1/5th Manchesters in front and 7th Manchesters in support marched in artillery formation to a position about 500 yards West of WARLENCOURT until contact with the enemy was gained. LIEUT. COL. E. V. MANGER returned from leave and resumed Command of the Battalion.	MHB
	25.		Brigade withdrawn from further advance and remains holding position around PYS and WARLENCOURT.	MHB
	26.		Heavy thunderstorm at night. The whole Division concentrates around PYS - WARLENCOURT - IRLES and MIRAUMONT in Corps Reserve. Casualties during operations	MHB

Killed   Wounded
Officers   1.   3.
Other Ranks   19.   129.

| | 27. | | Battalion in Bivouacs at IRLES. Marched out at 9 p.m. to take over Reserve line of Brigade position on LOUPART Road in M.5.d. and trenches advanced. | MHB |

WAR DIARY of 7th Bn. the Manchester Regt.

Army Form C. 2118.

INTELLIGENCE SUMMARY.

(Erase heading not required.)

Instructions regarding War Diaries and Intelligence Summaries are contained in F. S. Regs., Part II. and the Staff Manual respectively. Title pages will be prepared in manuscript.

Place	Date August	Hour	Summary of Events and Information	Remarks and references to Appendices
	27 (cont.)		Battalion H.Q. at M.S. a. 10.65. Trench Strength. 16 Officers 434 Other Ranks. Lieut. S.J. WILSON to U.K. on Leave. Lieut. H. ABBOTT to U.K. on Leave.	MR3
	28.		Holding same positions as on 27th inst. Positions for defence dug and prepared. Enemy shelling observed during night. 6 Officers reported:- Lieut. T. WOODS. 2/Lieut. H. PEARSON. 2/Lt. R.M. RAY. 2/Lieut. J.R. SIDDALL. 2/Lt. M.P.J.G. IAPP. 2/Lieut. W.H. MILNE. and 30 reinforcements.	MR3
	29.		Holding same positions. Enemy retreated during night from THILLOY. Patrols in front and his advanced about 2,300 yards to Bapaume Road in N.3.C. General retirement noticed in enemy positions.	MR3
	30.		Holding same positions. Bn. "Stood To" at 5 a.m. ready to move in Support to 1/5th & 1/6th Manchester Regt. in the advance on RIENCOURT and VILLERS au FLOS. Bn. moved up at 10 p.m. to occupy positions in N.2.B., N.2.d. and N.3.c. Battalion H.Q. at Burkfield N.R.d. Central. Lieut J.G. EVANS to U.K. on leave.	MR3
	31.		No further developments during the fight and Bn. in same positions. At 8.0 pm Corps mines forwarded orders to 75 Manchester Bgd. having reorganised by 48 Div. moving to N3 the Right, at N.3.c.3.4. 2 Coys in trenches in N3 cst. 1 Coy in shelters at M3a and M4E. Capt. F.G. BYRN to leave to U.K.	MR3

Capt. H. Manquel OC

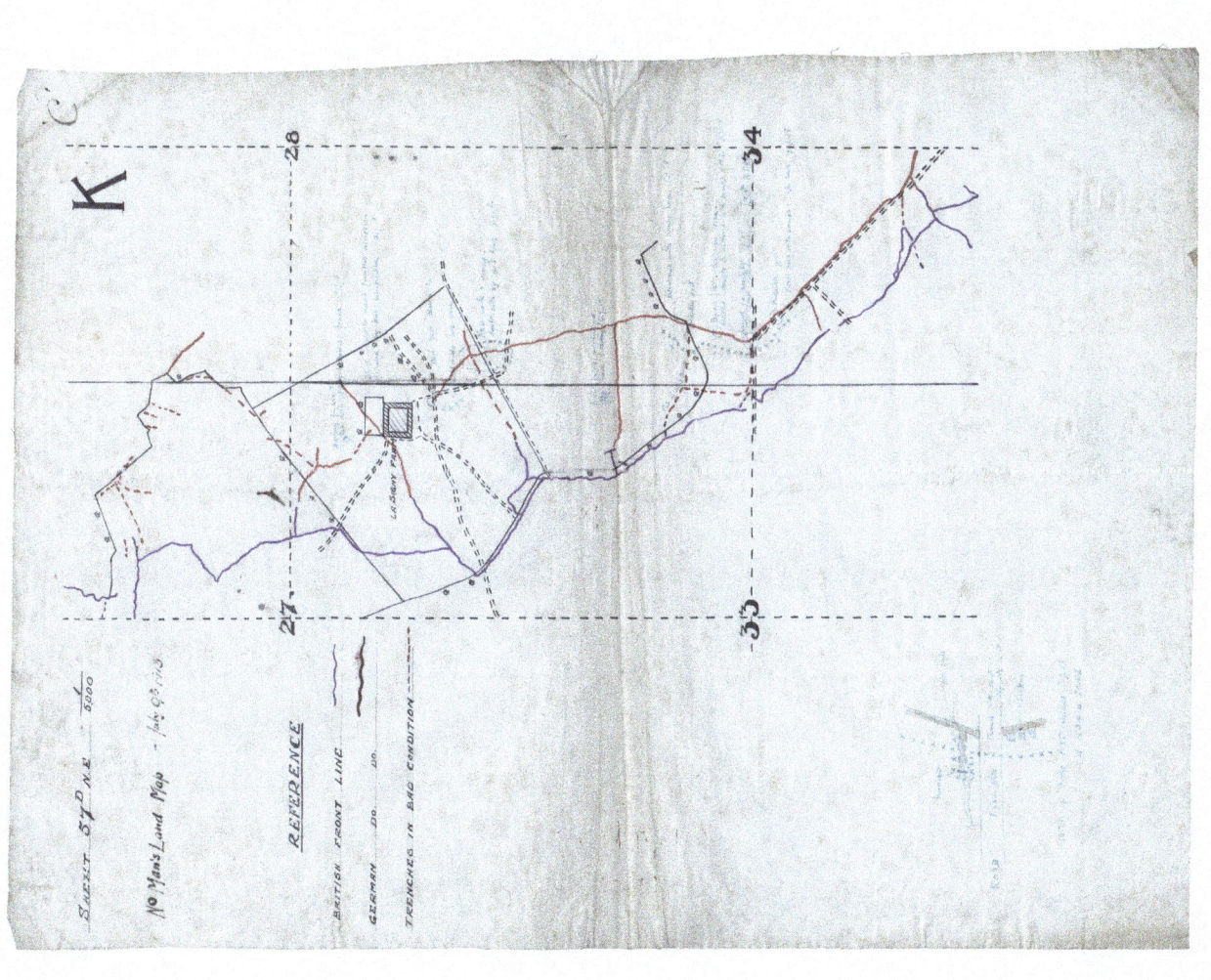

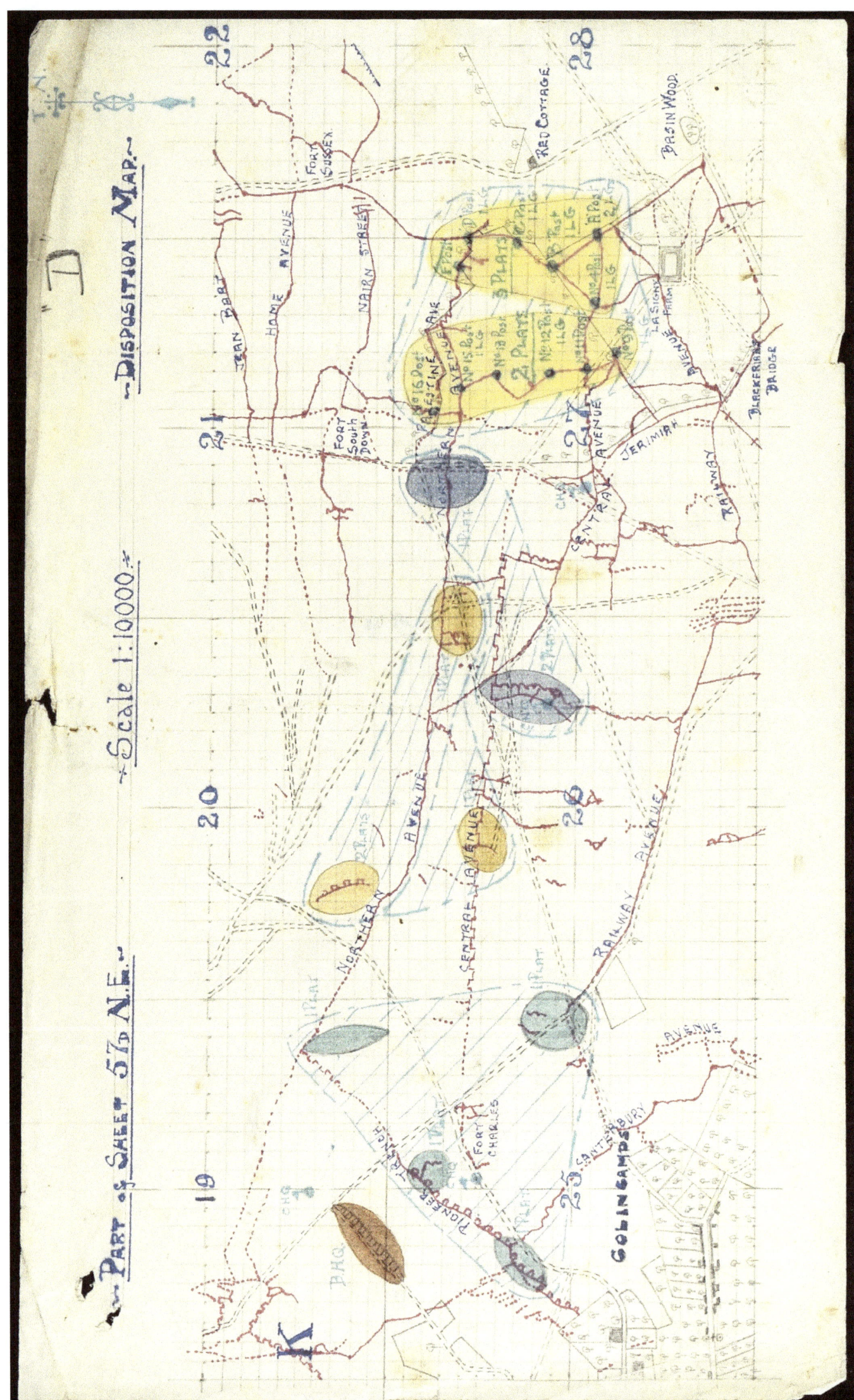

OPERATION ORDER 107.

Ref: 57 D.R.E. and S.E. Sheet, 1:20,000.   16/8/18.

1. The 7th. Battalion Manchester Regt. will relieve the 1/6th. Battalion in the Left Subsector of the Brigade Front on the night 17th./18th. August.

On relief Coy. Dispositions will be as under:-

                                                                Coy. H.qrs.

"A" Coy......LEFT FRONT   about   K.35.b.09.
"B" Coy......RIGHT FRONT   K.35.a.7.7.
"C" Coy......LEFT SUPPORT   K.27.d.1.1.
"D" Coy......RIGHT SUPPORT   K.33.c.4.6.
Battalion H.qrs. will be at K.33.a.2.2.

2. Relief will commence -
Rear Platoons of Support Coys. at 7-30 p.m., guides (guides for Forward Platoons will be met at 8-15 p.m.) 1 for Coy. H.qrs. and 1 per Platoon - will be at following rendezvous :-

For LEFT SUPPORT COY at EUSTON DUMP 7-30 p.m.
For RIGHT SUPPORT COY at SUGAR FACTORY 7-30 p.m.
Guides for Forward Coys- 1 for Coy. H.qrs and 1 per Platoon will be at the 1/6th. Manch. Regt Bn. H.qrs. (K.33.a.2.2.) at 8-30 p.m.

Left Front Coy. will proceed to relieve ahead of Right Front Coy.   The line of approach to Front Coys. is along CHURCH-HERUE road.

3. At least 100 yards distance between Platoons will be maintained throughout the move.

4. R.A.P. is situated at K34.b.9.0.
A runner Relay Post will be established at K34.a.2.0.

5. Water Bottles will be filled before Coys. move from their present positions.   Rations for the 18th. inst. will be carried on the man.

Spades and Picks, at least 25% of Coy. Strength, will be carried forward by Forward Coys.

6. Trench Stores, Defence Schemes, Maps, Aeroplane Photos etc. will be handed over to the representatives of the 1/6th. Manch. Regt. who will report to Coys. by 5-0 p.m. 17th. inst.

Similarly Trench Stores etc. will be taken over on relief. Copies of receipts will be sent to B.O.R. by noon 18th. inst.

7. The Signalling Officer will arrange that each Forward Coy. H.qrs. is supplied with a bicycle.

8. O.C. "A" Coy. will return to New Bn. H.qrs. K33.a.2.2. by 10 p.m. all Hot Food Containers for re-issue.

O.C. "A" and "D" Coys. will hand into New B.H.qrs. by 10 p.m. the 17th. all Petrol Tins on charge for the organisation of Water Supply.

9. Cookhouses for "A" and "D" Coys. will be established near Battalion H.qrs.   Coy. Cooks. will report to R.S.M. there for accomodation.

10 The Transport Officer will arrange to remove the spare limber from COLLINCAMPS tomorrow the 17th, and replace it with 2 additional pack animals.   Feeds will be brought up daily.

11 The Q.M. will send up any additional Food Containers with rations tomorrow the 17th. inst.

12 Completition of relief will be reported to Bn. H.qrs. by following codes :-
    "A" Coy......NELSON.   "B" Coy......WELLINGTON.
    "C" Coy......BRUTUS.   "D" Coy......CAESAR.

13 ROYD   ACKNOWLEDGE.

DISTRIBUTION :

Copies to :-

    NO 1.........A Company.
    NO 2.........B Company
    NO 3.........C Company.
    NO 4.........D Company.
    NO 5.........C.O.
    NO 6.........M.O.
    NO 7.........T.O.
    NO 8.........Q.M.
    NO 9.........1/8th. Manchester Regt.
    NO 10........War Diary.
    NO 11........War Diary.
    NO 12........File.

A/Adjutant   C. 127.   Lieut.

WAR 127/42
DIARY
(CONFIDENTIAL)
OF
17th BATTALION
MANCHESTER
REGT.

PERIOD

SEPT. 1st. 1918 to SEPT. 30th 1918

VOLUMN. 9.

Mss. 12000. 57c S.W. N.W.
FRANCE. 57c S.E. N.E.

WAR DIARY or **INTELLIGENCE SUMMARY**

Army Form C. 2118.

of 7th Bn. The MANCHESTER REGT.

SEPTEMBER 1918.

Place	Date	Hour	Summary of Events and Information	Remarks and references to Appendices
	1/9/18.		Bn. in trenches East of THILLOY in Bgde. Reserve. Moved up at 10.0pm to trench system in N.4.a and N.5.a & c. Bn. HQ. at N.4.a.0.7. Occupying positions vacated by 1/6 Bn. Manchester Regt. Orders received that 1/5 and 1/6 Manchester Regt. will attack and take VILLERS AU FLOS on the 2nd inst. 1/7 Bn. in close support; 1 company of 1/7 Bn. to be attached to and at disposal of 1/5 Bn. on Right flank of the attack.	Lt. GEE & MANGER 57265 Lof Bn reported from MACHINE GUN BATTLE SCHOOL attached to "C" Company of the Bn.
	2/9/18.	5.15am.	"C" coy attached to 1/5 Bn. on Right of the line. Heavy enemy shell fire on O.B.L. and caused 6 fire casualties. Lt. TONE and Lt. H.M. EVANS wounded. O.R. killed. O.R. wounded. Considerable opposition from enemy M.G. posts from high ground in O.2.a and b	Lt. TONE and Lt. THROTCHLEY and Lt. J.M. TONES at Regt. Aid Post. Lt. Gen. T.R. 12. Lt. H.W. GRESTY M.C. Lt. R.C. ALMONT Returned from leave to U.K.
		7.50am.	"A" coy moved forward to Kenterward through O.1.a and N.6.d. and "D" coy moved forward to occupy trenches vacated by "A" coy.	
		8.15am.	"B" coy moved forward to get in on trench S.E. and S.W. of RIENCOURT and that at that of 1/6 Bn. for support. Tactical Emergency.	Lt. F.A. SMITHIES ordered to U.K.
		9.45am.	Orders received that "A" coy in N.6.d come under the command of 1/6 Bn. 2 platoons reinforce 1/5 Bn. line on Right – 2 platoons and by 1/6 Bn. to form defensive flank on left about O.2.c and O.8.d.	
		Noon	"D" coy moved up to Luke Road in N.6.d and Bn. HQ. to N.5.d.9.8. Preparations made to relieve 1/6 Bn. Manchester Regt. in the line. "B" coy on 2nd Objective to take over back system through O.8.d.9.6.d. and O.14.b.c. and d. "C" coy on Right flank A. and D. coy on line of 1st Objective cyf. East of VILLERS AU FLOS. O.8.b.2.5. to O.13.b.8.2. Relief complete 2.45am. Sept. 3.	gre
	3/9/18.	6.30am	Bn. H.Q. at N.5.d.4.0. and Bn. in the line, holding positions as taken up on 2nd inst. Sent fwd patrols forward by "B" coy advance on relief towards BARASTRE. BARASTRE to find one of the enemy and occupied by patrols of "B" coy. Similar situation on the a.	gre

Army Form C. 2118.

WAR DIARY
or
INTELLIGENCE SUMMARY.
(Erase heading not required.)

Instructions regarding War Diaries and Intelligence Summaries are contained in F. S. Regs., Part II. and the Staff Manual respectively. Title pages will be prepared in manuscript.

Place	Date	Hour	Summary of Events and Information	Remarks and references to Appendices
	3/9/18	7.30am	Orders received that 18th Lancashire Fusiliers will advance through BARASTRE towards BUS as the advanced guard to the 127th Inf Bde on Hazebrouck Bde frontage. 17th Bn Manchester Regt to follow up as close supports. This order was later cancelled and 125th Inf Bde took over the disposition from 127th Inf Bde. Bn ordered to continue patrols when 18/5th L.F. have gone through and stand by for further orders. Bn. H.Q. moved back to N 5d 9 8. Capt F.G.BURN on leave to U.K.	ple

	4/9/18.	1.30pm	Bn holding same positions as advanced Bn of the Reserve Bgde. Standing by awaiting orders. Men resting, washing & making clear changes where possible. Hot meals provided. Total casualties during operations from Aug 21st to date.
			Officers.
			Killed 1
			Wounded 4 (accidentally)
			Missing —
			O. Ranks.
			   21
			   150 (including gassed)
			   —
			Bn H.Q. moved forward to O.8.d.2.0.
			Bn holding same position East of YTRES am. FLDS. Reconnaissance parties to examine likely new positions for the Bn. On high ground in O.9.c and O.14.d. sent to A. SMITHIES. 15th U.K. on leave
				ple

	5/9/18			ple
	6/9/18.		Bn moved at 8.0am with transport by main road to occupy bivouac area near MARLES COURT. Bn H.Q. at M.5.a.21. Corps to LOUPART Road M.5.c. and in Sunken Rd M.5. Central. Accommodation Tents and Bivouacs. Arrived in new area 10-45am. Remainder of day spent in cleaning up and making camp area. Lieut G.G.HAMMOND and 2/Lieut T.M.JONES to U.K on leave	ple
	7/9/18		Bn in occupation of same area. Bathing, Exchange of kit etc. 2/Lt W.B.SMITH to U.K. on leave 2/Lt L.T.GOODALL the Kens B. attached to 67th L.T.M.Battery.	ple

WAR DIARY or INTELLIGENCE SUMMARY

Army Form C. 2118.

Place	Date	Hour	Summary of Events and Information	Remarks and references to Appendices
	8/9/18		Position of Coy at Bn. H.Q. Same as for 7/9/18. Church Parade. Training area allotted by Bgde. to "E" M5, N16 and M11 and to "F" M5, N16 and M11 and to 9/9/18.	
	9/9/18		Training commenced. Hours 8 to 1. 2.6 to 3.30pm. Based on new 3 section formation. Capt. J.R. CREAGH returned from leave.	Appx I.
	10/9/18		Training. Hours 8 to 1. 3 to 5. Musketry Commenced on Range. N.C.O. Specialist Classes — Lewis Gun, Signalling, Scouts, Young N.C.O's.	
	11/9/18		Training. Same hours of parade. Machine gun on Musketry and Platoon Coys in Tactical Exercise — Embodying the 3 Section formation in Platoon. Coys battling at WARLENCOURT.	
	12/9/18		Shooting Competition during afternoon. Specialist Classes commenced viz. Lewis Gun, Signalling, Scout, Rifle Grenade. 2nd Lt. R.H. LYNN B to U.K. on leave.	
	13/9/18		Training as for 12th inst. Capt. M.A. TINTO proceeded to the Base (Aufsf).	
	14/9/18		Training as normal. Wilds G.V. WRIGHT and T.M. CARLEY reported from Base and taken on the strength. Lt. H. ABBOTT rejd. from leave in U.K. Lt. L.G. HARRIS taken on strength. 2/127th Lt. Bn. at Intelligence Officer took up post from 14/8/18.	
	15/9/18		Church Parade Service. Lieut. C.J. BRYAN to U.K. on leave.	
	16/9/18		"D" Coy gave demonstration of "a Company in the attack." Coys Commanders in attendance. Thirds T. LEVER and J.W. WILKINSON reported from Base and taken on strength. Lieut. N. EDGE M.C. from 3rd Army Musketry camp.	Appx II
	17/9/18		Training. Tactical Route march culminating in an attack. Formations of approach against defensive position carefully practised, viz Artillery formation to Platoon and section Extended order. Mutual Support. Reconnaissance of Coys R.V. rendezvous line during day by Coy Officers & relief by other Coys in Command.	

WAR DIARY or INTELLIGENCE SUMMARY

(Erase heading not required.)

Army Form C. 2118.

MAP 57 C NQ.OOO

Place	Date 1918	Hour	Summary of Events and Information	Remarks and references to Appendices
M.5.a	18/9/18		Training. Reconnaissance of the Corps Reserve line by O.C. Award of 1 Bar to M.M. and 13 M.M.'s announced in Divl Routine Orders. Major G.T.B.L. RAE on leave in France. Capt. A.H. BRAHAMS proceeded to the Base (Engl't.) 33 O.R. Reinforcements from the Base.	pc
	19		Training.	pc
	20		Bn: Preparing to move up to Line tomorrow.	pc
	21		Bn: relieve 1st Essex (37th Div) 2nd Wilts (65 Men: 10 R.E.) in Divisional Support. Bn location J.33 and 34. Role to garrison Corps Main Line of Resistance running S.E. from J.34.a. Light touring P.4. entire co. to re-inforce or counter-attack Divisional Line of Resistance running from S.W. to N.E. along east face of HAVRINCOURT WOOD. March of Bn with transport commenced 9 am. 11:30 am. 15 hour Rest for arrival day meal. Weather showery.	pc
J.27.d	22		Relief complete 3.30 hr. Reconnaissance very indifferent. Patrols from Bn H.Q. & coy. boys pushed to reconnoitre post. Garrison area. Lt. W.M. BARRATT departs for 1 month to III Army Officers Rest House PARIS PLAGE.	pc
	23		Mild form of training. Further reconnoitering parties to forward area S and E. of HAVRINCOURT. Lt. G.G. HAMMOND, Lt. A. SMITHIES and 2/Lt. J.M. JONES return from leave.	pc
	24		Training in attack formation. 2/Lt. W.B. SMITH from base.	pc
	25		Training & further reconnoitering front area. Big attack on our front pending shortly in which 127th Bde will take part. Receive Administrative Orders at 9.30 hrs.	pc
	26		Receive O.O. & O. for attack taken 9 am.	pc

Army Form C. 2118.

WAR DIARY
or
INTELLIGENCE SUMMARY.
(Erase heading not required.)

Place	Date	Hour	Summary of Events and Information	Remarks and references to Appendices
	26.9.18		All arrangements made for attack tomorrow. (See Operation Order No. 17) App III. The Battalion gets into preliminary assembly position in deep dug-out, without casualties by midnight.	App III
	27.9.18	5.20 am	Zero hour. 5.20 am. Morning fine and bright. Companies get into attack assembly position without casualties and were ready by 8.0 am. Companies moved forward to attack according to plan, i.e.	
		8.20 am	"C" Company. 8.20am, followed by	
		8.28 am	"A" " 8.28 am, 200 yards in rear.	
		8.50 am	"D" " 8.50 am. In Artillery formation of Sections.	
		8.56 am	"B" " 8.56 am. About 200 yards in rear in same formation.	
			"C" Company immediately came under heavy machine gun fire from BLACK LINE, but moved steadily forward and caught up some of the 5th Manchesters who were held up. Advance was checked here for a few minutes and casualties were numerous. CAPT. C.R. ALLEN was killed and LIEUT. NEDGE wounded. The O/C of the Company offered most of the platoons having only 4 men left. "C" Company then advanced and reached the trench CHAPEL WOOD SWITCH, capturing 2 Machine Guns and 25 prisoners. "C" Company continued under heavy Machine gun fire, chiefly from high ground East and S.E. and were pinned to this trench. "A" Company had a similar experience to "C" Company and arrived in the BLACK LINE in command of C.S.M. JOYCE, all their Officers being casualties.	
			LIEUT. G.G. HAMMOND. (WOUNDED)	
			" T. WOODS. "	
			2/LT. J. McALMONT. "	
			" T.M. CARLEY. "	
			KILLED	
			2/LT. J.M. JONES was now in command of "C" Company and took over command of "A" Coy. as well. He immediately set about reorganising both Companies which were very much depleted in numbers. 2/LT. JONES then led both Companies forward. The advance was checked by explosive bullets and machine gun fire from Maple High York Copses flank about 150AR COPSE. 2/LT. R.M. RAY was killed, leaving 1/LT. JONES the only Officer with both Companies.	

WAR DIARY
or
INTELLIGENCE SUMMARY.

Army Form C. 2118.

Place	Date	Hour	Summary of Events and Information	Remarks and references to Appendices
	27.9.18	10.30 am	About 10.30 am A and C Companies captured the Right Section of the RED LINE in Q.6.a and about 45 Prisoners. They immediately reorganised and commenced to consolidate. 2/Lt JONES found that the Right flank was in the air and formed a defensive flank with "A" Company on the high ground in Q.5.b. Touch was obtained with the 6th Manchesters on left in RED LINE.	
		11-0 am	2/LT JONES had under his command in the RED LINE :— "A" Company. 55 O.R. } NO OFFICERS. "C" " 32 O.R. } Under the circumstances he decided not to push on, but attack the BROWN LINE which was "A" Company's objective.	
		8.50 am	"D" Coy. At 8.50 am advancing in Artillery formation came under heavy Machine Gun fire from S.E. crossing Ridge in K.35.d and Q.5.a, but entered the "BLACK LINE". Rifle and Lewis without check. Advance in extended order was continued from there under heavy fire from about the BROWN LINE which checked the pace a good deal. A number of men that had been hit as well as 2/Lt G.V. WRIGHT and 2/Lt F.D. THRUTCHLEY a member of the enemy were still holding out on the RED LINE, but "D" Co.	
		9.40 am	rushed them any [how] captured about 50 Prisoners. Time about 9.40 am. Advance was checked in this line for about 15 minutes. LIEUT. GRESTY, M.C. commanding "D" Coy. was informed here that there were no troops in front of him on his Right flank. He determined to advance and capture the BROWN LINE.	
		9.55 am	Advance had to be continued, but had to be cautiously done as no troops were advancing on either of "D" Coys flanks. Opposition was met in the TRECAULT ROAD in K.36.d and about K.36 Central, in which series of fights ensued and about 100 prisoners captured. A good many enemy went RIGGIN here. Advance was continued from about K.36 Central down to HINDENBURG LINE and a good deal of fighting and mopping up was done, and a further 50 Prisoners captured.	

WAR DIARY or INTELLIGENCE SUMMARY

Army Form C. 2118.

Place	Date	Hour	Summary of Events and Information	Remarks and references to Appendices
	9/4/18	8.58 am	B.G. about 8.58 am advanced in artillery formation from assembly position Dog Yks where D Co. No serious opposition was encountered till the BLACK LINE had been reached. About him it became apparent that LIEUT. ST WILSON (Commander of D Co.) that his Right Flank had not been clear of the enemy, and he two Left Platoons commenced advancing again. Then his two Right ada to come under fire from M.G. in Q.5.d and outflank connected. No 5. Platoon encountered M.G. positions in Q.5.b and attacked them at once. PTE WHITE rushing forward disposed of 1 by himself, bayoneting the gunner and killing some of the remainder with his rifle. From this point fire was kept up the Right Brigade, and the Left of his Company was pushing ahead. The RED LINE was crossed without much obstacy. D Coy were encountered there. A/L passing K.36.d.0.5. the two Left Platoons came into action with the enemy immediately S.E. on the Spur in Q.6.b & a vigorous fire fight ensued from these two platoons lost heavily. 2/LT SIDDALL and both Platoon Sergeants being wounded. In spite of this the men pushed on and a few reached the trench running EAST in Q.6.b. The enemy them bringing up men from the valley to the S.E. and counter attacked. This was dealt off. LIEUT. WILSON then realised that the Right Brigade had been held up and having been informed by the 6th Manchesters with whom he was in touch in UNSEEN TRENCH that they were the most advanced troops he decided to form a defensive flank facing S.E. His Right Platoons were then moved to the left to support the other two.	

WAR DIARY
or
INTELLIGENCE SUMMARY.
(Erase heading not required.)

Army Form C. 2118.

Place	Date	Hour	Summary of Events and Information	Remarks and references to Appendices
	27.9.18		Enemy M.G. fire was very active from the E. and S.E. of the BROWN LINE, ie the Sunken Road running through K.31.c and K.36.a was eventually reached. As other British troops on the left flank on the BROWN LINE. About 25 mins later, 30 of the 6th Manchesters arrived in the BROWN LINE on the left flank. The advance was held up on this line by fire M.G. fire from the front and Right flank. LIEUT GRESTY sent a message back for a barrage to be put on the YELLOW LINE. This came down ¾ hour later, and LIEUT GRESTY immediately took his company forward to the attack in conjunction with the 6th Manchesters ie 50 O.R. of 11th Manchesters and 30 of 6th Manchesters. The advance was in a N.E. direction. TWO LIGHT GUNS, 77 mm and their crews were captured in RIBECOURT – VILLERS PLOUICH RD, running through L.31.d. and d.1 about L.31.c.1.1.	
		1.5 pm	At 1.5 pm D Coy, composed of 2 Officers LIEUT GRESTY & 2/LT. J.H. MILNE) and 38 O.R. charged and captured the YELLOW LINE, and killed many of the enemy. The 6th Manchesters who were advancing further on the left arrived in. The objective about 20 minutes later. D Coy's line now ran from L.31.c.5.8 – L.31.b.5.5. M.G.'s were firing on them from L.31.a.1.4. LIEUT GRESTY sent a message to the K.O.Y.L.I. who were apparently checked just EAST of RIBECOURT, that "the Manchesters were on their right". The K.O.Y.L.I. immediately advanced.	
		3.30 pm	About 3.30 pm the 16th Manchesters Platoons withdrew to SUNKEN ROAD in L.31.a. LT GRESTY's company was now without troops on either flank, and being fired on from his Right Rear, and suffering heavy casualties, so about ½ hour later he withdrew his men to SUNKEN ROAD in L.31.a again. Withdrawal was successfully accomplished under covering fire of 2 Lewis guns. B Co. formed up with B Co. on this line and were in touch with the 6th Man. on the Left.	

WAR DIARY
or
INTELLIGENCE SUMMARY.
(Erase heading not required.)

Army Form C. 2118.

Place	Date	Hour	Summary of Events and Information	Remarks and references to Appendices
	27.9.18		The attack the position was pressed on spite of the fact that the enemy was still holding ground on the Right flank since M.G. protection. The Company continued to lose heavily, and 2/LT M D T CAPP and 2/LT H PEARSON were wounded, leaving LIEUT. WILSON the only Officer with the Company. A line was eventually formed in Shell Holes from K.36.d.4.2 to K.36.d.0.1. There were not sufficient men to gain ground on the Right. In this position the Company checked the enemy's counter attack and held him to the French E and W. of Q.6.b.4.7. Touch with the 6th Manchesters was made on the left.	opp. IV
		11.30 a.m.	LIEUT. WILSON arrived in Conference with the 6th Manchesters Commander that in view of his small numbers and his Right flank in the air he could not continue the advance. Two Patrols S. along the road through Q.6.b. reported the enemy in strength in the trench. A number of sniping shells arrived and the position was rapidly consolidated. Constant touch was maintained with the enemy by patrols until night. 2 Platoons of 5th Manchesters came up to reinforce and were disposed along a line from K.36.d.0.1 to Q.6.a.3.5. The night of 27/28 passed quietly. The 10th Manchesters came through the Batⁿ during the night and reoccupied the YELLOW and took the BLUE LINE (See attached Map) shewing objectives.	

Army Form C. 2118.

WAR DIARY
or
INTELLIGENCE SUMMARY.
(Erase heading not required.)

Place	Date	Hour	Summary of Events and Information	Remarks and references to Appendices
	08/8/18		The Tanks did not prove of very great assistance during the advance. They were presently hurt from or were moving in front of the Infantry. A number of M.G. nests were left untaken by the Barrage or Tanks. These were moped up by the Battalion. There were great scarcity of Stretchers. The work of the Regimental Staff. Lieut TABUTERS was magnificent. The Signal arrangements under 2/Lt W.B SMITH worked without hitch. Battalion Signallers followed behind the 4th wave and maintained connection throughout.	
			CASUALTIES	
			OFFICERS	
			CAPT. C.R ALLEN. M.C. KILLED	
			2/LT T M EARLEY "	
			2/LT R M RAY "	
			LT. G.G. HAMMOND WOUNDED	
			" N. EDGE, MC "	
			" T WOOD "	
			2/LT J McALMONT " (since died)	
			" H PEARSON "	
			" J.R SIDDALL "	
			" MPJ GAPP "	
			" F.D THRUTCHLEY "	
			" G.V WRIGHT "	
			OTHER RANKS	
			KILLED 40	
			WOUNDED 159	
			MISSING 34	
			233	Appx V-XI
			Copies of messages and telegrams received and dispatched during operations attached	

Army Form C. 2118.

WAR DIARY
or
INTELLIGENCE SUMMARY.
(Erase heading not required.)

Place	Date	Hour	Summary of Events and Information	Remarks and references to Appendices
	28.9.18		Fine day. General position greatly improved. All ground on the Right now in British hands. WELSH RIDGE captured. Companies are withdrawn during afternoon to dug-outs in O.4.b. LT C.B. DOUGLAS rejoins Bn from leave.	9e
	29.9.18		Battalion is withdrawn during afternoon to Camp in P.11.c.	9e
	30.9.18		Battalion Resting.	9e
			2/LT A.A. LAMB rejoins from leave.	9c

E.H. Mangles Lieut Col
the 7th Manchesters
Commanding

App. V

To: ADJUTANT,
VEGE

The Spur in K.36.d was not cleared of enemy and I am held up there also.
6th MANCH. have not advanced beyond BROWN LINE. I am getting 6th. to counter attack advancing back southwards from K.36.b. with intention of cutting them off.

9.36. S.J. WILSON

App VI

To. The Adjt
C/127

A and C. Coys are at
K 36 b. 2 4
C. Coys Strength 1 Off 32 O.R.
A Coy " 55 O.R.

We are consolidating and
reorganising.

D and B Coys have
gone forward.

(Sgd) J. N. Jones
2/Lt
C. Coy.

Runner
B.M. 11.0 am

To Adjt. Sept 24.
C/124 App VII

Have just reached my
objective. and taken two light guns.
    I have only about 50 men
and they are in no condition.
You must send some men and L.
Gun drums Wright and
Stratchley are not with us
    A party of about 40
of the 6th are on our left.
    Nobody is on the Right.
    Also send me Water and
Rum if possible.
    Wilson I have not seen
for some time.
        (Sgd) W Bresty Lt
            O.C. D Co.
1.5 pm   C/117

TO VEGE   App VIII

BM 23   27

Place one Company at disposal of VEGE to act as a Reserve to meet counter attack. aaa. O.C. VEGE will report when O.C. Coy concerned has reported to him. aaa andsa. VERI reptd. VEGE

WULI 1.6 pm

To: "A" Co.
App IX

Repeated B, C & D for information.

Brigade on our Right are held up on line N and S. through BOAR COPSE in Q.6.c.

With a view to meeting counter attack from BOAR COPSE, one Company "A" Bn. will Garrison RED LINE.

You will furnish a defensive flank facing SOUTH along PLUSH TRENCH running forward from Right of RED LINE and the Switch running N.E. from Q.6.b.2.5. and gain touch with "D" Co. in Sunken Road running N and S in Q.6.b. also gain touch with B Co. located in R.36.d.

You will move at once when the relieving Company is in position, and be prepared to launch a counter attack.

(Sgd) J.R. Creagh
Capt. & Adjt.

The Bde on the Right are now established on the RED LINE. including BOAR COPSE. Try to get in touch

"D" VEGE   App. X

BM 30   27

VEZO and WEGE will hold the Bde line tonight and They will sort out their Coys so as to hold frontages in their respective sub sectors and One Coy VERI is placed at disposal of VEGE to meet counter attack and VERI less One Coy will be Support Battn about CHAPEL WOOD SWITCH and at an early hour VENU will pass through VEZO and VEGE and will capture YELLOW and BLUE LINES on WULI from under a Barrage and VEPO has been ordered to occupy old front line of WULI Sector.

WULI   6.50 pm

O.C. A. B. C. D. Coys.   App XI

A. 544.

1. Present Position.

(a). B. and D. Coys. with 2 Platoons A. Bn.
hold line of Sunken Rd. from Inter. Bn.
boundary on left to about its intersection
with Unseen Trench and thence a
defensive flank running due W and
facing S.

A. and C Coys with 2 Platoons of A. Bn.
Hold RED line Northern inter Bn. boundary
to about Q 6. a. 0. 0. with defensive flank
thrown forward facing S.E.

(b) 125th. Bde on right are in touch with
Coy. on RED line and have captured
BOAR COPSE.

(c) 6th. Manch. are in close liason
with us on left.

(2) Intention

With a view of capturing Blue Line
tonight on our Divisional Front the 125th
Bde. on right and the 10th Bn. Manch.
Regt. on 127th Bde front. will attack the
Yellow and Blue lines after m.n.
the 10th Manc. leapfrogging our Bn.

(3) C Bn. and attached troops will
consolidate and reorganise in depth
as much as possible on the lines
they now hold, giving special attention
to measures of protection on their

right flank with a view to preventing surprise.

C Bn. will give every assistance possible to 10th Manch. especially as regards maintainence of direction

Ammunition, Water, Food, Rum, and L.G. Drums are being pushed forward.

Coys. will look out for and help to direct Carrying Parties to the best of their means at their disposal.

Higher authority fully realize the splendid achievement of the 6th and 7th Bns. in making such a deep advance and retaining their gains so hardly won and with their right flank in the air.

(Sgd). E. V. Manger
Lt. Col.
Commdg 7th Manch. Regt.

Copy of Order to C and D Coys
"A" Battalion

App XII

A 543.   2/

1 Company to reinforce Garrison of RED LINE from SOUTHERN BRIGADE boundary to PLUSH TRENCH and be prepared to deal with any attack from direction of Q 6 Central.

The remaining Company will take up positions in the SUNKEN ROAD Q 6 b, SOUTHERN BRIGADE boundary to UNSEEN TRENCH. and be prepared to form a defensive flank forwards to meet enemy attack from direction of PLUSH TRENCH

Each man of both Companies will carry as much extra S A A from the troops holding the line and L.G. drums if available

VEGE.

(Sgd) J.B. Creagh
Capt

App XIII

7th. Bn. The Manchester Regt.

PRISONERS & BOOTY CAPTURED
DURING OPERATIONS
27/28. SEPT. 1918

PRISONERS .... 600.

GUNS
Heavy. M.G. 9
Light. M.G. 19
Trench Mortars 2
77 M.M. 2

O.T. Mangn Lieut-Colonel.
Commanding 7th Bn. The Manchester Regt.

War Diary
8 7/7 McKey

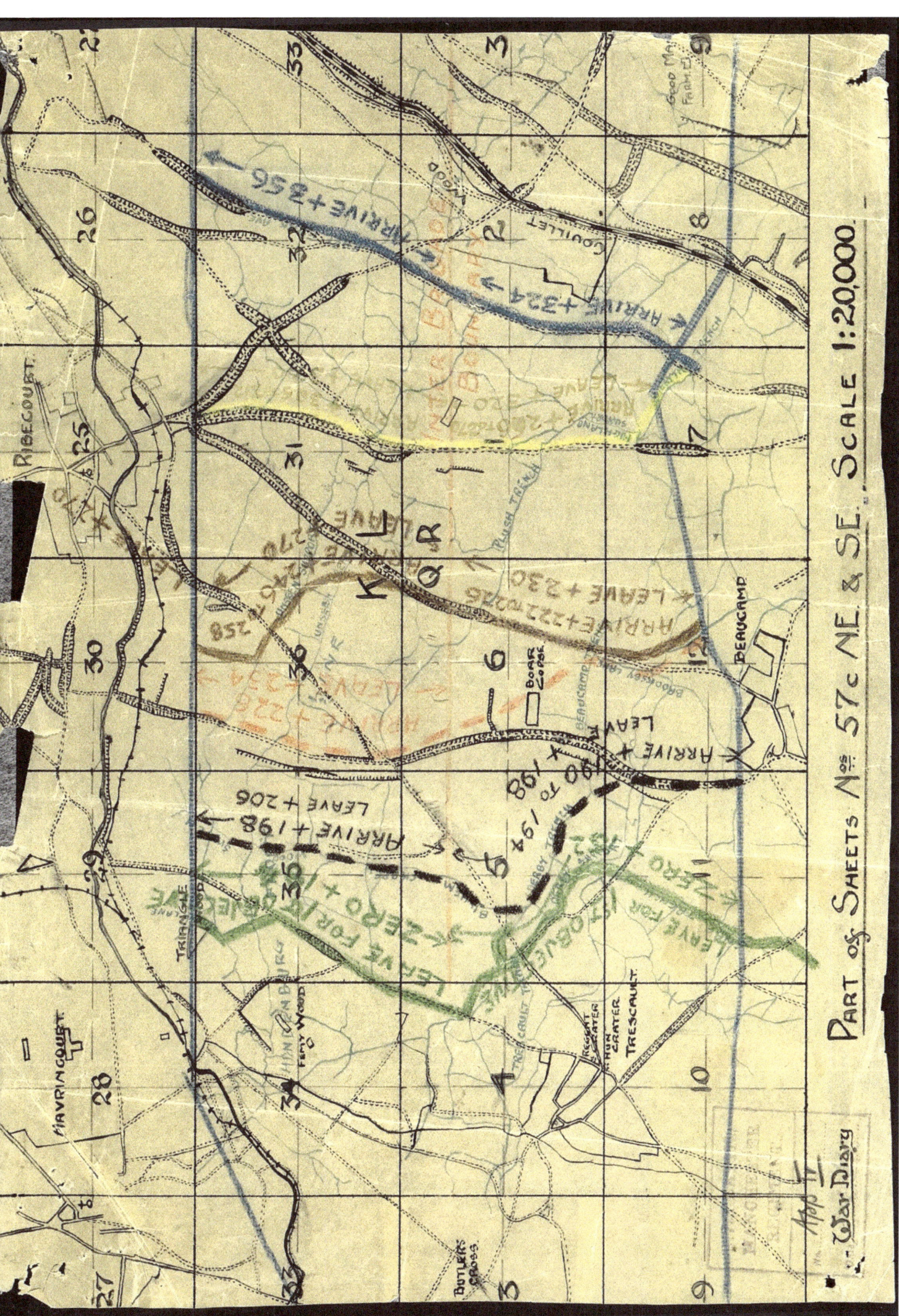

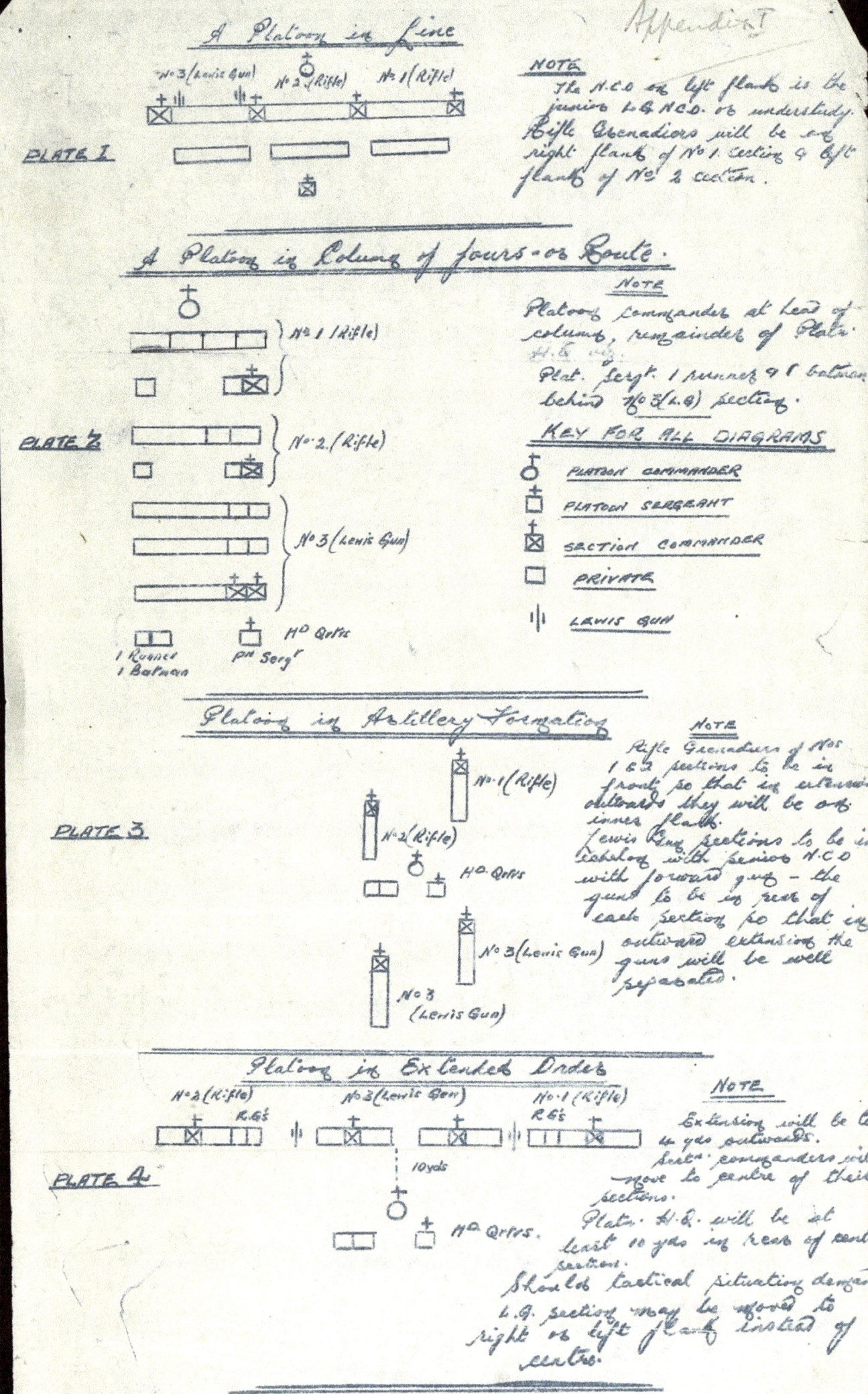

Appendix II

OPERATION ORDER No. 69
15th. Sept. 1918.
by
Officer Commanding C U B.

Ref. Map. 57c. S.W. 1/20,000

(1) The attack will be continued tomorrow at 10-30 a.m. against the enemy's positions in G.34. central including LOUPART WOOD, Loupart Road Exclusive.
X Bn. are attacking on our right.
Y Bn. on our left.

(2) A line will be consolidated in advance of the Northern edge of LOUPART WOOD.

(3) BARRAGE. Standing 4.5" and 6" Hows. on LOUPART WOOD, creeping 18 pounder shrapnel barrage advancing 100 yds. in 3 minutes to first objective in 3 lifts thence on to M.G. positions in front of Southern face of LOUPART WOOD for 15 minutes.

(4) OBJECTIVES.
The attack will be in 3 bounds which will be made as follows.-
1st. Bound. - Trench running E. and W. through M.4.a. and b.
2nd. Bound. - M.G. nests in G.34.c and d. southern face LOUPART WOOD.
3rd. Bound. - To positions of consolidation North of LOUPART WOOD.

(5) Capt. J. BAKER'S Company will lead the attack.

(6) Position of Assembly.- Trenches immediately in rear of our Outpost position running through M.4.c. and d.

(7) One section of "B" Coy M.G.Bn. and 2 3" Stokes mortars are attached to Capt. Baker's Company.

(8) 1st Line Transport will be ready to move up LOUPART Road when final objective has been taken.

(9) Bn. H.Qr. and R.A.P. will be in Crater M.5.c.6.0.

(10) All signal communication by Flapper and Lamp.

(11) ZERO hour - 10-30 a.m.
Watches will be synchronised at 10 a.m.

By Runner to.-
1   C.O
2   "A" Coy.
3   "B" "
4   "C" "
5   "D" "
6   T.O
7   Q.M
8   M.O
9   Sig. Officer
10 X Bn.
11 Y Bn
12 H.Q. 127th. Bde.
13 "B" Coy. M.G. Bn.
14 127th. L.T.M.B.
15 File.
16 and 17 War Diary.

W.H. Barratt Lieut.
Adjutant.
7th Bn. The Manchester Regt.

TACTICAL DEMONSTRATION.

(1) **General Idea.**

Enemy hold LOUPART WOOD and have held a British Attack from the West 400 yds. short of the Wood.

The enemy have been driven in from the spur running S.W. from the wood.

It has been decided to renew the attack from the South and SouthWest. The British hold WARLENCOURT with an Outpost Line running through M.4.d.c.a. and G.3 3.d.

(2) **Special Idea.**

The 7th. Man. Regt. has received orders to take part in a combined attack on the morning of the 16th. on the enemy's position the high ground in G.34 and 35 central.

7th. Bn's objective being the Western half of LOUPART WOOD, Loupart Road exclusive.

The flank Battalions will attack simultaneously, each Bn. on a 1 Coy. frontage.

(3) **Dispositions of 7th. Bn. Manchester Regt.**

1st. Phase.
Position of Assembly - reverse slope in old trenches M.4.d.
First Bound - to trench running East and West through M.4.a and b. under 18 pounder shrapnel barrage, standing 4.5" and 6" barrage on Wood and M.G. nests in front of it.
Second Bound - clear M.G. nests and capture Wood by Fire and Movement and Infiltration.

2nd. Phase.
Consolidation in advance on Northern Face of LOUPART WOOD prior to continuation of advance by moonlight.

By Runner to -
1 C.O
2 "A" Coy.
3 "B" "
4 "C" "
5 "D" "
6 T.O
7 Q.M.
8 M.O
9 Sig. Officer.
10 X Bn.
11 Y Bn
12 H.Q. 127th. Bde.
13 "B" Coy. M.G. Bn.
14 L.T.M.B.
15 File.
16 and 17 War Diary.

W.H.Barratt Lt.
Adjutant
7th Bn. The Manchester Regt.

Copy No......

APP III

Operation Order No...72.

by

Lieut.Col. M.V.Manger.　　　　　　　Commanding "C" Battalion.
　　In the Field.　　　　　　　　　　　　　　26/9/18.

Ref: Map. 57c S.E. and N.E

1. Operations are being undertaken by the VI Corps to secure FLESQUIERES and the high ground to the East. In conjunction, the 42nd.Div.are attacking with 125th.Inf.Bde. on the right and the 127th.Inf.Bde.on the left.

2. The objectives of 42nd.Div.,the 9th.Inf.Bde.and 187th.Inf.Bde.and our Bde. and Bn.boundaries are shown on the attached map.

3. The Black Line within the Bde.boundary will be captured by the 1/5th. Man.Regt.
The Red,Brown,Yellow and Blue Lines will be captured by the 1/7th. Man. Regt.on right and the 1/6th.Man.Regt.on the left.

4. On Y/Z night-
(a) the 1/5th.Man.Regt.will assembly 2 Coys.near present front line, assembly will be complete by 10 p.m.
(b) the 1/6th.and 1/7th.Man.Regt.will move to assembly positions West of 1/5th. Man.Regt., assembly to be complete by 12 mid-night.
(c) to cover the assembly of 127th.Inf.Bde.the 125th.Inf.Bde.are leaving Outposts to hold the Line and patrol the front.

5. "B" and "D" Coys.M.G.Bn. will co-operate with the 127th.Inf.Bde. "D" Coy. providing covering fire for the advance, and "B" Coy.co-operating in the consolidation of the captured lines.
　　The following points will be consolidated. -
　　　　(1) L.32.b.3.7.
　　　　(2) K.2.a.8.9.
　　　　(3) K.36.b.8.9
　　　　(4) L.31.a.2.2.

6. Six fighting Tanks are expected to co-operate,their objectives as follows -
　　　　(a) between starting line and Brown line.
　　　　1 Tank to PLUSH Trench.
　　　　1　"　to UNSEEN　"
　　　　1　"　to　"　Support.
　　　　(b) between Brown and Blue Lines.
　　　　1 Tank to Valley Trench and RIDGE trench.
　　　　1　"　to　"　support and　"　support.
　　　　1　"　to MOLE trench.

7. The attack will be carried out as follows:-
1/5th.Man.Regt.will form up under initial barrage by Zero plus 180 mins. and advance at Zero plus 186 minutes to Black Line.
Thence onwards the 1/7th.Man.Regt.on right and 1/6th.Man.Regt.on the left. will conform to the timings of the barrage keeping as close to the barrage as possible.
Barrage tables attached.
Coy."Leapfrogs" will be on Red,Brown and Yellow Lines.

8. Handshakes will be made between 1/6th.and 1/7th.Man.Regt.where the line of each objective cuts the Inter-Bn. boundary.
Handshakes with the 125th.Inf.Bde.on our right will be given later.

9. (a) Contact Aeroplane will call for flares at:-
   Zero plus 220 on Red Objective.
   Zero plus 300 on Brown objective.
   Zero plus 420 on Blue objective.
The signal to denote the assembly of the enemy to counter attack is the dropping of a Red smoke bomb over the place where the enemy are seen.
   (b) Tank signals shown from of Tanks:-
   Green and White flag.   indicated   "Come on"
   Red and Yellow   "   "   "Broken down"
   Red, White and Blue"   "   "Going Home"

10. Battle H.Q.
   127th.Inf.Bde. from 8 p.m. on Y day... Q.3.b.2.2.
   Bn.H.Q.   "   10 p.m. " "   Q.4.a.2.1

11. Two R.E. sappers will go forward when objectives are gained to examine Dug-outs.
On no account will dug-outs be used until passed as safe.

12. Watches will be synchronised at Bn.Battle H.Q. between 11 and 12 mid-night on Y day.

13. "Z" day and Zero hour will be notified.

14. MOVE.

   (a) The Battn.will parade at 7-0 p.m.in Coy.areas, ready to move at 7-15 p today.
   (b) DRESS. - "Fighting Order" with great coat round haversack.
   Each man will carry his complete ration for 27th. and filled water-bottle,170 rounds S.A.A. 2 Grenades in tunic pocket and 1 in haversack.
   N.C.O's will carry 1 "P" instead of grenades. 2 Verey Light pistols and Flares and full complement of wire cutters will be carried by Coys.
   (c) Coys move in following order:-
   "B" "D" "A" "C" Bn.H.Q.
   100 yds.distance to be maintained between Platoons.
   Route as on attached map.
   (d) Bn. less Bn.H.Q. will march to and assemble in Dug-out in Q.4.b.2.4.
   Assembly complete will be notified to Bn.H.Q. by Capt.ALLEN.
   (e) Hot tea and rum will be served to the troops about 3 a.m. 27th.
   (f) ASSEMBLY FOR ATTACK.
      At Zero ~~+~~ 100 minutes "C" Coy. followed by "A" will assemble along trench running N.and S. through Q.4.b. and K.34.d. between Bn. boundaries.
      At Zero plus 140 "D" Coy.followed by "B" will assemble in the 2 parallel trenches running E.and W. through Q.4.b.
   (g) ATTACK.
      "C" Coy.deploys on 4 Platoon frontage in 1 wave of 2 lines advances at Zero plus 180 keeping 150 yds. distance from "A" Bn. "leapfrog" Black Line and capture Red at Zero plus ~~234~~ 226
      "A" Coy.follow 2-0 yds.behind "C" Coy.in same formation "leapfrog" Black and Red and capture Brown Line at Zero plus ~~240~~ 246
      At Zero plus 210 "D" Coy advance from assembly positions on a 4 Platoon frontage in artillery formation "leapfrog" Black,Red,and Brown objectives and capture Yellow Line at Zero plus ~~300~~ 306
      "B" Coy.follow 200 yds. distance from "D" in same formation "leap-frogging" Black,Red,Brown,and Yellow lines and capture final objective Blue Line at Zero plus 356.
      Reconnoitering and protective patrols will be sent forward.

(h) The 2 drummers attached to each Coy.H.Q. will be sent back as guides to Bn.H.Q. at once when objectives are gained, they will report arrival to R.S.M.

(i) Advance Command Post will be about K.36.d. where UNSEEN Trench cuts sunken road.

(j) It is most important that direction is kept, each Platoon will be allotted a definite objective and compass bearing must be taken.
Flanks must be watched and protected.

15. SIGNALS.

The Signalling Officer will push forward the Signallers as soon as he possibly can.

16. MEDICAL ARRANGEMENTS.

The R.A.P. will be at Bn.H.Q. No. sound men except a S.B. will take wounded men to R.A.P.

17. Great-coats will be left under charge of a guard detailed by R.S.M.

18. PRISONERS.

Until Zero plus 360 no prisoners will be sent back. After this hour prisoners will be passed back from Coy. to Coy:.
Capt. ALLEN will be responsible for sending them under escort to collecting station at Q.10.a.4.6.

19. Detailed Administration Orders have been passed to all concerned.

20. Coys. will handshake on their right with the 1/8th.Lancs.Fus. at:-

   Q.6.a.2.5. (Sunken Road)
   Q.6.b.5.5. " "
   R.1.b.1.6. " "
   R.2.a.65.70.(Ridge trench.

21. Acknowledge.

 N.B. No.Telephonic Communication till Zero plus 180 Until this time telephones will not be connected up.

Copies to.-

1. C.O
2. "A"
3. "B"
4. "C"
5. "D"
6. T.O and Q.M
7. 127th.Inf.Bde.
8 and 9. "A" and "B" Bns.
10. War Diary.
11. File.

WAR DIARY
(CONFIDENTIAL)
OF
7th Bn. Manch. Rgt.

PERIOD

Oct. 1st to Oct 31st.
1918.

Volumn. 10.

MAPS - FRANCE
1:40.000
57C.
57B.

WAR DIARY of 7th Bn. The Manchester Regt.
or
INTELLIGENCE SUMMARY. October 1918.
(Erase heading not required.)

Army Form C. 2118.

Place	Date	Hour	Summary of Events and Information	Remarks and references to Appendices
	Oct 1st		Strength of Battalion. Officers 29 O.R. 704	
	2.		Battalion received cleaning and making out new. Capt. L.R.CREAGH proceeded to Senior Officers School Aldershot taken off the strength. Lieut. J. BARRATT from base Havre Training Commenced. Lewis Gun classes very necessary owing to numerous casualties amongst Lewis Gunners. Reorganisation troop per equipping attached to. Lt.& Lt. BARRATT assumed the duties of Adjutant.	
	3.		Training - including specialist classes. Lt. C. J. BRYAN from leave to England.	
	4.		Training - including Musketry on Range. Lt. Col. E. K. HANGER proceed on leave UK. Maj. G.B.L. RAE assumed Command of the Bn.	
	5.		Training as usual. Capt. F.G. BURY and Lt. C.B. DOUGLAS awarded the Military Cross 3 awards of D.C.M. 2nd Lt. H.V. SPREADBURY returned from LEBUCQUIERE. (Town Major).	
	6.		Church Parade. Reinforcement Training. Draft of 87 O.R. received. Mostly men of A.S.C. Remounts with only 14 to 16 weeks training - Coy Indents of 180 Rendezvous.	
	7.		Training. Reorganisation of platoons. New formations for attack practised with men of the draft. Draft shooting on the Range. Results not very satisfactory. Lt. ABBOTT (R.E.) Bn. moved forward in Bgd Group by March route to from RUYAULCOURT to Town Major of VILLERS PLOUCH. Bn. H.Q. at R24.d.4.0. During enemy bombing of the Bivouacs 2 men were killed and 3 wounded.	
	8.		Advance continued by march route to Bivouac area in LE GRAND PONT. Bn. H.Q. at H.33.d.25.30. Military Khel at CHENAUX WOOD M.16.a. Bn. Bivouaced in Sunken Road N.3.C. Bn. in same situation. No further Orders received to continue the advance. Modified training programme made out for tomorrow Bn. at Vilers notice to move	
	9.			
	10.			

MAPS FRANCE 1:20,000
57b. NW.SW.

Army Form C. 2118.

WAR DIARY
or
INTELLIGENCE SUMMARY.
(Erase heading not required.)

7th Bn. The Manchester Regt.

Place	Date	Hour	Summary of Events and Information	Remarks and references to Appendices
	11/10/18		Bn. in same position. Training during morning in open attack formation.	
	12/10/18		Bn in same position. Orders rec'd to move following morning. 2/Lt. W.R.INMAN-WRIGHT a. & M.F. BANKS joined the Bn. and take on the strength.	
	13/10/18		Bn. moved forward to Billets in BEAUVOIS en CAMBRESIS by march Route. Bn. Billets in the outskirts of the village in good accommodation.	
	14/10/18		Training recommenced. Musketry practice and open formation, Lewis Gun specialists classes formed.	
	15/10/18		Training continued. a/Major H.C.74th.	
	16/10/18		Training continued. (CAPT BRAITHWAITE, 2/Lts. McALESTER, Lieut STERN	M.M.I.
	17/10/18		Bn. Tactical Exercise as per a/b orders. Reg.tl. Reg. orders. Officers joined the Bn. & Lt. J. COOKSON, C.R.THORPE while 2/Lt. H.W. HARRIS, A.E. CARTWRIGHT, J.BREAKELL, H. RICHARDSON. and taken on the strength. Warning order rec'd to relieve 126th Inf Bde in L of Ctt to morrow.	
	18/10/18		Bn. moved up to HERPIGNY Farm arriving 5.15 p.m. 2/Lt. P.P. ILDERTON to U.K. on Leave.	
	19/10/18		Regt. order No. 36 issued to the Bn. to be pub in further advance of the Divn tomorrow. Bn. to be in Bn. support. Orders issued (No 74) at 3.0 pm to K Coop. left HERPIGNY Farm 11 pm to assemble position in Sunken Road through DRZA & C. Heavy shelling experienced but only 6 casualties. Hot meal provided before leaving. Entrained. Heavy barrage. 126th Inf Bde attacked under barrage and took its objective (Green Line). 127th Inf Bde replaced for their object after Bn. left the remainder of division. Bn. commenced the crossing of RIOM SELLE by the allotted bridge punctually at 5.40 am. Bn. Zero hour for the operation of the 127 Inf Bde. "D" Coy on Right were counter-attacked behind the Manch Regt. and "A" Coy on left behind 16 Manch Regt. B&C Coy in Reserve in Ravine at E20.a.15.95.	Mk.II 50.74
	20/10/18	2 am		

Maps. FRANCE 1:20000
57.3 N.E.

Army Form C. 2118.

WAR DIARY of 7th Bn. The Manchester Regt.
or
INTELLIGENCE SUMMARY.

(Erase heading not required.)

Place	Date	Hour	Summary of Events and Information	Remarks and references to Appendices
	20/10/18	8.40am	Message here head of at 7.15am by Capt BAKER was received, showing his Coy was located in Sunken road E.11.b. that he had returned to 2 officers and 30 O.R. and was very weak to establish a defensive flank in E.15.c.	
		8.45am	1 Platoon of "C" Coy under Mr RICHARDSON sent up to reinforce "D" Coy.	
		9am	15 Manch Regt reported situation on this front very obscure, but Capt BAKER had reported that 2 Platoons Coys approximately at this objective about MAROU. Nothing known of the other 2 coys but Casualties reported very severe. During this information "C" Coy was sent forward under command of Lt GRESTY M.C. was next found forward of Capt BAKER in forming the Defensive flank. The Right Division were reported to have been hung up at the Green line. Thus rendering the Right flank of the 7th Regt Bn unprotected. Attack by No Manch Regt reported to be succeeding on the Left flank.	
		11.45am	Lt DOUGLAS M.C. O.C. "A" Coy, where coy was now located, had reached their objective situation in E.8.f. "A" Coy reported the 11th Manch also in touch with 62nd Div on the left. Capt BAKER reported enemy collecting by double in E.16.a in Right Divl front, obviously for counter attack on our exposed flank. Priority telegram sent	
		11.53am	6/727 Lt Bell asking for Artillery assistance forward up the concentration.	
		2.10pm	Wire sent 6/727 Lt Bell that the enemy were moving from 3 or 4 high ground in E.10.c.d. on E.16.a. Very shortly afterwards our Guns put down an intense barrage on E.16.a. which lasted for half an hour. This intensely heavy bombardment the hostile enemy counter attack	
		4.0pm	The Right Division attacked and took Henin in E.22.a and E.15.b. Another barrage "C" Coy was instructed to exploit success and gain the spur in E.15.k. and establish	

(A8-04) WS W4771/M2031 750,000 5/17 Sch. 52 Forms/C2118/14

Maps FRANCE 1:20000
57.B N.E.

WAR DIARY of 7/7th Manchester Regt.
or
INTELLIGENCE SUMMARY

Army Form C. 2118.

Place	Date	Hour	Summary of Events and Information	Remarks and references to Appendices
	20/10/18		Outpost Positions. In conjunction with the movement "B" Coy under Capt F.G.BORN M.C. were ordered to occupy the outpost Road in E.14.a. Information received that 5th Div were on "C" ridge and he was in touch with them and had taken up an outpost position as ordered.	
	21/10/18	1·0 am	The Bn was organised in a defensive position in depth in the following localities:– "C" coy outpost in E.15.b. - "B" coy in E.15.a. 8.6. – "D" coy about E.15 cent. "A" coy moving from left flank of Bde to Sunken Road about E.15.b.3.6. to Cross roads E.15.d.8.2.	
		3·0 am	All coys reported in position successfully before dawn. Bn H.Q. moved up to Sunken Road E.14.a.4.1.	
		7·0 am	Orders received from 127 Inf Bde to push out contact patrols to gain touch with and locate the enemy. Hourly reports to be sent in.	
		10·30 am	Lt GRESTY M.C. reports that enemy was holding GRAND CHAMP ridge with M.Guns. Capt F.G.BORN M.C. reported that his patrol was fired upon at E.9.d.6.2. by M.Guns from GRAND CHAMP Ridge. Enemy also located 15 foot about E.16.c.2.8. and also showing keen on top of ridge in E.10 cent.	
		12 noon	During the whole of the operations of Oct 20th and 21st enemy artillery activity was extremely heavy, both with gas and H.E. The ground was sodden and very difficult to move over as on the night 19/20.10.08 and throughout 20th Oct. Here was very heavy rain. Enemy machine guns were very active throughout the day on 20th Oct only ceasing on the night Oct. The German Division opposed to this Div fought with great tenacity, supported by large numbers of M/Guns and unusually heavy artillery. Identification proved the enemy (to be the 238th Division (Infantrie Bodz guards). Communication and Medicine arrangements were quite satisfactory.	
		7·30 pm	Bn. relieved by the 1/7 Lancs Fus. and proceeded by march route to ROLLE at HERAGNY Farm.	

Army Form C. 2118.

WAR DIARY of 7th Bn. The Manchester Regt.
INTELLIGENCE SUMMARY

(Erase heading not required.)

Maps. FRANCE. 1:40000
578.

Place	Date	Hour	Summary of Events and Information	Remarks and references to Appendices
BEAUVOIS	22/10/18		Bn. moved to billets in BEAUVOIS at 2-30 p.m. Bn. Hd. at Bn. Hd. at planned Command. 2/Lt. E.V. MANGER returns from leave in U.K. and assumed Command.	
	23/10/18		Bn. cleaning up. Baths. Foot treatment. Men at weaker than condition and is want of a lot of attention.	
	24/10/18		Training Commenced - principally Musketry and Tactical formations. Men of recent draft & poor shooting classification put through special instruction. Battle Surplus rejoined the Bn. Capt & Qm H. WOODS joined the Bn. and taken on the strength.	
	25/10/18		Training continued. Capt. D. NORBURY joined the Bn. and taken on the strength.	
	26/10/18		Training continued.	
	27/10/18		Bn. on Bde. parade for presentation of Medal Ribbons by Div'l. Commander. Award of Military Crosses as follows announced:- Lt. M. GRESTY M.C.(Bar.) Lt. S.J. WILSON. 2/Lts. J.A. MILNE. J.R. SIDDAL. Lt. M. GRESTY and 2/Lt. M.C. WILSON to Paris on leave.	
	28/10/18		Training Continued.	
	29/10/18		Bn. Tactical Route march.	
	30/10/18		Field firing exercise carried out. Capt. F.G. BURN M.C. evacuated to 2/5th Bn. Lancs Fus. as 2nd in Command.	
	31/10/18		Training continued. Capt. D. NORBURY assumed command of "A" Coy. Capt. BRAITHWAITE assumed Command of "B" Coy.	

E.A. Munger Lieut-Colonel.
Commanding 7th Bn. The Manchester Regt.

SECRET   Appendix I

                    7th Battalion Manchester Regiment.   Copy No ..7..
                        OPERATION ORDER No. 10.
In the field,
   16.10.18.
Ref. Sheet 57 B.N.W.

INFORMATION.   An enemy rearguard is holding LIGNY en CAMBRÉSIS and HAUCOURT.
                Prisoners state he is preparing to retire a considerable
                distance, but that he has two Battalions Prussian Guards
                billeted at BEULLANY whose duty would be probably to deliver an
                immediate counter-attack to delay our troops.

INTENTION.   The 127th Inf. Bde., will advance from LE CATEAU – CAMBRAI ROAD
                and capture the high ground in I 14 c and d and I 20 a and b,
                and also in I 15 b c and d and exploit success as far as I 26 d
                and I 32 d, also in I 31 b and I 31 d where localities will be
                established.
                The 125th Inf. Bde., will advance on the EAST and 4th Inf. Bde.,
                on the WEST.

INSTRUCTIONS. (1) The 7th Battalion Manchester Regiment will be the leading
                  Battalion.
BOUNDARIES.   (2) Brigade boundary grid line between I 2 square and I 3
                  square running due SOUTH, and grid line between H 1 2 square
                  and 517 square running due SOUTH.
COMPANY   (3) "A" Company will capture high ground in I 20 a and b.
OBJECTIVES.   "D" Company will capture high ground in I 14 c and d. I.196 c
                  "B" Company will leapfrog through A Company and exploit
                      success to I 26 d and I 32 D where localities will be
                      established.
                  "C" Company will leapfrog through "D" Company and exploit
                      success to I 31 b and I 31 d forming a defensive flank
                      facing HAUCOURT.
ASSEMBLY.   (4) "A" and "B" Coys, at I 2 c 8,6
                  "C" and "D" Coys, at I 2 c 1,6
FORMATIONS & (5) The advance will begin in artillery formation of Coys with
DEPLOYMENT.   leading Coys. 500 yds. ahead of rear Coys.
                  Coys, will deploy into artillery formations by sections just
                  previous to reaching road running through I 7 a and b, and
                  I 8 c and d.
SCOUTS.   (6) With the exception of the Scout Sergeant and one Scout
                  remaining with Bn. H.Q., all Battalion Scouts will proceed with
                  their Companies.
ARMS.   (7) BATTLE ORDER, LEWIS GUNS WILL BE CARRIED.
SIGNALLING.   (8) This will be exclusively by visual.
B.H.Q.   (9) At I 2 c 9,4 and later about 400 yds. behind rear attacking
                  Company on left – White signalling flag will be kept hoisted
                  to shew position.
R.A.P.   (10) On Main Road at I 2 central.
RATIONS.   (11) Iron Rations only will be carried. Full waterbottles.
ZERO HOUR.   (12) 0900/17 Oct 18

Issued at 8.0.pm. by runner. 16.10.18.
Copy No 1 C.O.
  " "   2 A Coy.
  " "   3 B   "
  " "   4 C   "
  " "   5 D   "
  " "   6 Signalling Officer.   W H Barrett
  " "   7 Filed.
                                                   Capt & Adjt.
                                              7th Manchester Regiment.

Copy No. 10

7th. Bn. Manchester Regiment.
OPERATION ORDER NO. 74.

SECRET.

Appendix II

Maps : 1/20,000 57 B. N.E.   51 A. S.E.

INFORMATION :

(1) The 42nd. Division is continuing the advance on 20th. Oct. 1918.
The 62nd. Division will attack on the North and the 5th. Division on the South.

(2) Distinguishing Marks of Flank Divisions :
13th. Brigade 5th. Division will wear a white tape over the left shoulder under the right arm.
95th. Brigade will wear a white tape tied on the left shoulder strap.
62nd. Division will wear a white band on the left arm.

INTENTION :

(1) 126th. Inf. Brigade will lead the attack and will take and consolidate the line of the Sunken Road in E.14.a. and c. and E.20.b. ("B" Ridge)

(2) The 127th. Inf. Brigade will then pass through 126th Inf. Bde. and consolidate the following line -
Spur in E. 15.b. and E.9.d. - Hamlet of MAROU - Sunken Road in E.3.b. and d. with the high ground about the Cross Roads in E.3.b.

1. INSTRUCTIONS :

The 1/5th. Manch. Regt. will attack on the Right.
The 1/6th. Manch. Regt. will attack on the Left.
The 1/7th. Manch. Regt. will be in Support.

The leading wave of the 5th. Division on our right will be echeloned slightly in advance of the 1/5th. Manch. Regt.
Leading troops of 62nd. Division are timed to start in line with 1/6th. Manch. Regt.

2. ASSEMBLY POSITIONS :

The 1/5th. Manch. Regt. D.29.b. (127th. L.T.M.B also)
The 1/6th. Manch. Regt. D.17.c. ("B" 42nd. M.G.Bn lso)
The 1/7th. Manch. Regt. D.22.c.

3. BRIDGES :

Coys. of the 1/7th. Manch. Regt. are allotted bridges across the river SELLE Nos. 1 to 12.
No Coy. will cross the river until Zero plus 220.
Coys. have this day reconnoitred bridges by which they propose to cross.
"A" followed by "B" Coy. will commence crossing at Zero plus 220.
"D" followed by "C" Coy. will commence crossing at Zero plus 220.
Distance :- 100 yards between Platoons, 500 yards between Coys.

4. DEPLOYMENT :

After crossing the river and before arriving at the BELLE VUE - SOLESMES Road Coys. will "shake out" into Artillery Formation.
"A" Coy. will move at a distance of at least 500 yds. behind the 1/6th. Manch. Regt. followed by "B" Coy. echeloned 300 yds. to the South and at a distance of 500 yds.
"D" Coy. will move at a distance of at least 500 yds. behind the 1/5th. Manch. Regt. followed by "C" Coy. echeloned 250 yds. to the North and at a distance of 500 yds.

Sheet 2.

5. BOUNDARIES :   Boundaries have been marked on the maps of all Coy. and
Platoon Commanders.

6. BOUNDS :   Lines at which leading troops arrive at and leave
their successive lines are as per attached time table.

7. BATTALION   Battalion H.Q. will cross the river after the rear
H.Q.   Coys. and will be established in Sunken Road at approx.
E.20.a.4.7. where all Coys. will report where they are
situated after crossing the river and if in touch with leading
Battalions and each other. They will eventually move forward
in rear of the Support Coys.

8. ADVANCE :   When the leading Battalions of the Brigade move across
"B" Ridge "A" Coy. and "D" Coy. will follow 1/6th. Manch.
and 1/5th. Manch. Regt. respectively at a distance of 500 yds.
and open out in Artillery Formation of Sections before crossing
the Ridge. These Coys. will be responsible for mopping up
any of the enemy that may be left in the Sunken Roads etc.
behind the leading Battalions.
"B" & "C" Coys. will keep touch with "A" & "D" Coys.
respectively but will not move forward over "B" Ridge until
instructions are received from Bn. H.Q.
(N.B. It appears from recent information, Road running
through E.15.c. - E.14.b. and E.8.c. is a Sunken Road and
not as shown on maps 57 B. N.E.)

9. OBJECTIVES
 OF   The localities to be captured and held by the leading
 BRIGADE :   Battalions of the Brigade are shown on maps already
issued to Coys. as also the localities where "D" & "A" Coy.
are to form Defensive Flanks for the protection of the two
leading Battalions.
"B" & "C" Coys. will be held in reserve and will
probably be sent to localities indicated on the maps issued.

10. MACHINE   Two Coys. of the 42nd. M.G. Battalion will be in
 GUNS :position on Ridge E.14 and will support the advance of the Brigade
In addition "B" Coy. 42nd. M.G. Bn. will advance behind the
Infantry and act with 1/6th. Manch. Regt. for the final
consolidation.

11. TRENCH
 MORTARS :   Two Mortars and 80 rounds of ammunition are being
sent forward to assist the advance of the leading Battalions.

12. COMMUNICATION :
A Brigade Forward Report Centre will be established in
E.14.d. The Battalion Signalling Officer will endeavour to
establish a Battalion Forward Report Centre at E.8.d.7.0. in
the Sunken Road. Messages will be sent to the Forward
Report Centre.

13. MEDICAL :   The Medical Officer will establish a R.A. & D.S. in
Sunken Road E.20.a.

Sheet 3.

14. **RATIONS AND WATER** : All water bottles will be filled before leaving camp and men warned to use the water as sparingly as possible to last them until the night of 20/21st. Oct.
    Iron Rations and the unexpended portion of the ration for 0th. Oct. will be carried on the man.
    Hot Tea and Rum will be issued in the Assembly Position about 0300 on the 20th.

15. **S.A.A. BOMBS ETC** : 120 Rounds S.A.A. and an extra 50 rounds in Bandolier will be carried on the man.
    16 filled Magazines per Gun will be taken by all Lewis Gun Teams.
    Each Coy. will take the following :-

    No. 36 Rifle Grenades..................36.
    S.O.S. Grenades........................6.
    Ground. Flares........................48.
    Very P.A. 1" White....................24.
    Shovels...............................20.

16. **DRESS :-** Battle Order including the Blanket.

17. **ZERO HOUR :** 0200 Hours, 20th. Oct. 1918.

18. **ACKNOWLEDGE.**

                                    W H Barratt
                                    Capt. & Adjutant
                                    7th. Bn. Manchester Regt.

Copies to :-

 (1)...........C.O.
 (2)..........."A" Coy.
 (3)..........."B" Coy.
 (4)..........."C" Coy.
 (5)..........."D" Coy.
 (6)...........T.O.
 (7)...........Q.M.
 (8)...........M.O.
 (9)...........S.O.
✓(10)
 (11).........War Diary.
 (12).........File.

Operation Order No. 74.
....

TIME TABLE.
....

1. 5th. and 6th. Manchesters arrive Sunken Road the first objective at plus 310   7-10 a.m.

2. 5th. and 6th. leave Sunken Road at plus 325   7-25 a.m.

3. 5th. reach "C" Ridge Spur at plus 360   8-0 a.m.

4. 5th. and 6th. reach BEARD BROOK at plus 360   8-0 a.m.

5. MAROU is assaulted at plus 370   8-10 a.m.

6. 5th. and 6th. leave MAROU at plus 390   8-30 a.m.

7. 5th. and 6th. assault last objective at plus 430   9-12 a.m.

8. 5th. and 6th. arrive at last objective at plus 442   9-22 a.m.

NOTE :-   5th. last objective is in valley V astride the Sunken Road.
6th. last objective is Cross Roads E.3.b.

Contact Aeroplanes will call for Flares at :-

    0830.
    1030.
and at other hours as required.

M H Barratt

19th. October 1918.

Captain & Adjutant
7th. Bn. Manchester Regiment.

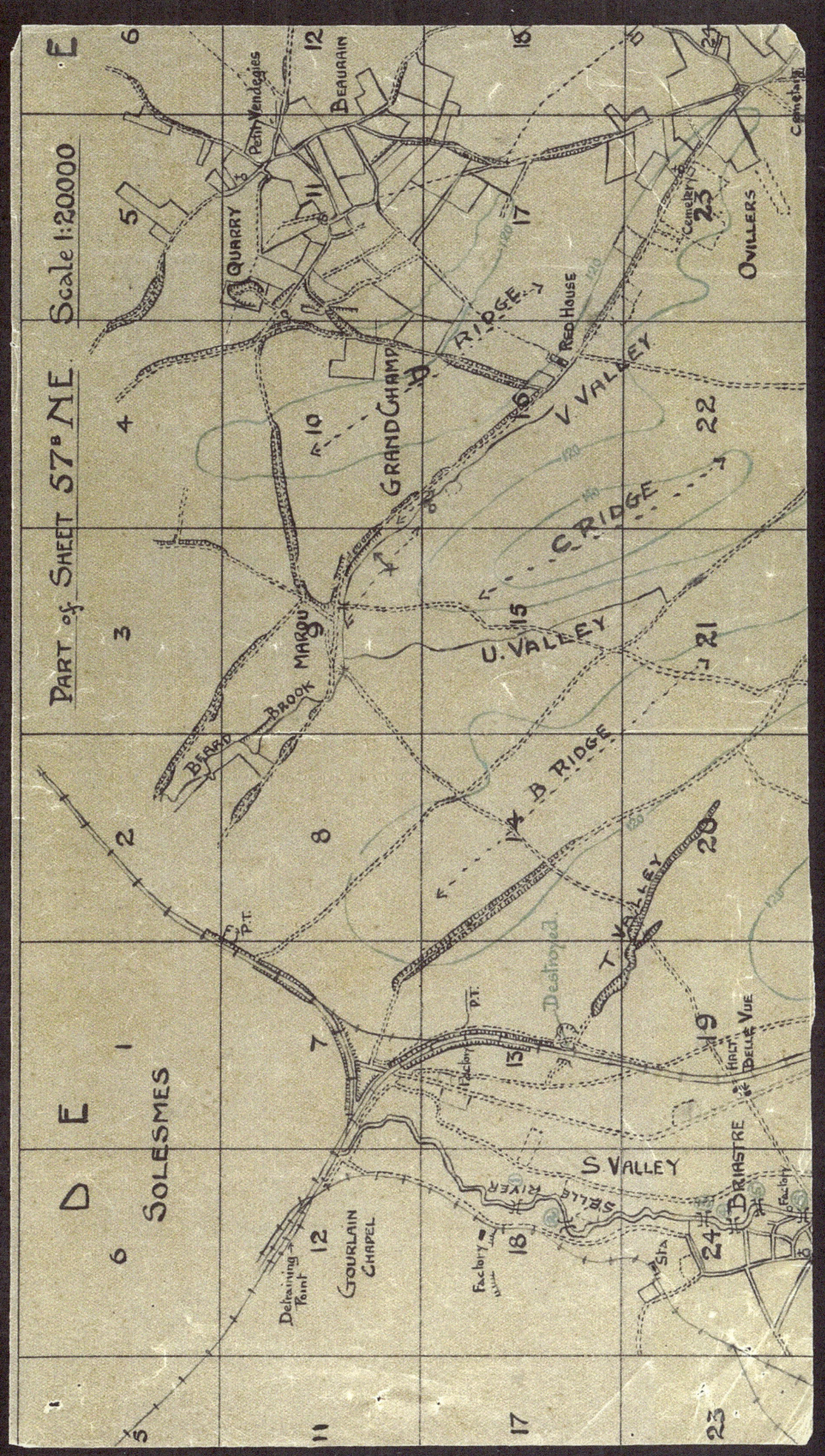

NOTES ON OPERATIONS.

During the two day's operations, the fighting was continuous and severe every type of Infantry weapon being used. The enemy was very thick on ground chosen by himself and carefully prepared for defence, i.e. the thickly wired HINDENBURG LINE. The troops fought their way forward to a depth of 5,000 yards through this HINDENBURG SYSTEM. It was a soldiers' battle which necesitated initiative, resourse, determination, and endurance on the part of subordinates leaders and men. All these qualities were displayed by all Units of the Division. The resistance offered by the enemy M.G's. was particularly stubborn, they unlike his Infantry, invariably fought until they were killed. After the enemy M.Gunners had been put out of action the Infantry resistance in most cases weakened and prisoners wre taken. The nature of the fighting can be gauged by the fact that on the ground covered by first 1,500 yards of the attack, on a front of 2,500 yards, over 350 enemy dead were afterwards buried, and 1,015 prisoners and numerous M.G's were taken. Two strong enemy counter attacks were repulsed on Divisional front during 27th. September.

The tanks of "C" Coy. 11th. Bn. Tank Corps were of great assistance in overcoming the resistance of M.G. nests. Tank K.42, commanded by 2/Lt. T.C.WILSON, was handled with great skill and dash and accounted for many enemy M.G.Nests.

The work of the Artillery continued to be excellent and the rapidity with which Batteries moved into action in new advanced positions were remarkable.

On the only occasion Cavalry were used they were well handled and reached their objective on WELSH RIDGE.

The Guns of the 42nd. Bn. M.G. Corps were boldly and skilfully handled. In some cases they advanced with leading Infantry, and during the whole operations were most successful in overcoming the enemy resistance and in co-operating with the Infantry.

In the course of these two days operations, 42nd. Division captured 24 Officers and 1,588 other ranks (from 5 different enemy Divisions) one 4.2." How., six 77 m.m. guns, 70 Light M.G's., 22 Heavy M.G.'s., and a considerable quantity of other war material.

Casualties were as follows :-

Officers.			Other ranks.		
Killed.	Wounded.	Missing.	Killed.	Wounded.	Missing.
12.	33.	-.	179.	781.	93.

4th. Oct. 1918.

(Sd) A. SOLLY-FLOOD.
Major-General,
Commanding 42nd. Division.

42nd. (EAST LANCASHIRE) DIVISION.

SUMMARY OF OPERATIONS.

21st. to 28th. September 1918.

1. After a fortnight in Corps Reserve in the THILLOY - FYS Area, 42nd. Division relieved 37th. Division in the left sector of the IV Corps Front on the night 21st/22nd. September.

The front held was of 2,500 yards and comprised part of the HINDENBURGE SYSTEM of trenches immediately S. of HAVRINCOURT, and the defences of the village of TRESCAULT. 126th. Inf. Brigade was leading Brigade with all three Battalions in the front line. 127th. Inf. Brigade, less one Battalion was in support near RUYAULCOURT with one Battalion attached to 126th. Inf. Brigade holding the Divisional Main Line of Resistance on the E. edge of HAVRINCOURT WOOD. 125th. Inf. Brigade was in reserve in the LABUCQUIERE - BEUGNY Area.

From 22nd. to 26th. September there was no event of importance to report on the Divisional Front, except for the very heavy gassing of HAVRINCOURT Wood on the night of 21st/22nd. Sept. about 2,000 to 3,000 Yellow Cross Gas Shells being used.

Active patrolling was carried out, resulting in the capturing capture of a few prisoners, and the material improvement of our positions in front of BILHEM FARM. The enemy was very active on all back areas with H.V. Guns.

2. Supported by 6 Brigades R.F.A. and one Brigade H.A. the enemy was attacked on the morning of 27th. September, the 125th. Inf. Brigade being on the right and 127th. Inf. Brigade on the Left. 126th. Inf. Brigade was withdrawn on the night 26th/27th. Sept. the front of the Division being covered by three outpost companies of this Brigade. Although presenting considerable difficulties owing to the attack of the Division not coinciding with the main attack further north, the assembly was successfully carried out.

The attack of the 125th. Inf. Brigade took place at 7-52 a.m., and the 127th. Inf. Brigade at 8-20 a.m., both some two hours later than the Third Division on our Left.

The attack was preceded by an intense Artillery and T.M. Bombardment lasting 10 minutes and Infantry advanced under a creeping barrage which lifted at the rate of 100 yards in 4 minutes.

"C" Coy. 11 Battalion Tank Corps co-operated in the attack. Out of the 8 Tanks allotted to the Division 2 were placed under orders of right Brigade and 6 of Left Brigade.

2 of the 8 Tanks failed to start owing to breakdown and one tank was put out of action by enemy shell fire before reaching first objective. The other tanks were of considerable assistance in overcoming the resistance of enemy M.G. Nests.

The attack of the 127th. Inf. Brigade progressed favourably - the BROWN LINE - vide attached map - being reached in scheduled time. 125th. Inf. Brigade, however, met with considerable resistance in the neighbourhood of BEAUCAMP and could not get further than the RED DOTTED LINE owing to Hostile Machine Gun Fire from that village. The line of BOAR COPSE VALLEY was reached at 1-0 pm.

The fact of the 125th. Inf. Brigade not being able to advance left 127th. Inf. Brigade with an exposed right flank: 7th. Bn. Manchester Regt. on the right having many casualties from enfilade M.G. Fire from neighbourhood of VILLAGE TRENCH and the north west slopes of HIGHLAND RIDGE. 127th. Inf. Brigade had kept in touch with 62nd. Division on the N. who had passed through 3rd. Division.

WAR DIARY
(Confidential)
OF
7th Bn. Manch. Regt.

PERIOD

Nov. 1st to Nov 30th 1918.

Volumn 11.

Maps 1:40000 57b. 51a. 51.

WAR DIARY of 7th Bn. The Manchester Regt.
or INTELLIGENCE SUMMARY.   November 1918.

Army Form C. 2118.

(Erase heading not required.)

Place	Date	Hour	Summary of Events and Information	Remarks and references to Appendices
BEAUVOIS.	1/11/18.		Training Continued. Strength of Bn. Total Strength. Officers. Other ranks. 39 748	M32
	2/11/18.		Training. 21 608	M32
	3/11/18.		Tactical route march including practice in wood fighting formations.	M32
			Orders received to move to MESLY. Move complete 11p.m. Bn. in billets. 2/Lieut T.LEVER joined.	M32 M32
	4/11/18.		Returned from II Corps School.	M32
	5/11/18.		Move continued to billets in PONT A PIERRE.	M32
			Move continued to billets in HERBIGNIES (Sheet 51). Lt A.DAVIES joined the Bn. and	M32
‡‡ A130	6/11/18.		took on the strength.	
			Bn. did a turning mvt. to N.Bank of RUISSEAU du PONT of I26 S.E. Rd. to FORET DE NORMAL to Roumigny T3f and N.35. a & c.E. Very heavy driving rain all day. Bn. bivouacked	M32 M32
LE CARNOY.	7/11/18.		Roumigny and Bivouaced through T3f and Division Reserve ntl billets at 6pm. Billets LE CARNOY. N19a.	M32 M32
VIEUX MESNIL	8/11/18.		Bn. Battalion moving by march route to VIEUX MESNIL (O2&d) into billets. Move completed by 16.00	M32
	9/11/18.		Day spent in cleaning up billets & equipment. Lieut W.GREESTY & 2/Lt M.C.WILSON	M32
			Arrived from PARIS/SEINE.	
	10/11/18.		Bathing & foot treatment carried out in billets area. Five companies detailed as	M32
			relief to working parties on bridge at HAUTMONT (P23 c 53)	
	11/11/18.		Telephone message received this morning at 0900 that hostilities will cease at 11.00	M32
			today. On the march of the signing of an armistice. The Bn. paraded in front of the Church at VIEUX MESNIL where the Band carried in a "Cease fire" followed by "No Parade".	
	12/11/18.		2 Coys companies securing tanks or bridge at HAUTMONT. Remainder taking	M32
			& preparing for an early move.	

Ref. Sub. 51.
40.000

Instructions regarding War Diaries and Intelligence Summaries are contained in F. S. Regs., Part II. and the Staff Manual respectively. Title pages will be prepared in manuscript.

Army Form C. 2118.

WAR DIARY of 7th Bn THE MANCHESTER REGT
or
INTELLIGENCE SUMMARY.
(Erase heading not required.)

November 1918

Place	Date	Hour	Summary of Events and Information	Remarks and references to Appendices
HAUTMONT	13/11/18		The battalion marched into billets in HAUTMONT (P29 d) move completed by noon. Lieut T.P. WILKINSON rejoined from PARIS Leave.	
"	14/11/18		The morning spent in cleaning up (i) Personnel (ii) Billets. Afternoon devoted to recreational training.	
	15/11/18		Coy Commanders Inspection. Steady Drill. Inspection by the Commanding Officer. 2/Lt W.B. SMITH rejoined the Bn from PARIS Leave.	
	16/11/18		Stairs Drill. Equipment fitting. Inspection. Divine Service to precede arrival of Captain & Group K the town of HAUTMONT. R represented by 1 Coy. 2/Lt W.F. BANKS rejt from Corps Gas School. Divine Service. Lt. H.S. STERN from G.H.Q. Lewis Gun School.	
	17/11/18		Route March in full marching order 8 mile.	
	18/11/18		Section & Platoon Company Drill. N.C.O.'s School commenced. 2/Lt W.C.WILSON appointed Employment Officer	
	19/11/18		Capt J. BAKER appointed Education Officer for the Bn. Route March in full marching order. 10 miles. Capt. SERGEANT RAMC (T.C.) taken on attached strength as Medical Officer vice Capt M.E. DELAFIELD rett to Field Ambce.	
	20/11/18		The Coy on Range. 200 yds practice. Remainder Platoon Company drill.	
	21/11/18		Kit Inspection by Coy Commanders. Commanding Officer.	
	22/11/18		Bgde Route March. Full marching Order. N. Transport. (8mile) Divine Service. Lt J.G. EVANS appointed Asst Transport Officer of 127 I.L.f Bde. Inoculation T.A.B.	
	23/11/18		by the M.O.	
	24/11/18			
	25/11/18		Coy training indoors owing to wet weather.	
	26/11/18		Parties musketry & electrical training. One company firing practice on the range.	

WAR DIARY of 7th Bn. THE MANCHESTER REGT
or
INTELLIGENCE SUMMARY. November 1918

Army Form C. 2118.

Place	Date	Hour	Summary of Events and Information	Remarks and references to Appendices
HAUTMONT	27.11.18		Companies at the Plateral & Company commanders. Cadre. Baker rejoined from III Army L.G. Course. Lieut. V.G. Smithies rejoined from Paris Leave. The following Officers reported for duty, were taken on strength. 2nd Lt. J.G. LUCAS; F.W. PALMER; W.R. HOPNER; F.C. CURREY, F. HARGREAVES; S.W. POLLINGTON. Capt. C. NORBURY rejoined from 1st Royal Scots Fus. (Intelligence Officer)	L. L. L.
	28.11.18		Bathing; Platoon practice and specialist training. Capt. S.J. WILSON MC. and 2 Lt. J.H. MILNE MC Reported for leave to PARIS.	L.
	29.11.18		Company drills 2 Companies; 2 Companies firing practice on range.	
	30.11.18		Battalion took part in Brigade route march, about 12 miles. Full marching order. Midday meal on the march.	L.
			Casualties for November NIL	
			Strength of Battalion 30.11.18 = 39 Officers 869 other ranks.	

E A Murray
Lieut Colonel
Commanding 7th Bn. The Manchester Regt

WAR DIARY.
(CONFIDENTIAL)
OF
4th Bn. MANCH. REGT.

Period: Dec. 1st to 31st 1918

Volume 12.

WAR DIARY or INTELLIGENCE SUMMARY.

Army Form C. 2118.

of 1/7th Bn THE MANCHESTER REGT

DECEMBER 1918

Place	Date	Hour	Summary of Events and Information	Remarks and references to Appendices
HAUTMONT	1.12.18		The Division were inspected on the MAUBEUGE – AVESNES Road at about 9pm R70 a 9c. by Oen. THE KING. The troops were lined up on either side of the road when His Majesty was conducted between the lines by the C.O. Lt Col E.V. MANGER (O.L.I.), being the senior officer present in the Division. The whole battalion were working on a systematic salvage scheme. A Coy cleared square P24; B Coy P29; C Coy P22; D Coy P23. CSM/Sgt S.J. & L/Sgt taken by 2nd Lieut C. Norbury (all 12:10 to 368) admitted to hospital. Part of 77 Bn entered Bay	S/S
"	2.12.18			S/S
"	3.12.18		Salvage scheme continued. A Coy cleared square P28; B Coy P30; C Coy 9.19; D Coy P25. Draft of 77 O.R. arrived today.	S/S
"	4.12.18		Two companies continued salvage work + two companies on range. Capt D. NORBURY and Lieut C.B. DOUGLAS M.C. left for Paris leave.	S/S
"	5.12.18		Two companies on range and 2 companies on salvage. Elementary education work started in the battalion. Amount of salvage collected valued at £1628.0.0. Recreational training in the afternoon.	S/S
"	6.12.18		Barking and training by companies also elementary educational training. Recreations in the afternoon. Lieut C.E. THORPE to 2nd Dec H.Q. for Traffic Control duties.	S/S
"	7.12.18		Inspection of kit, barrack rooms etc.	S/S
"	8.12.18		Church parades in the Drill Shed.	S/S
"	9.12.18		The day being wet, companies were at the proposal of company commanders for training. After Paris leave is inspected on parade by the C.O. in the square at HAUTMONT. Guard of 24 O.R. Service forward to HANUR area for duty.	S/S
"	10.12.18		Brigade route march. F.S.M.O. About 9 miles. Day wet. Recreational training in the afternoon.	S/S
"	11.12.18		Cleaning up. Inspection of barrack rooms & equipment by Commanding Officer. Educational training still in progress. Lieut L. PELL ILDERTON left battalion to report to 119th Railway Coy. R.E. at ROISEL for duty. Church of England of 2 wings of Battalion.	S/S

By VALENCIENNES 1/100.000
NAMUR 1/100.000

Army Form C. 2118.

Instructions regarding War Diaries and Intelligence
Summaries are contained in F.S. Regs., Part II.
and the Staff Manual respectively. Title pages
will be prepared in manuscript.

WAR DIARY 7th Bn. The MANCHESTER REGT.
INTELLIGENCE SUMMARY.
December 1918

(Erase heading not required.)

Place	Date	Hour	Summary of Events and Information	Remarks and references to Appendices
HAUTMONT	12.12.18		Companies training under Coy. Commanders. Elementary Education classes.	
	13.12.18		Preparing for move tomorrow. Fatigues, cooking etc.	
	14.12.18		The battalion moved with 127th Inf. Bde group by march route to ASSEVENT. being in billets for the night.	
ASSEVENT	15.12.18		Moved by march route into billets at MERBES STE MARIE	
MERBES, STE MARIE	16.12.18		Move continued to LEVAL TRAHEGNIES where the battalion was accommodated in billets.	
LEVAL TRAHEGNIES	17.12.18		Halt for the day at LEVAL TRAHEGNIES. Capt. W.H. BARRATT and LIEUT. W. GREGSTY left with colour party to proceed to ENGLAND to bring out Colours. LIEUT. C.B. DOUGLAS returned from PARIS	
	18.12.18		Move continued to-day to MARCHIENNE au PONT where the night was spent in billets.	
	19.12.18		Move to FLEURUS completed. Battalion accommodated in billets.	
FLEURUS	20.12.18 to 23.12.18		All companies munching or firing up of conferences, canteens, making tables etc. for men's messes. Organising billets etc.	
	24.12.18		Bathing and decorating mess Rooms. 2/Lt MILNE proceeded as conducting officer to containing Leave parties.	
	25.12.18		Xmas parades today. All companies had Xmas dinner today.	
	26.12.18		Battalion route march in fighting order, about 10 kilometres. Very wet day.	
	27.12.18		Simple tactical exercise, educational training etc.	
	28.12.18		Weekly inspection of billets, equipment by commanding officer. Recreation in the afternoon.	
	29.12.18		Church Parade.	
	30.12.18 31.12.18		Companies occupied in platoon training, bathing, recreation etc.	

E.F. Mergat Lt Col
Comdg. 1/7th Bn. Manchester Regt

WAR DIARY
or
INTELLIGENCE SUMMARY.
(Erase heading not required.)

Army Form C. 2118.

1-7 Man 42

Instructions regarding War Diaries and Intelligence Summaries are contained in F.S. Regs., Part II. and the Staff Manual respectively. Title pages will be prepared in manuscript.

Place	Date	Hour	Summary of Events and Information	Remarks and references to Appendices
FLEURUS.	1/1/19.		Education in the school. History, reading & writing, Arithmetic, Geography. No.1090. R.S.M. W. ANLEZARK. mentioned in despatches.	Hrs. appx.
	2/1/19.		The day was devoted to training. Guard mounting. Physical drill &c. Education. Capt. Poker proceeded to England for leave & demobilisation. Lt. SMITHES took command of "D" Coy. Lt. W.B. SMITH took over the duties of Adjutant.	Hrs. Hrs.
	3/1/19.		Capt. T.R. CREAGH having returned the Bn. from Senior Offrs School, Aldershot is taken on the strength and assumes the duties of 2nd in Command. Major. C.B.L. PAE to hospital dated 12/11/18.	Hrs. Hrs. Hrs. Hrs.
	4/1/19.		Capt. D. NORBURY. Arrived from Hospice, PARIS. NEW YEARS DESPATCH.	Hrs.
	5/1/19.		Training during the day. Church Service in the CINEMA. Fleurus.	
	6/1/19.		The day was devoted to Education & Baths.	
	7/1/19.		Training. Officers monthly Mess meeting. Football match with the Machine Gunners at VELAINE. 7/Lt. Col. E.V. MANGER to be Brevet Lt Colonel.	
	8/1/19.		Education. Bn. for duty.	
	9/1/19.		Training. Rugby Football match with Machine Gunners. "B" Coy. medical inspection.	
	10/1/19.		Capt. W.H. BARRATT. & Lt. W. GRESTY. return from ENGLAND with colours & colour party. 1 Platoon per coy. acted as Colour escort under Capt. S.T. WILSON & one officer from each Coy. The Bn. lined the sheets of FLEURUS. 2nd/Lt. T. LEVER. to U.K. for leave & demobilisation. a/Capt. T. BAKER. to awarded the MILITARY CROSS.	Hrs.
	11/1/19.		Training. Platoon training & recreational training.	Hrs.
	12/1/19.		The following Officers & O.Rs proceeded to England for DEMOBILISATION:-	Hrs.
			A/CAPT. W.H. BARRATT.	
			CAPT. R.N. BRANTHWAITE.	
			" D. NORBURY.	
			LT. C.B. DOUGLAS.	
			2nd/Lt. A.E. CARTWRIGHT.	
			" A. DAVIES.	
			41. O.Rs.	

Army Form C. 2118.

WAR DIARY
or
INTELLIGENCE SUMMARY.
(Erase heading not required.)

Instructions regarding War Diaries and Intelligence Summaries are contained in F. S. Regs., Part II. and the Staff Manual respectively. Title pages will be prepared in manuscript.

Place	Date	Hour	Summary of Events and Information	Remarks and references to Appendices
FLEURUS	12/1/19		CHURCH SERVICES. Outlying guards on Barges etc. found by "A" Coy. relieved by "B" Coy. "B" Coy dance at the HOTEL DE VILLE. LT. W. B. SMITH assumes duties of Adjt. 2nd LT. H. V. SPRENDBURY appointed ASST. ADJT. LT. A. SMITHIES takes command of "B" Coy. LT. W GRESTY takes command of "D" Coy.	Hrs.
	13/1/19		Education. The day was devoted to training & Baths. "A" Coy on the range.	Hrs.
	14/1/19		Education. M.O. inspected "A" Coy. "C" Coy dance at the HOTEL DE VILLE.	Hrs.
	15/1/19		Football match. V. 6th MANCHESTERS on Battalion Ground.	Hrs.
	16/1/19		Route march. "B" Coy on Range. LECTURE by Mr E. Halsfield. Turbulara game of "Basket Ball"	Hrs.
	17/1/19		Education. Rugger match V. 6th MANCHESTERS on their ground. Football match. V. L.T.M.By. 127 Bde. on their ground.	Hrs.
	18/1/19		C.Os. Inspectors. Coy. Commanders Conference. Baths.	Hrs.
	19/1/19		Church Services. M.O. inspected the Battn. Outlying guards on barges etc relieved by "C" Coy. Fire broke out near Battn. transport lines. Owing to the energy of the Battn. Fire Picquet & the transport section. The was kept within bounds. LT. T. COOKSON. to U.K. Draft Conducting Officer.	Hrs.
	23/1/19 24/1/19		The day was devoted to training & G.O.C Inspection. Baths.	Hrs.
	20/1/19		Education. "A" Coy. on Range. Baths. Lecture by Lieut. Col. Apsin. D.S.O. The Battn. concert party gave a concert which was a great success.	Hrs.
	21/1/19		Training. Corp. Commander's Lecture at WATERLOO. Concert by Battn. Party	Hrs.

Army Form C. 2118.

WAR DIARY
or
INTELLIGENCE SUMMARY.
(Erase heading not required.)

Instructions regarding War Diaries and Intelligence Summaries are contained in F. S. Regs., Part II. and the Staff Manual respectively. Title pages will be prepared in manuscript.

Place	Date	Hour	Summary of Events and Information	Remarks and references to Appendices
FLEURUS.	22/1/19		Presentation of Medal Ribbons by G.O.C. The following officers & O.R.s received decorations.	H.S.
			CAPT. B. J. WILSON. M.C.	
			LIEUT. W. GRESTY. Bar to M.C.	
			C.S.M. W. TABRON. D.C.M.	
			277007 PTE. A. GREER. Bar to M.M.	
			275173 SERGT. W. FIDLER. M.M.	
			276887 PTE. T.E. WILLIAMS. M.M.	
			275963 SGT. A. SCHOFIELD. M.M.	
			275782 " . BARNHAM. M.M.	
			276882 " H. TITTERINGTON M.M.	
			276482 " H. LYNN. M.M.	
			276245 " W. COFFY. M.M.	
			275201 C/SGT. A. GAMMOND. M.M.	
			300991 " F. EASTWOOD. M.M.	
			51634 " J. WILKINSON. M.M.	
			276430 L/CPL. W. TOPLIS. M.M.	
			295704 PTE. C. MULLEN. M.M.	
			2/5726 " S. BAYLEY. M.M.	
			Lt. A. SMITHIES. proceeds to U.K. on leave.	
	23/1/19.		The day was devoted to training & C.O.s inspection.	
	24/1/19.		Battalion parade with Colours. Outlying Guards relieved by "D" Coy.	H.S.
	25/1/19.		Brig. General Henley inspected the Battn. Messes, Billets & Regimental Books.	H.S.
	26/1/19.		CHURCH SERVICES. The C.O. congratulated all ranks on their excellent turnout & smartness on parade the previous day.	H.S.
			270495. C.S.M. T. SHIELDS. awarded the M.S.M.	
	27/1/19.		This day was observed as a holiday. CAPT. C. NORBURY proceeded to U.K. on leave.	H.S.
	28/1/19.		The day was devoted to training & Baths. CAPT. & QM. H. WOOD proceeded to U.K. on leave.	H.S.

Army Form C. 2118.

WAR DIARY
or
INTELLIGENCE SUMMARY.
(Erase heading not required.)

Instructions regarding War Diaries and Intelligence Summaries are contained in F. S. Regs., Part II. and the Staff Manual respectively. Title pages will be prepared in manuscript.

Place	Date	Hour	Summary of Events and Information	Remarks and references to Appendices
FLEURUS.	29/1/19.		Education. Capt. W.B. Smith. proceeded on Course. 2nd Lt. H.V. SPREADBURY. took over duties of O/Adjt. Boxing at Divisional Tournament. CHARLEROI.	Hrs.
	30/1/19.		The day was devoted to training. Bn. for duty. Boxing at Divisional Tournament. CHARLEROI. Bn. took 1st prize. BANTAMS. & second prize in FEATHER weights and LIGHT weights.	Hrs.
	31/1/19.		Education. Baths. "B" Coy on range. Outlying guards relieved by "A" Coy. The good feeling existing between the troops & the inhabitants is very evident. The health of the men is excellent. Rations everything very good. All ranks very contented & show no anxiety for early demobilization with the exception of married men, & those who have land employment to go to. The fairness of demobilization arrangements is fully appreciated by all ranks.	

E.F. Manops Lieut-Colonel.
Commanding 7th Bn. The Manchester Regt.

WAR DIARY (Confidential) OF 7th. Manchester Regiment.

Period.

Feb. 1st. to Feb. 28th

Volume 2

Army Form C. 2118.

WAR DIARY
INTELLIGENCE SUMMARY.
(Erase heading not required.)

Instructions regarding War Diaries and Intelligence Summaries are contained in F. S. Regs., Part II. and the Staff Manual respectively. Title pages will be prepared in manuscript.

Place	Date	Hour	Summary of Events and Information	Remarks and references to Appendices
FLEURUS	1.2.19		C.O.'s Inspection. Severe frost sets in. 28.O.Rs to U.K. for demobilization	M.S.
	2.2.19		Bn. for duty. Divine Service. 9 German prisoners arrive for duty with the Bn. Frost continues	M.S.
	3.2.19		Education. A Coy on Range. Frost continues	M.S.
	4.2.19		The Day was devoted to Training. B. Coy on Range. Frost continues	M.S.
	5.2.19		Education. Bn. for duty. Lecture by Rev. Stoddart Kennedy. C. Coy on Range. Frost Continues	M.S.
	6.2.19		Training. Lecture by Rev. Stoddart Kennedy. D. Coy on Range. Slight fall of snow. Frost continues. D. Coy's dance at Hotel de Ville. Capt. J.S. Wilson & 210 O.Rs to U.K. for demobilization.	M.S.
	7.2.19		Education. Baths. Lecture by Rev. Stoddart Kennedy. Heavy fall of snow. Bn. Officers dance at Hotel de Ville. Outlying guards relieved	M.S.
	8.2.19		Training. Bn. for duty. A. Coy on Range. Frost continues. C. Coy dance at Hotel de Ville. 3.O.Rs to U.K. for demobilization	M.S.
	9.2.19		Divine Service. On account of decreasing strength A & B Coys + C & D Coys amalgamate. Frost continues. 46 O.Rs to U.K. for demobilization	M.S.
	10.2.19		Education. C.O.'s Inspection. 127 Brig. Musketry Competition. Sgt. Files (5 chevrons) + Cpl. TRANTER (4 chevrons) win first prizes, Cpl. TRANTER making highest score in Bde. Frost continues	M.S.

WAR DIARY
or
INTELLIGENCE SUMMARY.

Army Form C. 2118.

Place	Date	Hour	Summary of Events and Information	Remarks and references to Appendices
FLEURUS	11.2.19		Bn. for duty. Baths. Frost continues	Hrs.
	12.2.19		Education and Training. C.O. inspects the draft proceeding to 2nd Bn. Manchester Regt. Frost continues. A. Coy. dance in Sgts. Mess.	Hrs.
	13.2.19		The day was devoted to training. C. Coy. dance at Hôtel de Ville. Frost continues. 30 Rs. to UK for demobilization. This day a Frost set in.	Hrs.
	14.2.19		Bn. for duty. Baths. Up to this date 31 N.C.Os & men of this Bn. have re-enlisted for the Regular Army, provided that they can serve in the unit which they wish to join. It is essential that men should have the choice of unit with which they desire to serve otherwise very few will re-engage for future service. The number re-engaging is small & likely to decrease at leave. 17 others 30 O.Rs. to UK for demobilization. Outlying guards relieved by A Coy.	Hrs.
	15.2.19		The day was devoted to training. C Coy on Range. Lt. Col. E V Mayer to UK on leave. Major J.R. CREAGH assumes command of the Bn. 2 Officers & 150 men proceed to MONTIGNIES D'UNE Service	Hrs.
	16.2.19			Hrs.

WAR DIARY

INTELLIGENCE SUMMARY.

(Erase heading not required.)

Army Form C. 2118.

Place	Date	Hour	Summary of Events and Information	Remarks and references to Appendices
FLEURUS	17.2.19		Education, Training & Baths. 42-Div Boxing Tournament CHARLEROI	H.S.
	18.2.19		The day was devoted to Training. 42nd Div. Boxing Tournament CHARLEROI. The Bn team scored 15½ points & win silver cup. LT. Heavy Weight contest won by C.S.M. Branchflower. Runners up in Bantam & Welter weights 4/CPL NYLAND & PTE CAMPBELL. 3 medals awarded. A. Coys dance Hotel de Ville	H.S.
	19.2.19		Education. Training. 41 O.Rs for demobilization. 2LT HARGREAVES to U.K. as draft conducting officer	H.S.
	20.2.19		Training Training & Baths. C. Coys dance at Hotel de Ville	H.S.
	21.2.19		Training. C. Coy on Range. Guard at MONTIGNIES relieved by 37th Div. Capt. B. Smith to U.K. on leave	H.S.
	22.2.19		Training. 100 O.Rs to U.K. for demobilization. LTS. STERN & 2 LT. H. RICHARDSON to U.K. as draft conducting officers.	H.S.
	23.2.19		Divine Service	H.S.
	24.2.19		Training. A. Coy on Range.	"H.S.
	25.2.19		Training. The Div Commander inspects Bn. Transport. A. Coys dance at Hotel de Ville	H.S.

Army Form C. 2118.

WAR DIARY
INTELLIGENCE SUMMARY.
(Erase heading not required.)

Instructions regarding War Diaries and Intelligence Summaries are contained in F. S. Regs., Part II. and the Staff Manual respectively. Title pages will be prepared in manuscript.

Place	Date	Hour	Summary of Events and Information	Remarks and references to Appendices
FLEURUS	26.2.19		Training + Baths.	N.T.S.
	27.2.19		Training. Bn. awarded second prize in Div. Transport Competition. 11 Bronze medals. C. Coy on Range. 2 Lt. WAINWRIGHT to U.K on leave.	A.T.S.
	28.		Training. C. Coy dance at Hotel de Ville	N.T.S.

J Palmer Capt.
for Lieut-Colonel
Commanding 7th Bn. The Manchester Regt

WM 26

Confidential

War Diary
1/7th Manchester Regt.

1st - 31st March 1919.

Volume 3.

Army Form C. 2118.

WAR DIARY
or
INTELLIGENCE SUMMARY.
(Erase heading not required.)

Instructions regarding War Diaries and Intelligence Summaries are contained in F. S. Regs., Part II. and the Staff Manual respectively. Title pages will be prepared in manuscript.

Place	Date	Hour	Summary of Events and Information	Remarks and references to Appendices
FLEURUS	1.3.19		Training & Baths. No.275252 Sgt. HARDY died at 20th. C.C.S. Bn. for duty	A.V.J.
	2.3.19		Divine Services. 2 LT LUCAS to U.K on leave	A.V.J.
	3.3.19		Training	A.V.J.
	4.3.19		Training & Baths. A. Coy dance at Hotel de Ville. Bn for duty.	A.V.J.
	5.3.19		Training	A.V.J.
	6.3.19		Training. 62 O.Rs to U.K for demobilisation. 2 LT W. F. Banks to U.K as draft conducting officer. C. Coy dance at Hotel de Ville.	A.V.J.
CHARLEROI	7.3.19		The Bn. moves to billets in Charleroi. 1 Off + 62 O.Rs proceed to MONTIGNIES for guard duties. Bn. for duty	A.V.J.
	8.3.19		Training	A.V.J.
	9.3.19		Divine Services. LT COL E. K. MANGER resumes command of the Bn. on return from leave to U.K.	A.V.J.
	10.3.19		Training.	A.V.J.
	11.3.19		Training. The Divisional Commander presents Transport Competition Medals. The B.g. General inspects billets. Capt. Smith resumes duties 8 days on returning from leave. Battalion dance at Philharmonic Hall. Bn for duty.	A.V.J.

Army Form C. 2118.

WAR DIARY
INTELLIGENCE SUMMARY
(Erase heading not required.)

Instructions regarding War Diaries and Intelligence Summaries are contained in F.S. Regs., Part II. and the Staff Manual respectively. Title pages will be prepared in manuscript.

Place	Date	Hour	Summary of Events and Information	Remarks and references to Appendices
CHARLEROI	12.3.19		Training. LT. SPREADBURY & 2 LT. PALMER to U.K on leave. Officers N.C.Os men to last performance of Divisional Pantomime.	HVS.
	13.3.19		Training. Officers & Sgts dance at Philharmonic Hall.	HVS.
	14.3.19		Training. Guard at MONTIGNIES relieved by 5th Division. Bn for duty.	HVS.
	15.3.19		Training. LT. Cookson. R.S.M. Arlorark, & 6 O.Rs to U.K. for demobilization	HVS.
	16.3.19		Divine Services.	HVS.
	17.3.19		Training. A & C Coys amalgamate. Bn. dance in the Philharmonic Hall. Bn for duty.	HVS.
	18.3.19		Training & Baths. 1 O.R. to U.K. for demobilization	HVS.
	19.3.19		Training. LT. SMITHIES to UK for demobilization.	HVS.
	20.3.19		Training. Bn for duty. The Bn. provide a firing party and escort for Belgian Officers funeral.	HVS.
	21.3.19		Training. LT. C. BRYAN to U.K on leave.	HVS.
	22.3.19		Training	HVS.

Army Form C. 2118.

WAR DIARY
INTELLIGENCE SUMMARY.
(Erase heading not required.)

Instructions regarding War Diaries and Intelligence Summaries are contained in F. S. Regs., Part II. and the Staff Manual respectively. Title pages will be prepared in manuscript.

Place	Date	Hour	Summary of Events and Information	Remarks and references to Appendices
CHARLEROI.	23. –26.		Preparations for departure of Cadres for U.K. Major J.R.Cheyt. Capt. C. Horbury } Proceed to U.K. for demobilization on 25/3/19. Capt. J.C. Palmer	4435. 4073 S
	27th		G.O.C. Bde farewell to U.K. Bde farewell dance at the Café de la Philharmonie	4073 S
	28th		The Bn. less Cadre handed over to Lt. F.L. Staith.	4073 S
			The following officers will proceed home with Cadre Lt. Col. E.V. MANGER, Capt. H.B. SMITH, Capt. & Qmr. H. WOOD, Lt. H.Y. SPREARBURY, Lt. T.R. WILKINSON, Lt. J. MILNE. Officers to carry Colours.	
			Many more men would have re-engaged for the regular army had those who volunteered been sent on leave more quickly. The unaccountable delay in dealing with the cases of these men undoubtedly prejudiced recruiting. In this unit alone there are now twenty eight men waiting to be sent home on leave. These men finally approved five men have not as yet been demobilised for (attestation papers) difficult was experienced in obtaining enlistment forms

E.V.Manger Lt-Col. 1/7 D.A. Lieut-Colonel.
Commanding 7th Bn. The Manchester Regt.

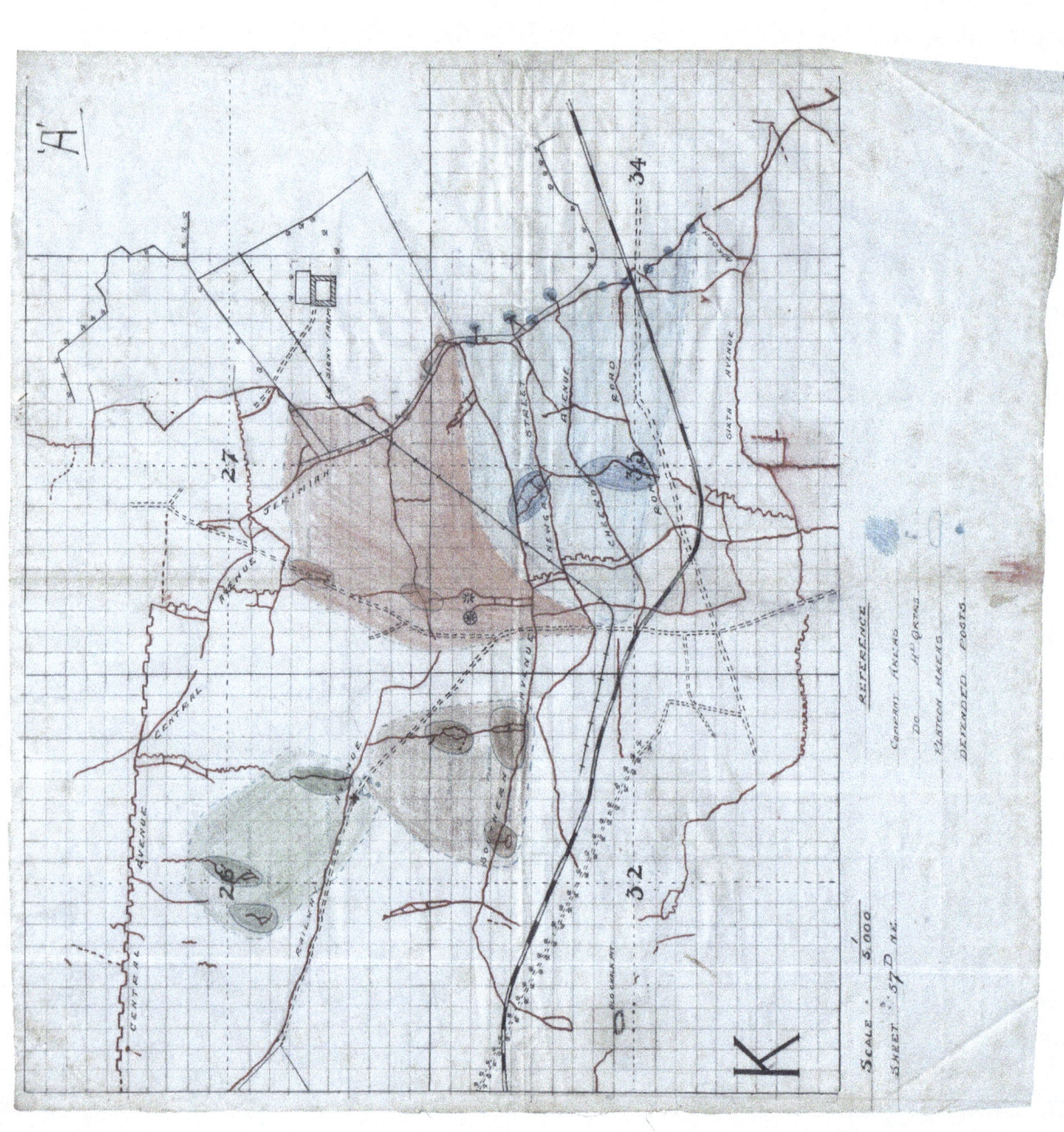